Paradox and Power in Caring Leadership

NEW HORIZONS IN LEADERSHIP STUDIES

Series Editor: Joanne B. Ciulla, *Academic Director, Institute for Ethical Leadership and Professor of Leadership Ethics, Department of Management and Global Business, Rutgers Business School, USA*

This important series is designed to make a significant contribution to the development of leadership studies. This field has expanded dramatically in recent years and the series provides an invaluable forum for the publication of high quality works of scholarship and shows the diversity of leadership issues and practices around the world.

The main emphasis of the series is on the development and application of new and original ideas in leadership studies. It pays particular attention to leadership in business, economics and public policy and incorporates the wide range of disciplines which are now part of the field. Global in its approach, it includes some of the best theoretical and empirical work with contributions to fundamental principles, rigorous evaluations of existing concepts and competing theories, historical surveys and future visions.

Titles in the series include:

Paradox and Power in Caring Leadership

Critical and Philosophical Reflections

Edited by

Leah Tomkins

Senior Lecturer in Leadership and Organization Studies, The Open University, UK

NEW HORIZONS IN LEADERSHIP STUDIES

Edward Elgar
PUBLISHING

Cheltenham, UK • Northampton, MA, USA

Published by
Edward Elgar Publishing Limited
The Lypiatts
15 Lansdown Road
Cheltenham
Glos GL50 2JA
UK

Edward Elgar Publishing, Inc.
William Pratt House
9 Dewey Court
Northampton
Massachusetts 01060
USA

A catalogue record for this book
is available from the British Library

Library of Congress Control Number: 2019954469

This book is available electronically in the **Elgar**online
Business subject collection
DOI 10.4337/9781788975506

ISBN 978 1 78897 549 0 (cased)
ISBN 978 1 78897 550 6 (eBook)

Printed and bound by CPI Group (UK) Ltd, Croydon, CR0 4YY

This book is dedicated to my father, Michael Tomkins – my own blueprint for caring leadership

Contents

Contributors

The late **Gerardo Abreu Pederzini** was formerly Assistant Professor (Lecturer) of HRM/Organizational Behaviour at Kent Business School, University of Kent, UK. He was also Adjunct Fellow at Universidad de las Américas Puebla in Mexico. His research focused on using unconventional and critical theories, such as psychoanalysis, evolutionary theory, complexity theory, Bourdieu, or the philosophy of science, to understand leadership and strategy. His work has been published in world-leading journals, including the *Academy of Management Learning & Education* and the *Journal of Management Inquiry*.

Carol Atack is a bye-fellow and Director of studies in Classics at Newnham College, University of Cambridge, UK. Her research on ancient Greek political thought explores intersections of power and ethics, and theories of political change. Her doctoral thesis on the philosophy of monarchy is being published as *The Discourse of Kingship in Classical Greece* (Routledge, 2020). As a postdoctoral researcher, she co-authored *Anachronism and Antiquity* (Bloomsbury, 2020) with colleagues at the University of Oxford, the aim of which was to offer a new conceptual map of antiquity through the notion of anachronism.

Dr Vinca Bigo is Associate Professor in Embodied Leadership and Corporate Liberation at KEDGE Business School, France, a post she has held since 2010. She holds a PhD from Cambridge University after a career in finance. Her current research centres on embodied learning, the ethics of care, philosophy of science, leadership, silence, and liberated entrepreneurship. Her teaching commitments include Embodied Leadership, Liberated Entrepreneurship, Yoga and Philosophy. Recent publications include: On Silence, Creativity and Ethics in Organization Studies in the journal *Organization Studies* (2017).

Dr Peter Bloom is Professor of Management at the University of Essex, UK. His books include: *The Bad Faith in the Free Market: The Radical Promise of Existential Freedom* (2018); *Beyond Power and Resistance: Politics at the Radical Limits* (2016); *The Ethics of Neoliberalism* (2017); and with Carl Rhodes, *The CEO Society: The Corporate Takeover of Everyday Life* (2018). He has served as lead academic on a range of recent BBC programmes, including *The Bottom Line* on Radio 4 and *Can Britain Have a Pay Rise?* on BBC2.

Joanne B. Ciulla is Professor of Leadership Ethics and Director of the Institute for Ethical Leadership at Rutgers Business School and Professor Emerita of the Jepson School of Leadership Studies, at the University of Richmond, USA. A philosopher by training, her research focuses on Leadership Ethics, Business Ethics, and philosophy of work. Her books include: *The Working Life: The Promise and Betrayal of Modern Work*; *Ethics the Heart of Leadership*; and a co-edited 3-volume reference work, *Leadership Ethics*.

Ann L. Cunliffe is Professor of Organization Studies at Escola de Administração da Fundação Getulio Vargas, Brazil and Visiting Professor at the Università Cattolica, Milano, Italy and Aalborg University, Denmark. Her current research interests include ethical leadership, embodied sensemaking, qualitative research, and reflexivity. Recent publications include articles in *Organizational Research Methods*, the *British Journal of Management*, and *Organization Studies*. She organizes the biennial Qualitative Research in Management and Organization Conference in New Mexico, USA.

Matthew Eriksen is Professor in and Chair of the Department of Management at Providence College, Providence, Rhode Island, USA. His research interests are in the areas of leadership, leadership development, and management education. His publications include the articles: Relational Leadership in *Human Relations* (2011), On Developing Responsible Leaders in the *Journal of Management Development* (2018), and Shared-Purpose Process: Implications and Possibilities for Student Learning, Development and Self-Transformation in the *Journal of Management Education* (2017).

Yiannis Gabriel is a social psychologist, currently Professor Emeritus at the University of Bath, UK and Visiting Professor at Lund University, Sweden. Yiannis has researched organizational storytelling and narratives, leadership and followership, management learning and contemporary consumption. He is co-author of *Return to Meaning: A Social Science with Something to Say* (with Mats Alvesson and Roland Paulsen, OUP, 2017) and maintains an active blog on www.yiannisgabriel.com, in which he discusses his academic interests as well as musical, political and other issues.

Dr Rita A. Gardiner is Assistant Professor in Critical Policy, Equity and Leadership Studies, Faculty of Education, Western University, Canada. An Arendtian scholar, she sees leadership as an affective, embodied and relational experience. Her publications include *Gender, Authenticity and Leadership: Thinking with Arendt* (Palgrave Macmillan, 2015), and articles in *Business Ethics Quarterly*, *Leadership*, *Organization*, and *Gender, Work and Organization*. She is currently working on a Social Science and Humanities funded project that examines the implementation of sexual violence policies in Canadian universities.

Dr Liz Gloyn is Senior Lecturer in Classics at Royal Holloway, University of London, UK. Her research interests explore the intersection between Latin literature, the Roman family and ancient philosophy, with a particular focus on how relationships of care are modelled and idealised. She also works on classical reception and how the past infuses contemporary sensibilities, experiences and understandings. She is the author of *The Ethics of the Family in Seneca* (Cambridge University Press, 2017) and *Tracking Classical Monsters in Popular Culture* (Bloomsbury, 2019).

Jen Jones, PhD, is Associate Professor and Department Coordinator in the School of Business at Seton Hill University, USA. Her research attends to ethics in leadership and communication from a humanities perspective. Recent publications include: Empathic Leadership: Saint Edith Stein's Phenomenological Perspective in Denison's *Women, Religion, and Leadership: Female Saints as Unexpected Leaders* (Routledge); and The Derivative Organization and Responsible Leadership: Levinas's Dwelling and Discourse; and Leadership Lessons from Levinas: Revisiting Responsible Leadership in *Leadership & the Humanities*.

Donna Ladkin is Professor of Leadership and Ethics with Antioch University's Graduate School in Leadership and Change, USA. A philosopher and musician by background, Donna's work explores leadership as a lived phenomenon, focusing particularly on its aesthetic and embodied aspects. Her philosophically informed approach to leadership has been published in journals such as *Leadership Quarterly, Business Ethics Quarterly, Journal of Business Ethics* and *Leadership*. The second edition of her book, *Rethinking Leadership: A New Look at Old Leadership Questions* will be published by Edward Elgar in 2020.

Michèle Lowrie, Andrew W. Mellon Distinguished Service Professor of Classics, University of Chicago, USA, works on Latin literature and Roman political thought. She is currently writing a monograph on security, a concept through which people and leaders reimagined their relationship during the transition from the Roman Republic's distributed leadership to monarchy under the Empire. Publications include: *Writing, Performance and Authority in Augustan Rome* (2009); Roman Law and Latin Literature, *Oxford Handbook of Roman Law and Society* (2016); and Political Thought, *Cambridge Critical Guide to Latin Literature* (forthcoming).

Iain Munro is Professor of Leadership and Organization at Newcastle Business School, University of Newcastle, UK. He has previously worked at the universities of Warwick (1994–2000), St Andrews (2000–2009), and Innsbruck (2009–2013). Iain is engaged in research in the fields of business ethics, power in organizations and information warfare. He has written a research monograph, *Information Warfare in Business: Strategies of Control and Resistance in the Network Society* (Routledge).

Dr Helen Mussell is Lecturer in Management, Employment and Organisation at Cardiff University, and Research Associate at the Centre for Business Research, University of Cambridge, UK. Her interdisciplinary research spans business ethics, gender, power and leadership, and also includes corporate governance issues, specifically fiduciary duty and trust in organizations. Publications include: Who Dares to Care? (In the World of Finance) in *Feminist Economics*, Special symposium edition on Sustainability, Ecology and Care (2018); and The Nature of Social Responsibility: Exploring Emancipatory Ends in the *Journal for the Theory of Social Behaviour* (2017).

Major Ben Sawyer left the British Army in 2017 after 16 years' service. Ben's career centred on counter-terrorism bomb disposal and leadership. His experience has included multiple tours in the Balkans, Northern Ireland, Iraq and Afghanistan, four of which were as a bomb disposal operator with special operations task forces. Ben has personal experience of PTSD, moral injury and its connections with care/carelessness, and is interested in what the business world can learn from the military about leadership and moral injury, and vice versa.

Dr Liz Sawyer is an Associate Researcher at the Ioannou Centre for Classical and Byzantine Studies at the University of Oxford, UK. Her primary interest is the use of classical literature in spheres outside the academy, especially in public discourse, and in the use and transmission of quotations from classical writers. Upcoming publications include co-editing *Brill's Companion to the Legacy of Greek Political Thought* (forthcoming, 2020) with David Carter and Rachel Foxley.

Peter Simpson is Associate Professor in Organization Studies at Bristol Business School, UK. He has published widely in international journals on leadership, change management, organizational complexity, group dynamics, and workplace spirituality. He co-authored with Robert French *Attention, Cooperation, Purpose: An Approach to Working in Groups Using Insights from Wilfred Bion* (Karnac, 2014) and co-edited *Worldly Leadership: Alternative Wisdoms for a Complex World* (Palgrave, 2011) with Sharon Turnbull, Peter Case, Gareth Edwards and Doris Schedlitzki.

Amanda Sinclair is a writer, teacher and researcher in leadership, change, gender and diversity. Currently a Professorial Fellow, Amanda held the Foundation Chair of Management (Diversity and Change) at Melbourne Business School, the University of Melbourne, Australia (1995–2012). Her books include: *Doing Leadership Differently* (1998); *Leadership for* *the Disillusioned* (2007); *Leading Mindfully* (2016); and, with Christine Nixon, *Women Leading* (2017). Also a yoga and meditation teacher, Amanda encourages care and self-care as central to effective and sustainable leadership.

Torkild Thanem, PhD, is Professor of Management and Organization Studies at Stockholm Business School, Stockholm University, Sweden. Torkild has a longstanding interest in the ethics, politics and philosophy of leadership and organization, and he is currently completing an ethnographic project on life and work in a corporate performance culture. His recent work appears in journals such as *Leadership, Organization,* and *Business Ethics Quarterly.* Torkild's most recent book is *Embodied Research Methods* (with David Knights, published by Sage in 2019).

Dr Leah Tomkins is Senior Lecturer at the Open University, UK. Originally a classicist and linguist, her research explores the enduring themes of organizational experience, especially in connection with leadership ethics and the meanings of work. Having spent twenty years in the corporate world, she looks to bridge gaps between academia and practice. Other books include *Health at Work: Critical Perspectives* (Routledge, 2019), and she has published articles in *Organization Studies, Business Ethics Quarterly,* and *Leadership.* Forthcoming work examines caring leadership as slave morality through the prism of the philosophy of Nietzsche.

Charlotte von Bülow is founder and Director of the Crossfields Institute Group, an awarding organization, HEI and research institute for social innovation established in 2007. Crossfields Institute focuses on education, professional practice and leadership that facilitate transformative ways of life and working practices in a complex world. Charlotte has held a range of senior leadership positions and her global consulting practice is currently focused on the USA, Scandinavia and the UK. She registered for a doctorate at Bristol Business School in 2014, studying 'The Practice of Attention in Workplace Experience.'

Acknowledgements

This book has been a true labour of love. It would not have been possible without the support, enthusiasm and hard work of many people, some of whom have contributed chapters to this collection, whilst others have been cheer-leading from the side-lines.

A special thank you goes to Joanne Ciulla, who invited me to contribute to this Edward Elgar series on *New Horizons in Leadership Studies*, and who has given me guidance, encouragement and the occasional kick up the backside ever since! I cannot think of a better exemplar of the 'caring leader'!

My sincere gratitude, appreciation and respect go to all those whose work appears in this volume. I have hugely enjoyed discussing matters of leadership and care with them, and have learned a great deal in the process. Based on these experiences, I would particularly like to commend working across disciplinary boundaries. The contributors here come from the fields of ancient and modern philosophy; critical organization and leadership studies; language and literature studies; psychology; sociology; psychoanalysis; legal studies; military studies; and management education. They draw on sources as diverse as Addams, Adi Shankara, Arendt, Barnes, the Bible, Darwin, Foucault, Freud, Heidegger, Homer, Hume, Jung, Kafka, Kant, Keats, Kierkegaard, Lucretius, Merleau-Ponty, Plato, Ricoeur, Sartre, Seneca, Socrates, Spinoza, Vergil and Xenophon, as well as the ground-breaking work of Gilligan, Held, Kittay, Noddings, Tronto, and others in the modern care ethics movement. This is a deliberately broad sweep, highlighting that the interplay of leadership and care – and the power dynamics, dilemmas and agonies it brings forth – is not some new fad on the business school curriculum. Rather, as the historical and multi-disciplinary focus of this book underscores, the idea of caring leadership has been exercising philosophical, literary and political minds for thousands of years – its costs and its benefits; its sources and its effects; its dangers and its allure.

I have become increasingly conscious that such a multi-disciplinary approach provides a particular space and impetus for *care*. The editor/author relationship demands a special attentiveness when one is aware of the differences between subjects, perspectives, ideologies and disciplinary conventions and lexicons. If care ethics' potential to enhance institutional life will only be realized by loosening the hold of the familiar in order to actively seek out difference – as some of the chapters in this collection insist – then working across normally silo-ed disciplines feels like an excellent place to begin.

Amongst the cheer-leaders I mentioned, I would like to single out Ed Bispham, with whom I have been debating the resonance of classical scholarship for modern experiences and sensibilities for over thirty years. Ed kept assuring me that this book was both a good idea and possible to pull off, for which I am very grateful. I hope that Don Fowler – our former classics tutor and a staunch advocate for blasting through disciplinary barriers – would have been chuffed with us!

Thanks finally to the team at Edward Elgar for their enthusiasm for the book, their endorsement of its approach, and their excellent steering of the production process.

Leah Tomkins
Oxford, 2019

Postscript: As this book was being prepared for publication, news came of the untimely death of Gerardo Abreu Pederzini. Gerardo was a scholar with piercing insight and originality, and he was both willing and able to demolish what we take for granted about leadership and care. To my mind, the contribution his chapter makes to this book is enormous. I send my deepest condolences to his family and loved ones.

Introduction

Leah Tomkins

WHAT DOES IT MEAN FOR A LEADER TO CARE?

There is nothing new about a concern that our leaders may not be doing everything we expect or hope from them, whether in the institutions of public life or behind the closed doors of corporate organisations. For millennia, philosophers, poets, historians and artists have held up a mirror to leadership behaviour, and admired, but more often criticised, mocked or despaired of what they saw. What leaders do is significant, because of the power invested in them and the ability they have to affect people's lives – materially, politically and psychologically. Moreover, leadership is not something bestowed only on the very few at the top of society or on a single CEO of an organisation. Leadership is something in which most of us engage from time to time, whenever goals need to be set, actions need to be co-ordinated, and people need to be mobilised and motivated. In short, leadership matters.

In recent years, scholarly interest in leadership has focused increasingly on the notion of an ethics of care. When we think of popular archetypes of leadership, we often invoke leaders who seem to care – like Nelson Mandela, Mother Theresa, or even Princess Diana, all of whom were able to *connect* with people, willing to share both literal and metaphorical hugs. Such leaders inspire enormous devotion from those around them, who repay the care invested in them with often unquestioning support, adoration and even idolisation. In contrast, leaders who do not care suffer from a moral illegitimacy which tarnishes their other accomplishments and qualities (Gabriel, 2015). Not caring – or perhaps more accurately, *appearing* not to care – is an almost unforgivable transgression for leaders to make.

This was starkly brought to life in UK politics in the aftermath of the Grenfell Tower disaster in London. In June 2017, a fire broke out in a 24-storey apartment block in a relatively poor area of West London. With 72 deaths and more than 70 serious injuries, it was the most devastating residential fire in the UK since World War II. The fire's rapid spread was attributed to cheap building cladding, which contributed to the sense of outrage amongst the public and social and political commentators. The then Prime Minister, Theresa May, was roundly criticised for her very low profile visits to the scene, and her apparent refusal to meet the families of the dead and the missing. In contrast, the leader of the opposition Labour party, Jeremy Corbyn, won praise for the personalised attention he gave to individual survivors and relatives, and the way he seemed to roll up his sleeves to take an active role in the search for the missing. His very visible, hands-on presence at the scene of the disaster was interpreted to mean that he was deeply and genuinely affected by what had happened; that he was able to acknowledge, but also contain, both his own and other people's distress. In this instance, Corbyn seemed to epitomise the 'caring leader' as someone who puts human beings and human relationships first. This meant being personally invested in other people's concrete experiences, in contrast to the behind-the-scenes, ivory-tower strategising associated with Theresa May, or indeed, to her successor, Boris Johnson's notorious preference for rhetorical flourishes over actual facts. Whatever one thinks of their politics, Corbyn seems to fit the template of 'caring leader' more readily than May, with her unease with people, or Johnson, with his unease with detail.

Care and caring leadership are attractive ideas, because they trigger associations with closeness, belonging and mattering to one another. In academic studies, care has been linked to increased organisational commitment (Lilius et al., 2012), enhanced workplace self-esteem (McAllister and Bigley, 2002) and improved organisational performance (Cameron et al., 2003). Focusing on care in organisational relations seems consistent, therefore, with leaders having (or developing) emotional intelligence and good relationship management skills. This tallies with a 'common sense' view of care as being associated first and foremost with emotions, and with the good emotions of love, empathy and compassion, rather than the bad emotions of disappointment, envy or hostility.

However, care is more complex than simply being kind or sympathetic to people, or being personally interested and invested in their affairs. Instead of always being expressed in niceness, care can manifest as sorrow, anger, frustration and anxiety. We see this shadow side of care in common expressions such as 'take care', which implies caution and the acknowledgement of threat and danger. Moreover, if we scratch beneath the surface of our understandings of care, we find that it challenges some of the things we take for granted about leadership – indeed, about organisational and institutional life in general. Some of care's strongest associations, for example, with feelings, femininity and domesticity, are extremely problematic for an institutional world which appears to value success, efficiency and delivery above all other qualities, and is often suspicious of emotions (except when they are the achievement-orientated emotions of pride or ambition). So, when we admire apparently caring leaders, we do not usually suspend our expectation that they should actually be able to *do their job*. We may crave warmth and compassion from our leaders during moments of crisis and distress, but over the longer term, care is not usually a proxy for leadership competence.

CARING LEADERSHIP: AN ETERNAL REFRAIN

Over the course of this book, we will be pushing past the surface rhetoric of care to uncover some of the tensions and paradoxes of caring leadership, particularly in the context of leaders' relationships with other people. This will mean resisting the tendency to see care as simply another skill on the long list of attributes that leaders are expected to hone. In other words, the message of this book is not that leaders should aim to *be more caring*, as if care were merely a quantifiable commodity of unquestionable moral virtue. Rather, we hope that by exploring the dynamics of care, we might expose some of the often hidden dilemmas of institutional life, as well as highlight some as yet unfulfilled possibilities.

To do this, we will connect with debates in the modern care ethics movement and with philosophies of care which go back much further in the history of ideas. From a range of critical and philosophical perspectives, we will examine the moral and emotional politics of institutional relationships, focusing on how leaders both influence, and are influenced by, the people around them. For millennia, the dynamics of care have been helping *and* harming both those who give and those who are in need of care. In both its presence and its absence, care is implicated in our deepest concerns about the safety, protection and development of self, community, institution and nation.

Much of the rhetoric in leadership studies gives the impression that things are uniquely difficult or uniquely awful right here, right now, and that the solutions we come up with must, therefore, be based on discovering some hitherto secret or magic ingredient for leaders' greater effectiveness. Alvesson and Einola (2019) offer a timely reminder that the leadership models that come (back) to the fore at particular points in history say as much about the *Zeitgeist* as about the models *per se*. Certain approaches to leadership become particularly attractive during periods of social, economic and political turmoil as part of a relatively predictable identity crisis amongst the business and/or political elite. So, rather than assuming that caring leadership is the latest fad on the business school curriculum, this book encourages us to ask what it is about care that makes it surface as a priority at particular periods in time. What might our current age have in common with earlier times when the paradoxes of care have previously exercised intellectual, political and artistic minds?

Care goes to the heart of the relationship between those in charge and those in need. Decisions about how care should manifest are, therefore, enmeshed in the eternal fluctuations between strong, individualist leaders and more collaborative and participative forms of governance. Thus, whilst contemporary organisational scholarship might assume that the call for 'leadership, not leaders' (Crevani et al., 2010) is a radical new departure, the broader historical sweep of this book would suggest otherwise. It invites us to reflect on the tides of political and institutional energy that have been ebbing and flowing for thousands of years, and the role of care in both galvanising and disturbing them.

CARE AS SOCIAL AND INSTITUTIONAL PHILOSOPHY

When I have discussed this book with friends and colleagues, they have often initially interpreted the idea of 'caring leaders' as meaning leadership of the caring professions, that is, they have assumed that it applies principally to the management of institutions providing health-care, social-care, elder-care and/ or child-care. In this book, however, we are interested in how care ethics might be extrapolated from the spheres of domesticity and health/illness and into the wider world of organisation and institution. We use theorisations of care to frame negotiations between human beings in multiple walks of life, wherever these are between those able to provide support and those who need or desire such support, whether short- or longer-term.

We tend to use the term 'followers' to describe those in receipt of such care in organisational relations, because this is how the relationship is usually framed in leadership theory, despite the fact that most organisational practitioners do not think of themselves in such terms. The leader/follower distinction is useful simply as a heuristic to highlight the dynamics of organisational power; and the way these are usually assumed to be *asymmetrical*, positioning leaders as care-*givers*, who are the powerful, and followers as care-*recipients*, who are the relatively powerless.

Our extrapolation of care goes beyond the boundaries of individual organisations and into the wider social and political realm. The leadership we consider in this book is also leadership in the public arena, and we explore some of the ways in which both elected and non-elected leaders affect us as citizens. In short, we are interested in the challenges and opportunities for caring leadership as they apply to relations of authority and responsibility in any sector, occupation or realm of coordinated, organised activity. In this book, these include business, finance, law, higher education, leadership development, politics, the military, the prison service, social policy and social movements, as well as the more overtly caring contexts of health services and the family.

One way to extrapolate care into this broader realm is via care ethicists' distinction between caring-for and caring-about. Caring-for occurs in the face-to-face encounter between care-giver and care-recipient, that is, in the activities of tending directly to another person's needs, often within the intimacy of the domestic sphere. Caring-about, on the other hand, takes us away from the face-to-face encounter and into the broader social, cultural and institutional world. Caring-for prioritises action and the meeting of another person's particular needs, and does not necessarily have anything to do with feelings or principles. By contrast, caring-about usually does involve feelings, and probably principles, but need not have anything to do with either action or needs. For instance, we may care-for another person's child when we baby-sit, because both parents and child need someone to just be there; but when we care-about the state of our politics, say, this takes us beyond the meeting of specific, immediate needs, and says something about who we are and how we relate to the world. So, the distinction between caring-for and caring-about suggests how care might generalise from the home and into the wider social and institutional world, for: 'Chronologically, we learn first what it means to be cared for. Then, gradually, we learn both to care for and, by extension, to care about others. This caring-about is almost certainly the foundation for our sense of justice.' (Noddings, 2002, p. 22).

THE KEY THEMES OF THE BOOK: PARADOX AND POWER

As the authors in this collection illustrate, caring leadership is a concept which juxtaposes what we admire most (agency, authority, control) with what we fear most (vulnerability, incapacity, dependency), highlighting the paradoxes which infuse our everyday experiences of our social, institutional and political worlds. Care entails, but also complicates, emotions. It exceeds, but also naturalises, gender. It demands that we acknowledge the sometimes excruciating choice between what is best for one particular person and what is best for everyone. With its links with compassion and empathy, care may seem a highly attractive quality but, with its roots in the family and the familiar, it involves the somewhat less attractive trait that we are usually more comfortable with who/what we know than with who/what we do not know.

Above all, care's significance for leadership rests on the suggestion that care is a relationship of *power*. This might initially seem surprising, because the concept of the 'caring leader' probably conjures up a world far removed from popular conceptualisations of power as Machiavellian manoeuvring and greasy poles. But, as these chapters highlight, power is everywhere implicated in relations of care, whether through the dynamics of the family as archetypal organisational entity, as exemplified by *Yiannis Gabriel*; or through the power of discourse to construct and constrict our understandings of the leader identity, as considered from a range of different perspectives by *Vinca Bigo, Joanne Ciulla, Ann Cunliffe* and *Matthew Eriksen*.

In terms of familiar framings of power in organisation studies, the dynamics of care reveal elements of power-over, power-to and power-with. *Liz Gloyn*'s chapter on caring leadership through the prism of Roman Stoicism offers us the idea of the power-to-not. *Liz* and *Ben Sawyer* suggest caring leadership as the power-to-not inflict moral injury, and to restore justice where such injury occurs. The power-to-not damage or disadvantage others is often a kind of power-over the self. This emerges in *Peter Bloom's* interlinking of care and existential freedom; *Michèle Lowrie's* control of the self for the sake of a necessary yet impossible security; *Charlotte von Bülow* and *Peter Simpson's* exploration of negative capability as the power-to do without; and *Donna Ladkin's* caring leadership as resilience, fortitude and absorption of criticism. *Carol Atack* emphasises followers' power-to either give or withhold the consent to be led; and *Helen Mussell* suggests that increasingly active shareholders in business are exercising the power-to demand to be consulted.

Through the prism of care, we confront the power of emotions to both enhance and distort our organisational experiences. *Amanda Sinclair* and *Donna Ladkin* explore the power of embodied feelings and intuitions to guide us towards moral maturity. *Iain Munro* and *Torkild Thanem* consider the power of affect to mobilise collective leadership within and beyond the realm of formal organisation. In contrast, both *Jen Jones* and *Gerardo Abreu Pederzini* emphasise the power of feelings of love and altruism to deceive us, with quite startling implications for leaders and followers alike. As *Rita Gardiner* suggests, the seductive powers of transformational leaders are something to be especially wary of, especially when associated with Philosophers of Care!

Where the authors connect explicitly with other leadership models, these are seen through the prism of the power and paradoxes of care – its deceptions and dangers as well as its attractions and potential. Whether servant leadership, authentic leadership, transformational leadership, relational leadership, charismatic leadership, or indeed, any other prevailing theory, analysing leadership through the lens of care emphasises that power relations are never stable, settled or one-dimensional. In the dynamics of care, we see the shifting politics of privilege and disadvantage, of obligation and need; and we are forced to confront both the security we crave and the vulnerability we fear.

THE ORGANISATION OF THE BOOK

The chapters are organised into the following sections:

I. Setting the scene: Power, privilege and disadvantage;
II. The roots of care: Kinship, feelings and bodies;
III. The risks of care: Dependency, exploitation and vulnerability;
IV. The caring leader at work: Security, sacrifice and self;
V. Reshaping the contours of leadership: Relationship, community and democracy.

These are by no means discrete categories, of course, and the individual chapters overlap and criss-cross with each other. There are other ways in which these chapters could have been clustered, and I am sure readers will find their own threads and patterns amongst the various discussions and perspectives.

I have avoided creating mini disciplinary ghettos by grouping, for instance, all the classical scholars' contributions together. As Tronto (1993) suggests, care ethics demands that we redraw conventional boundaries between politics and morality, between abstract ethical theory and grounded, idiographic approaches, and between public and private life. In my view, this also means challenging the contours of disciplinary boundaries to benefit from the insights of those working in different disciplinary silos but on similar moral, political and intellectual problems. Working with these authors from very different fields has been hugely rewarding, and I hope that readers get a sense of the joy of these cross-disciplinary collaborations.

Part I: Setting the Scene: Power, Privilege and Disadvantage

In the opening chapter, I deepen the analysis of the power relations of care to create context for the chapters to come. Connecting with care ethicists' elaborations of the relationship between care and justice, I explore some of the ways in which care can involve and inscribe *in*justice for both leaders and followers. Through the prism of care, I challenge some prevailing assumptions about who is privileged and who is disadvantaged in leader/follower relations.

Part II: The Roots of Care: Kinship, Feelings and Bodies

The authors in this part of the book consider the complex relations between caring leadership and emotions, especially feelings of closeness and familiarity which stem from the origins of care in the home, the family and the body. Connecting with real and metaphorical families, the authors reflect on the deceptive and the productive power of feelings.

Joanne Ciulla asks whether leaders need to feel warm emotions when discharging their duties towards others. Suggesting that the ethical distinctiveness of leaders may lie in the question of who has first claim on one's care, she reflects on the tension between looking after family (whom one knows and supposedly loves) and looking after followers (whom one may not know or like, let alone love). Leaders can honour their duties towards followers even if they do not like them all that much. This might mean that, in order to care-for an unlikeable follower, one gets strength from caring-about one's duty and identity as leader. Proposing that duty-based care is probably morally sufficient for leaders (though not as emotionally satisfying for followers), Joanne suggests that leaders' moral conflicts reflect the ways in which leadership itself is socially constructed. Ultimately, leading with care means acting in accordance with constructions of social and institutional duty more than by the dictates of the heart.

In our next chapter, *Yiannis Gabriel* presents a psychodynamic view of caring leadership through the eyes of followers, proposing that followers' expectations are rooted in fantasy and myth, along with early-life experiences that leave enduring, if mostly unconscious, traces. The caring leader is associated with the maternal archetype, evoking followers' desire to feel connected, cherished and special. Like good mothers, caring leaders are expected to be genuinely concerned with followers' well-being, and prepared to go beyond the call of duty on their behalf. In family and organisation alike, too intense a care for one's children can stifle their growth and lock them in dependency, apathy and immaturity; and too much favouritism for one's own children over others can result in nepotism. The maternalist roots of care may appeal to our primal need to belong, but they also invoke the distortions and abuses of familial power.

The connection with the archetypal family also underpins *Gerardo Abreu Pederzini's* chapter on caring leadership through the prism of evolutionary theory, whereby life evolves as the endurance of some genetic instructions over others. From this perspective, attentiveness from parent to offspring – from leader to follower – is seen as one of the behavioural traits selected for its strategic evolutionary usefulness. Any connection between caring leadership and genuine feeling or concern is, therefore, a trick of nature. This trick is played on both leaders and followers, making the former able and willing to care and the latter open to receiving and responding to care. In a phenomenal feat of magic realism, we are drawn to the idea of caring leadership, because we have to try to make sense of reality in ways that make its evolutionary brutality tolerable. However, the feelings associated with both giving and receiving care are genetic ruthlessness masquerading as love.

Amanda Sinclair and *Donna Ladkin* explore the embodied dimensions of caring leadership. If care involves anticipating and meeting the needs of both self and others, then many of these needs originate with the gendered body. Caring leaders tap into the wisdom of their bodies through experiences such as gut-feel, and use this corporeal data to guide their actions and decisions. Connecting with feminist care ethics, Amanda and Donna argue that attending to the body is not some 'airy fairy' alternative to 'proper' leadership in the cut and thrust of the institutional world. Rather, feelings of care foster meaning, connection, common purpose and moral maturity, especially during times of trouble. Through embodied care, we might disrupt what the authors call the disembodied logic and mental mastery of mainstream leadership discourse, which privileges tools and checklists over an appreciation of the visceral demands of being a leader, and the often gut-wrenching conflicts between claims on a leader's care.

Part III: The Risks of Care: Dependency, Exploitation and Vulnerability

The chapters in this part consider whether care creates, reinforces and legitimises inequality or disadvantage for followers, exposing the problems of both too little and too much care. They reflect on the possibilities for a leadership which recognises differences of capability and experience, but without impoverishment or exploitation.

Carol Atack draws on Plato and Xenophon to explore the analogy of the shepherd king and his flock – a relationship depicted explicitly as one of caring, but potentially exploitative, leadership. Reflecting on the eternally complex interplay of power, agency and well-being, she asks how much followers can and should exchange autonomy and agency for the experience of being led well. The contrast between human and animal flocks exposes crucial issues for leader/follower relations, including the significance of consenting to be led and the distinction between articulated and assumed needs. Carol highlights the intriguing paradox of Athenian society, notionally based on equality (amongst free men, that is), being more, rather than less, concerned with the qualities of the individual leader: the more we seek to distribute power, the greater the requirement to examine what we need from our leaders. And in the Socratic shift from the person of the leader to the craft of leadership, there is a fascinating foreshadowing of contemporary debates about 'leaders' versus 'leadership'.

Mapping the leader/follower dynamic onto the relationship between legal trustees and beneficiaries, *Helen Mussell* highlights how the fiduciary relationship – often referred to as a duty of care – is premised on an unequal distribution of power. Trustees have traditionally not been required to consult with their beneficiaries, but can simply assume what their needs might be, reflecting a benign paternalism at best and a profound exploitation of the already disenfranchised at worst. Through a fiduciary lens, care is implicated *both* in subjugation (through its historical association with women and children, deemed incapable of economic agency and hence in need of care) *and* in the possibility of liberation. Drawing on feminist legal philosophy, Helen explores leaders' obligation to *care well*, that is, to exercise their influence in ways which neither assume nor institutionalise the beneficiary's inferiority. With increasing shareholder activism demanding greater consultation in legal and financial fiduciary matters, this is a call for care ethics without exploitation.

Liz and *Ben Sawyer* focus on the costs for followers of insufficient or inadequate care. Drawing on Ben's first-hand experiences of army leadership, including in Northern Ireland, Iraq and Afghanistan, they reflect on what it means for military leaders to care, both in and beyond combat. They connect with the psychiatrist, Jonathan Shay's work with soldiers with post-traumatic stress disorder (PTSD), which juxtaposes the ancient myth of Homer's *Iliad*, and the figure of Achilles in particular, with modern veterans' narratives of vulnerability. From this standpoint, they suggest that one of the most damaging aspects of followers' experiences is the notion of 'moral injury', which can occur when carelessness is intertwined with injustice. Caring leadership involves the ethical responsibility to prevent, or at least minimise, moral injury; and, if someone has suffered such injury, the caring leader must help them towards recovery by ensuring that justice is both done and seen to be done.

In the final chapter in this part, *Jen Jones* presents a reading of Kafka's *Metamorphosis* to underscore the dangers of the power asymmetries of care. Kafka's protagonist, Gregor Samsa, wakes up one morning to find himself transformed into an enormous insect. Drawing on Hazel Barnes' existentialist philosophy, Jen explores this development as Gregor's punishment for having cared-for his family in bad faith. As leader of the family unit, he has made them unhealthily dependent on him, denying them the space to work things out for themselves. What has been delivered in the name of care, and presumed, therefore, to be for the sake of others, has turned out to be precisely not in their interests. Paradoxically, Gregor becomes ethically human and able to relate to others only when he is ontologically no longer human. Despite his apparently good intentions, Gregor's fate reveals the agony and absurdity of the distortions of care, and of having cared-for, but not really cared-about.

Part IV: The Caring Leader at Work: Security, Sacrifice and Self

These chapters consider how leaders' care both underpins and undermines their own and other people's security – political, physical and psychological. Recalling care ethicists' discussions of the morality of self-sacrifice, they reflect on care as a kind of power-over self.

Michèle Lowrie explores the relationship between care, security and power in Vergil's epic poem, the *Aeneid*. Aeneas, the Trojan prince and founder of Rome, is a paradigmatic leader, whose successes and failures stand for the moral, political and psychological challenges of empire. With Aeneas' leadership, national security is at once pursued and undermined through care; the Latin for security (*securitas*) means being without care (*se* + *cura*). Exposing the force of care in its absence, that is, as the care*less* opposite of tending and the care*free* opposite of anxiety, Aeneas' leadership reveals security to be at once necessary, impossible and dangerous. Although national security is at stake, it is impossible to be permanently care*free* and dangerous to be care*less*. When Aeneas sacrifices both his own and Queen Dido's feelings for the sake of the mission, this 'se + curity' sows the seeds for Rome's future political crises. The warning that security measures may backfire – and precisely because of the conflict of cares within – has an arresting contemporary resonance.

In our next chapter, *Charlotte von Bülow* and *Peter Simpson* use Keats' concept of negative capability and a particular reading of Foucault's care of the self to discuss the leadership of a prison governor, responsible for the security of prisoners, officers, public and self. Connecting with care ethicists' accent on attentiveness, they emphasise the *quality* of this attention, seeing care as an attitude of both receptiveness and inquiry which entails living with paradox, uncertainty and mystery. Effective leadership involves visceral attunement to atmosphere, and the containment of people's emotions, including anger and despair. Through the prism of self-care, this requires an asceticism which is not about abstinence, so much as honing the capacity to *be or do without*. This means leading without the power-to remove anxiety and risk, and sacrificing the security afforded by so-called best, that is, universal, practice. For Charlotte and Peter, this is leadership 'on the pulses', not 'by the book'.

Liz Gloyn draws on Seneca's Stoic philosophy to consider the relationship between care and *clementia* (an idea more nuanced than the English clemency), on which Seneca bases his 'leadership development' of the Emperor Nero. For Seneca, *clementia* is crucial as a check on absolute power, that is, as a way for power to unfold, somewhat counterintuitively, through not being exercised. Connecting with distinctions between power-over and power-to, Liz proposes the power-to-not as a way of crystallising the interplay of *clementia* and care. Such power-to-not is nurtured through care (both for/about and from others), and practised through the self-restraint of *clementia*. Care is thereby implicated in symmetry, because it helps to deliver fairness and justice, but also in asymmetry, because it reinforces the absolute dominion of the Emperor, keeping him secure from the threat of rebellion or assassination. Both *clementia* and care are thus vital, if paradoxical, sources and stabilisers of power.

In the final chapter in this part, *Peter Bloom* draws on the philosophy of Jean-Paul Sartre to reflect on leadership, care and existential freedom. Taking care is the ability to choose how one lives in a socially and institutionally constructed world, and not be trapped in a socially prescribed identity or condition. This existential care of the self is contrasted with Sartre's particular articulation of bad faith, which is the continual embrace of a life and a self that one has not chosen freely. From this perspective, the caring leader is not some pastoral figure associated with religion or any other prohibition on morality. Rather, caring leaders use care as *resistance* to proscription, leading the way for both themselves and others to explore their own evolving priorities and concerns. Taking care of our existential self means securing the freedom to choose both who we are today and who we could be in the future.

Part V: Reshaping the Contours of Leadership: Relationship, Community and Democracy

The chapters in this part see care as fundamentally relational. This refers to relationships between people, but also between ideas, highlighting that the way we structure and legitimise knowledge is itself a practice of power. The authors engage with care ethics to cross boundaries and dissolve binaries, including binary distinctions between leaders/followers, ethics/politics and particular/ universal.

Ann Cunliffe and *Matthew Eriksen* discuss the education of caring leaders, suggesting that the way we organise knowledge about human beings is fundamental to management education as a moral endeavour. An objectivist approach, seen in discourses of Human Resources and typologies of leadership competences, means that we categorise, generalise and measure people in ways that are care*less*. A more care*ful* approach is subjectivist, focusing on the human being as a person, not a resource, a role or a thing. Ann and Matthew argue for an *intersubjective* approach, which focuses not only on the human being, but the human being in relation with others. Crystallising this as 'relational leadership', they suggest that care invigorates leaders' efforts to be attentive to others as they individually *are*, rather than in terms of their categorisation. An ethics of care emphasises our collective uniqueness, where each person is seen as deserving of particularised attention, but is also embedded in community, with responsibilities towards, and expectations of, others.

Collective responsibilities also underpin *Rita Gardiner's* chapter on the contrasting care philosophies and experiences of Hannah Arendt and Martin Heidegger. Rita makes Heidegger her 'fall guy', suggesting that his stint as university leader made him the ultimate 'transformational leader' in his emphasis on mission and vision, drawing on discourses of excellence and ambition which feel strikingly contemporary. But Heidegger's leadership was an unqualified disaster, for he was unable or unwilling to put his majestic vision to one side to attend to the human and the mundane. Rita considers

Arendt a better exemplar of caring leadership, with her concern for collective well-being over singularity of vision. From an Arendtian perspective, deconstructing our institutions into the binary of 'leaders' and 'followers' is a particular risk for 'followers', who are assumed to be more interchangeable than 'leaders', who are supposedly more special. But it creates categories out of all of us, denying us the possibility of giving and receiving care as humans, each of us unique in a plural world.

Vinca Bigo examines three persistent binaries in Western conceptualisations of leadership and care: mind/body, self/other and action/non-action. She engages with Eastern philosophies of non-separation in the Advaita Vedanta, a school in Hinduism, to explore caring leadership as a way of being, a practice of self and a profound commitment to others. This involves accepting that distinction and polarity are illusionary and temporary representations of a single underlying consciousness. From this perspective, leaders are inseparable from followers, which means caring for both ourselves and others without differentiation. Tracing connections between Vedantic philosophy and the European phenomenologists, Heidegger and Merleau-Ponty, along with other Eastern traditions of Daoism and Zen Buddhism, Vinca argues that transcending binaries is particularly challenging in a world which privileges the mind and those senses which are apparently located in the head. Through Advaita Vedanta, grasping the deeply relational nature of the world is a very real condition for caring both for and about it.

Engaging head-on with the 'leadership, not leaders' debate, *Iain Munro* and *Torkild Thanem* consider the possibility of care and organisation without leaders. They are critical of the ways in which the 'caring leader' has been absorbed into managerialist ideology, reinforcing hierarchical organisation and a paternalist, pastoral and exploitative understanding of care. Drawing on the philosophy of Spinoza, they explore the idea of 'affective leadership', which involves fostering our collective capacities to act and care for one another. Such capacities are stifled by an emphasis on the qualities of individual leaders, and more likely to flourish in leader*less* organisations. Grounding their arguments in social movements, including the anti-Vietnam protests, the Occupy movement, and Black Lives Matter, they argue that these organisations may have been formed in response to injustice, but they transform the pain of injustice into joyous affect and action. For Iain and Torkild, this shows what the relationship between care and justice can be when it is leader*less*.

Donna Ladkin draws on the work of social reformer, Jane Addams, to consider an ethics which is not universal in the sense of abstract principles, but rather, a universal commitment to social justice. For Addams, care is not care unless it results in action. Moreover, action should be based on a genuine attempt to discover, not assume, what other people need, want or would find comforting. This entails loosening the hold of the familiar to actively seek out difference, thereby breaking the connection between particular and familiar which harks back to care's roots in the family. Rather than seeing equality and particularity as binary opposites, caring leadership involves working with what makes people *both* equal *and* special. This takes curiosity, creativity, courage, resilience and, as Addams' own experience suggests, an acceptance that care does not necessarily make one popular. This final chapter in our collection offers a hard-hitting, but profoundly optimistic take on caring leadership. In suggesting that any one person's problem is a problem for us all, Addams' care ethics becomes the very life-blood of democracy.

REFERENCES

Alvesson, M. and Einola, K. (2019). Warning for excessive positivity: Authentic leadership and other traps in leadership studies. *The Leadership Quarterly*, **30**(4), 383–95.

Cameron, K.S., Dutton, J.E. and Quinn, R.E. (2003). *Positive Organizational Scholarship: Foundations of a New Discipline*. San Francisco, CA: Berrett-Koehler.

Crevani, L., Lindgren, M. and Packendorff, J. (2010). Leadership, not leaders: On the study of leadership as practices and interactions. *Scandinavian Journal of Management*, **26**(1), 77–86.

Gabriel, Y. (2015). The caring leader – What followers expect of their leaders and why? *Leadership*, **11**(3), 316–34.

Lilius, J.M., Kanov, J., Dutton, J.E., Worline, M.C. and Maitlis, S. (2012). Compassion Revealed. In K.S. Cameron and G.M. Spreitzer (eds), *The Oxford Handbook of Positive Organizational Scholarship* (pp. 273–88). Oxford: Oxford University Press.

McAllister, D.J. and Bigley, G.A. (2002). Work context and the definition of self: How organizational care influences organization-based self-esteem. *Academy of Management Journal*, **45**(5), 894–904.

Noddings, N. (2002). *Starting at Home: Caring and Social Policy*. Berkeley, CA: University of California Press.

Tronto, J.C. (1993). *Moral Boundaries: A Political Argument for an Ethic of Care*. New York: Routledge.

PART I

Setting the scene: power, privilege and disadvantage

1.   Leadership, care and (in)justice

Leah Tomkins

In this chapter, I deepen the exploration of care and caring leadership as relationships of power. Connecting with care ethicists' discussions of the interplay between care and justice, I probe some of the ways in which care can involve and inscribe *in*justice. This provides some scene-setting for the book as a whole, because many of the chapters engage both explicitly and implicitly with the risk and/or reality of injustice, and how the dynamics of care can bring about advantage and disadvantage for both leaders and followers.

CARE AND JUSTICE

In recent decades, care theory has mostly been developed by feminist philosophers. Carol Gilligan is generally held to have mobilised contemporary interest in care ethics, portraying care as a feminine moral voice, which is grounded in commitment to relationship (Gilligan, 1982). This is contrasted with an ethics of justice, which involves an abstract, universal morality and a distinctively masculine voice. With Gilligan's moral voice of care, actions are motivated by a concern for how they will affect other people (will this person be upset by what I do?), rather than a concern for universal justice and impartiality (is this right or wrong?).

For many feminist writers in the 1970s and 1980s, interest in care arose from a concern about the amount of unpaid and unacknowledged work performed by women within the family. This work prevented women from pursuing careers outside the home and hence denied them access to economic and professional identity and autonomy. Such a state of affairs allowed care to be cast as a 'labour of love', and care-giving to be associated with material and political disadvantage. As Finch and Groves (1983, p. 2) suggest, the feminist writing in this era focused on 'the tension between women's economic independence (actual, potential or desired), and their traditional role as front-line, unpaid "carers"'.

With this association with women's unpaid labour, care ethics has a strong maternalist aspect, at least in its origins. However, care's roots in the home and with the mother-figure do not mean that this is the only domain it can either illuminate or inform (Noddings, 2002). The suggestion in the Introduction of Jeremy Corbyn as an apparently caring leader helps to make this point. Thus, the gender associations of care-giving are not uniquely maternal or even female. In several chapters in this book, care-giving is associated with (a usually, but not always, benign) paternalism, both at the level of society and at the level of the family. When care is cast as paternalism, the injustices experienced by women shift from the disadvantages of care-giving to those of care-receiving; women move from being trapped in the home because they are *needed too much* to being trapped in socially constructed identities of inequality, where they are positioned as *being in need*. Whether giving or receiving care, justice seems to be particularly illusive for women.

Gilligan's distinction between the female and male moral voice put the relationship between care and justice onto centre stage of social and institutional theory. Gilligan originally developed care ethics explicitly in contrast to justice, highlighting care as a concern for the particular, as opposed to justice as a concern for the universal. Others have queried such a contrast, arguing that emphasising care as a wholly particularist, contextual morality deprives both care-givers and care-recipients of their rights, making it difficult to disentangle care, exploitation and even abuse. Theorists of care as political orientation, such as Tronto (1993) and Held (2006), argue that valorising personal caring without simultaneously attending to issues of social justice means naturalising and legitimising women's place within the home, without the opportunities that should be afforded to all. Instead, care should be seen as an overall framework of social morality and maturity, within which justice is also applied. For instance, Engster (2007, p. 13) sees care as a general moral and political theory of obligation, which is 'equally accessible to both men and women and universally obligatory for all capable human beings'. From this perspective, justice is enabled through our attentiveness, appreciation, and feelings of commitment towards other people.

The interplay between the particularity of care and the universality of justice highlights the significance of power, not least because it highlights the power dynamics of the choice over who receives our attention and solicitude. Power is, of course, central to the question of leadership, and arguably the core concern of critical organisational scholars (Collinson, 2011). In exploring the nuances of power, critical scholars and care ethicists alike distinguish between a commandeering power-over, a facilitative power-to and a more collaborative power-with (Hartsock, 1983; Haugaard, 2012). There is also much contemporary interest in the Foucauldian notion of bio-power, in which power (and subjugation) are enmeshed with prevailing norms about the sort of person we are supposed to be, and where discourse regulates our internal feelings, not just our external performances as 'good leaders', 'good employees', 'good citizens', and so on (Alvesson and Willmott, 2002). All these aspects of power find an expression in the ways in which care is experienced, felt, resisted, normalised and legitimised, and in particular, whether it incorporates or stands in contrast to justice. Care can both empower and disempower care-givers and care-recipients. Care both gives and saps energy and the power-to make things happen; and it both grants and denies access to power in the form of resources. This takes us way past any sense that care is just about nice feelings, and into a world where care can make a forcible difference to how events unfold: 'Those adept in the skills of care, of defusing conflicts before they become violent, of settling disputes among those who cannot just leave but must learn to get along with one another, have much to teach peacemakers and peacekeepers in other domains.' (Held, 2006, p. 151).

CARE AND (IN) JUSTICE

Of crucial concern to these debates is the argument that care ethics produces and reinforces a power imbalance between those who provide and those who receive care, thereby creating a kind of *in*justice. Such injustice is usually assumed to be disadvantage or denigration for care-recipients who, by extension, are usually deemed to be followers in the leader/follower relationship. This concern is exacerbated by definitions of care based on identifying and addressing people's *needs*, and the often negative connotations of needs and neediness.

Reflecting on the issue of needs in relation to care and justice, Noddings (2015, p. 72) suggests that: 'Justice is a rights-based ethic and care is needs-based ... the concept of needs is more basic than that of rights. Indeed, it seems that rights begin as expressed needs (or wants) and become rights when claimants finally can exercise the power to satisfy their needs.' From this perspective, needs are the property of the disempowered, at least whilst they are experienced and perhaps acknowledged, but as yet unmet. Once a way has been found to satisfy such needs, the previously disempowered become empowered, and needs become rights. But care is thus a kind of *pre-justice*.

Of course, much depends on what we mean by 'needs'. One person's need is another person's wish, hope or expectation. As we know from the ubiquitous Maslowian hierarchy, not all needs have the same quality or motivational value: some are basic, and overlap with universal human rights, whereas others are more orientated towards individual satisfaction or fulfilment. And lest we assume that care is *necessarily* needs-based, we should remember the distinction between caring-for and caring-about. The former has strong associations with need (though not necessarily with morality, principles or love); the latter is not so clearly based on need (though more easily associable with morality, principles and love).

Grounding care in the concept of needs begs the question of how we truly *know* what other people need. It highlights the importance – and complexity

– of distinguishing between expressed and inferred or imagined needs. As Tronto (2015, p. 34) explains, 'there is a "politics of needs interpretation" that makes some needs politically disabling compared to others'. Several of the chapters in this book engage with the politics of a care which is offered – however good the intentions – based on the assumption rather than establishment of other people's needs, and with the risks thereof for both care-givers and care-recipients, both leaders and followers.

Tronto (1993), amongst others, emphasises that care-recipients should be involved in identifying and articulating their *own* needs, rather than having them assumed by others. This is an attractive argument, but it raises significant questions for how care ethics might inform relations between leaders and followers, or indeed, between other groups of people with unequal experience or capability, such as parents and children. As any parent will tell you, relying on a child's identification of need is likely to result in ice-cream, not broccoli! My six-year-old nephew, Charlie, frequently assures me that he *really needs* chocolate!

Bubeck (1995) argues that the needs which are met through care are precisely those things that a person cannot do for him/herself. An activity – however kind or considerate – does not count as care if it is something which a healthy adult is capable of doing for him/herself, at least in principle. For Bubeck (1995, p. 132), this means that:

> The housewife cooking a meal for her husband is providing a service, whilst her cooking the same meal for an infant would be care ... [The needs of care] are absolute in that they make those in need necessarily depend on others. Thus a child cannot bring herself up, nor can a bedridden person provide food for herself, nor can somebody in need of talking a problem over with somebody talk to herself.

Bubeck's definition causes difficulties for the concept of self-care, which becomes oxymoronic; but it helps to ground discussions of care in the concept of dependency, highlighting the power dynamics of a relationship where one person depends on another for things that he/she perhaps cannot do alone. On the surface, at least, such dependency dynamics seem to lead inescapably to relations of inequality and disadvantage, with care-givers necessarily more powerful, privileged, capable and/or insightful than care-recipients. The emphasis on care-recipients' dependency triggers associations with inadequacy or inferiority, especially when applied to adults (for infants and, to a lesser extent, the elderly, are somewhat more exempt from the stigma of dependency). This is one of the most persistent concerns amongst theorists working with care ethics, both in the specifically caring professions and in broader social, political and institutional relations.

INJUSTICE FOR FOLLOWERS?

Associations between care, needs/neediness, dependency and inferiority help to explain the caution, even suspicion, that some critical organisational scholars have about applying care ethics to leadership relations. The concern is captured in the notion of 'asymmetry' in the relationship between leaders and followers, which is usually assumed to invoke privilege for the former and injustice (whether actual or potential) for the latter.

For many critical scholars, one of the biggest problems in contemporary institutional life is that individual leaders have been given too much power and licence, and allowed to believe that the rules which apply to others do not apply to them. Tourish (2013) highlights the particular case of 'transformational leadership' as an approach which legitimises an extraordinary concentration of power and agency in the hands of the special few, who accept their mission to 'transform' the world and the people around them. Such concentrated, almost messianic power makes it more likely that relations between leaders and followers will involve exploitation of the latter by the former. From this perspective, *any* theory that formalises, strengthens or naturalises the individual leader's superior position is bound to come under suspicion from critical scholars. The asymmetries of care feed such suspicion in spades.

Concerns about the ethical ramifications of leader-centric approaches have contributed to a burgeoning 'post-heroic' perspective in leadership studies, including 'distributed' (Gronn, 2002) and 'shared' (Pearce and Manz, 2005) leadership. They have inspired calls for the study of 'leadership, not leaders' (Crevani et al., 2010) and the 'leaderful' organisation (Raelin, 2011). Such approaches urge us to see organisational power as something which unfolds in interactions *between* people, suggesting that leadership involves something other than simply what an individual leader does (or is). Both tacitly and explicitly, they problematise asymmetry between leaders and followers.

The contributors to this book take different positions on this issue of care's asymmetry and its disadvantages for followers as care-recipients. Some are sceptical about any ethical system based on the assumption of need/neediness, however benignly felt or expressed. In this, they connect with social theorists, especially those concerned with disability rights, who contest the concept of care for valorising those who provide care over those who receive it, and for the resulting pernicious construction of care-recipients as lacking agency, that is, as not quite fully human.

Others – myself included – engage with care ethics precisely to expose and scrutinise the asymmetries of power, and to frame our thinking in ways which *recognise* differences of capability, expertise, experience and need, but without impoverishment or exploitation of the care-recipient, or follower.

An ethics of care should not have to either assume or reinforce the passivity or inferiority of the care-recipient; that is, the need for (or indeed, enjoyment of) care does not necessarily have to be equated with inadequacy. From this perspective, care ethics might help us to move past simplistic binary assumptions of leaders with all the power and privilege, and followers with all the disadvantage and exploitation.

Amongst care ethicists, a range of propositions have been offered for a care which is fundamentally empowering rather than disempowering. For instance, Tronto (2015) sees care as a political philosophy geared towards social transformation, which is less heroically constructed than its organizational counterpart, 'transformational leadership'. Because care is something we *all* need and experience at some stage in our lives, it is precisely through care that we approach the question of democracy. In other words, the very nucleus of care is something universal and equal, and therefore potentially a force for, not against, fairness, equivalence and justice.

Confronting the apparent paradox of democracy's emphasis on equality and care's emphasis on inequality, Tronto suggests that any *particular* act of care is necessarily unequal between care-giver and care-recipient, but that we should hope and expect to even this out across a life-time:

> What makes care equal is not the perfection of an individual caring act, but that we can trust that over time, we will be able to reciprocate the care we received from fellow citizens, and that they will reciprocate the care we've given to them. In such an ongoing pattern of care, we can expect moral virtues to deepen: We will trust in one another and in our social and political institutions. (Tronto, 2015, p.14)

For Tronto, therefore, the path to justice lies in acknowledging that we *all* have a right to receive care, not just in the obvious sense that we all need care in infancy and old age, but more broadly, that we deserve to be cared-for/ cared-about even as adults who are also capable of independent agency, responsibility and indeed, leadership.

In a complementary vein, Kittay (2013) argues that policies based on principles of equality have not actually helped to lessen disadvantage or injustice, and that we should develop more nuanced understandings of human dependency rather than trying to theorise or wish it away. She challenges us to interrogate why we so despise dependency, recalling how, when US presidential candidate, Mitt Romney, labelled roughly half the population 'dependent', 'the remark was widely perceived as an insult significant enough to negatively influence the outcome of his presidential bid' (Kittay, 2015, p. 54). In denying that we are sometimes dependent on others, 'we might as well decry our dependence on air' (*ibid.*). This is not to romanticise dependency, nor to deny that the experience of dependency often involves anger, frustration and helplessness. However, there are also positive aspects, such as the way in which dependency can be enmeshed in feelings of belonging. Dependency is not always easy, but it is not to be denied.

Kittay proposes the expression 'dependency work' to capture the experience of attending to those who need us. 'Dependency work' is less emotive than 'care', and perhaps more accurately and pragmatically focused on what is actually involved. When cast as 'dependency work', the dynamic is one of responsibility towards the other person, but one which differentiates between power and domination. Recalling the notion of power-with rather than power-over, harm can be done if *either* partner in the relationship abuses this moral and emotional contract, highlighting the vulnerability of *all* our human relations – both in dependency and in 'dependency work'. Rather than presuming, asserting or hoping that everyone is always equally capable and independent, Kittay's challenge is to distinguish between those inequalities that are inevitable and possibly productive, and those which are not inevitable and should therefore be resisted.

Both Tronto and Kittay offer a powerful counterbalance to assumptions that the vulnerability of care only applies to the less overtly powerful in social and institutional life. Both highlight the *mutual* responsibility for care which, extrapolated into the realm of organisations, means that followers are also accountable for how care is – or is not – put into practice, and whether its manifestation is closer to justice or injustice. Moreover, their work draws attention to the care that leaders themselves need, and poses important questions for how we might even out the experiences of giving and receiving care for everyone in our organisations and institutions.

INJUSTICE FOR LEADERS?

Instead of assuming that asymmetry automatically privileges leaders, we should reflect on how care might involve disadvantage, even injustice, for leaders. Seen in terms of Kittay's 'dependency workers', leaders are not only required to respond sensitively and capably to followers' dependency, but can themselves be made dependent by virtue of their dedication to this work; and it is conceivable that we might call this exploitation, even abuse. This is a somewhat contentious line to take in critical organisational theorising, but it is one worth examining if we are to work towards more collectively satisfying organisational relations.

Here, discussions amongst care ethicists help to frame the issue very powerfully. It is much easier to envisage how care-givers in the domestic sphere might be exploited in their care work than to suggest that organisational leaders might be exploited or exploitable in a similar way. Whilst we rarely, if ever, hear commentators say 'oh, that poor leader', thinking or hearing 'oh, that poor carer' feels much more likely. That care can be a burden which risks erasing a care-giver's sense of independent self is hardly news to anyone who has ever been in a care-giving role, whether for a child, an elderly parent or somebody else in our lives who is in need of help, especially of the hands-on, caring-for variety.

Indeed, one of the earliest objections in the modern care ethics movement was that care-giving is a kind of 'slave morality', which legitimises the oppression of women and other socially or economically disadvantaged groups. The notion of care as 'slave morality' draws on the philosophy of Frederick Nietzsche, who held that oppressed groups often develop moral theories that construct their own subservience and self-sacrifice as virtue. Drawing on this Nietzschean theme, Card (1990) argues that a sharp differentiation between care (valorising the particular and the proximal) and justice (venerating the universal) can distort ethics by endorsing closeness, familiarity, similarity and relatedness and thereby promoting racism, xenophobia and a disregard for the Other. Rather than encouraging an openness to the world, therefore, care ethics can *isolate* the care-giver from the world, practically, psychologically and politically. This pushes what happens between care-giver and care-recipient 'behind closed doors' and subject to idiosyncratic, private rules rather than general standards of relationship and behaviour. When we are enveloped in such idiosyncrasy and particularity, the idea of care-giving as being so attuned to another person that we can see the world through his/her eyes no longer feels like the mark of healthy empathy, emotional generosity and mutual understanding. Instead, it reminds us of what slaves and servants do: 'We can take up the perspective of others out of sheer necessity for survival, the necessity to anticipate others' needs in order to be a good servant or slave, for example. Women learn well to do this with men; slaves have learned well to do it with masters.' (Card, 1990, p. 106).

Seen this way, extolling care as an ethical ideal risks trapping people in unhealthy relationships from which neither side can escape, at least, not without censure. A relationship's positive public face can mask misery behind the scenes. Walking away from care may feel like it is a personal, ethical failure, but it is better to do this than allow oneself to be exploited through the relationship. Leaders can walk away more readily than domestic 'slaves', of course, but it is probably never easy. Thus, care-giving may only superficially be something that enriches our relationship with the world, and instead may operate as a kind of false consciousness that equates virtue with self-sacrifice.[1]

Within contemporary organisations, how might such slavery, self-sacrifice and false consciousness come about for caring leaders who, by virtue of their position, are supposed to be the ones with power, and sometimes too much of it? As I suggested above, it is unusual to detect much sympathy for leaders, especially in critical scholarly circles. In my view, however, we should suspend our hostilities towards leaders and try to understand the complexities of their work, rather than continue to use leaders as handy scapegoats for all our projected disappointments and frustrations with the world. Leaders are not an economically or politically disadvantaged group in the same way that women have historically been oppressed through the gendered domesticity of care-giving; but leaders might well be *emotionally* exploited through the care relationship. The 'slavery' experiences of care-givers brought to life by Card (1990) and others illuminate the isolation and stress that leaders can experience, but which usually go unremarked. Just as care-givers sometimes live in survival-mode, trying to anticipate and meet a care-recipient's demands, reasonable or otherwise, so leaders are often also in survival mode, especially in regimes of extensive employee consultation, engagement and empowerment.

Elsewhere (Tomkins, 2019), I argue that promoting 'leadership, not leaders' in theories such as distributed and shared leadership feeds a therapeutic fiction. It heralds the possibility of collective empowerment amongst all organisational members, and the creativity and innovation that such empowerment is said to foster. However, it also masks the considerable work undertaken *by leaders* to make distributed leadership seem possible. Invoking Badaracco's (2002) 'quiet leader', who implements strategy through barely noticeable nudges rather than grand gestures, I argue that just because such efforts are subtle or surreptitious does not mean that 'leadership' has replaced 'leaders'. Indeed, discourses of follower empowerment and inclusivity risk creating another kind of disadvantage, namely leaders who, when exercising their responsibility and expertise, must *also* make the workings of at least some of this responsibility and expertise invisible. So, whilst critical colleagues argue that 'employee empowerment' is a neo-liberal fiction, whose victims are organisational members absorbing an excessive, individualised pressure and guilt, I suggest that this is a fiction which panders to fantasies of symmetry and equality, whose victims are often leaders.

Just as care-givers may feel trapped and unable to walk away from relationships of abuse (because care is such an unimpeachable moral good), so leaders (and leadership scholars) risk censorship if they do not support 'leadership, not leaders' (because employee empowerment is such an unimpeachable and progressive institutional good). Just as Card's (1990) servants are hyper-alert to the mood-music of their masters, so contemporary 'masters' of organisation must stay hyper-alert to the mood-music of their increasingly empowered stakeholders. The therapeutic fiction of 'employee empowerment' allows us to critique care's asymmetry on behalf of followers, but often masks the costs of asymmetry for leaders.

Many of the chapters in this book wrestle with the power asymmetries of caring leadership. Particularly relevant for my argument here is Yiannis Gabriel's discussion of leaders as the product of followers' projections and fantasies, based on archetypes of father and mother (Chapter 3). From this perspective, followers' demands of their leaders are based on primal emotions, and have no obligation to be reasonable, logical or mature. Followers' anxieties and fantasies often collide, leaving both parents and leaders having to absorb and contain whatever emotional theatrics are projected onto them.

It strikes me that the loneliness – indeed, slavery – of the leader lies in having to sustain and tolerate followers' fantasies of symmetry and empowerment (fuelled by discourses of 'leadership, not leaders'), whilst remaining able and willing to restore fantasies of containment and protection, as required. Followers enjoy symmetry *qua* empowerment when things are going well, and asymmetry *qua* protection when they are not. If leaders get this protection/ emancipation balance wrong, they either become too interventionist and directive, shattering fantasies of equality; or they become too distant and *laissez-faire*, leaving them vulnerable to the charge of not caring (Tomkins and Simpson, 2015). For me, the central paradox of caring leadership is enveloped in these constantly shifting dynamics of symmetry/asymmetry, indeed, of justice/care. Caring leaders have to be hyper-alert to this mood-music, making their 'dependency work' complex, exhausting and lonely.

Moreover, if the roots of care lie in the family, then followers may unconsciously feel entitled to special benefits of family membership, such as unconditional loyalty, favouritism and patronage. Through this prism, followers not only expect their leaders to be genuinely concerned for their well-being; they also expect to be given preferential treatment over those who do not belong to this particular family unit. If organisational members, encouraged by discourses of distributed and shared leadership, absorb the specialness of care *and* the equality of justice, no wonder our organisations are spaces of such conflict, contradiction and disappointment, with ample opportunity for *in*justice throughout.

Furthermore, I think that care ethics helps to make sense of some of the antipathy towards leaders in certain academic quarters. By highlighting care as attention to the particular and the proximal, care emphasises the comfort of relationships of familiarity. Just as Card (1990) worries that care ethics promotes xenophobia, so critical scholars' hostility to corporate leaders may be because, by dint of their unfamiliarity, these leaders are cast as Other. This is one of many arguments for greater dialogue between academia and practice, so that scholars might develop greater empathy for the challenges of leadership in practice, and practitioners might benefit from the ways in which critical scholarship can expose their taken-for-granted assumptions, and foster potentially more ethical and more meaningful conversations about organisational dilemmas.

Leaders must, of course, take their fair share of the blame for what is wrong in our organisations and institutions. The experience of following can be intensely frustrating, disappointing and infantilising, and followers have to absorb their leaders' unresolved emotional theatrics as much as vice versa. But just as leaders should not be given all the credit for organisational success, they should also not be given all the blame for organisational failure. An ethics of care highlights the paradoxical and often unreasonable and irreconcilable demands of leadership, and the ways in which the dynamics of leader/follower relations involve continual tension between justice and injustice for all of us in institutional life.

NOTE

1. Whilst most commentators probably view self-sacrifice as problematic, Van Nistelrooij (2014) sees positive aspects of the sacrifices of care. If the self is ontologically one of interrelationship, then self-sacrifice can be part of a dignified and fulfilling identity construction. Self-sacrifice is no longer devotion to another person, but to the relationality that constitutes the care-giver's own self.

REFERENCES

Alvesson, M. and Willmott, H. (2002). Identity regulation as organizational control: Producing the appropriate individual. *Journal of Management Studies*, **39**(5), 619–44.

Badaracco, J. (2002). *Leading Quietly: An Unorthodox Guide to Doing the Right Thing*. Cambridge, MA: Harvard Business Press.

Bubeck, D.E. (1995). *Care, Gender, and Justice*. Oxford: Oxford University Press.

Card, C. (1990). Caring and Evil. *Hypatia*, **5**(1), 101–108.

Collinson, D. (2011). Critical leadership studies. In A. Bryman, D. Collinson, K. Grint, B. Jackson and M. Uhl-Bien (eds), *The SAGE Handbook of Leadership* (pp. 181–94). London: Sage.

Crevani, L., Lindgren, M. and Packendorff, J. (2010). Leadership, not leaders: On the study of leadership as practices and interactions. *Scandinavian Journal of Management*, **26**(1), 77–86.

Engster, D. (2007). *The Heart of Justice: Care Ethics and Political Theory*. Oxford: Oxford University Press.

Finch, J. and Groves, D. (1983). *A Labour of Love: Women, Work and Caring*. London: Routledge.

Gilligan, C. (1982). *In a Different Voice*. Cambridge, MA: Harvard University Press.

Gronn, P. (2002). Distributed leadership as a unit of analysis. *The Leadership Quarterly*, **13**(4), 423–51.

Hartsock, N.C.M. (1983). *Money, Sex, and Power: Toward a Feminist Historical Materialism*. New York: Longman.

Haugaard, M. (2012). Rethinking the four dimensions of power: Domination and empowerment. *Journal of Political Power*, **5**(1), 33–54.

Held, V. (2006). *The Ethics of Care: Personal, Political, and Global*. Oxford: Oxford University Press.

Kittay, E.F. (2013). *Love's Labor: Essays on Women, Equality and Dependency*. Abingdon: Routledge.

Kittay, E. (2015) Dependency. In R. Adams, B. Reiss and D. Serlin (eds), *Keywords for Disability Studies*. New York: NYU Press.

Noddings, N. (2002). *Starting at Home: Caring and Social Policy*. Berkeley, CA: University of California Press.

Noddings, N. (2015). Care ethics and 'caring' organizations. In D. Engster and M. Hamington (eds), *Care Ethics and Political Theory* (pp. 72–84). Oxford: Oxford University Press.

Pearce, C.L. and Manz, C.C. (2005). The new silver bullets of leadership: The importance of self- and shared leadership in knowledge work. *Organizational Dynamics*, 2(34), 130–40.

Raelin, J. (2011). From leadership-as-practice to leaderful practice. *Leadership*, 7(2), 195–211.

Tomkins, L. (2019). Leadership and the Art of the Invisible. In G. Abreu Pederzini (ed), *Considering Leadership Anew: A Handbook on Alternative Leadership Theory* (pp.59-72). Cambridge: Cambridge Scholars Publishing.

Tomkins, L. and Simpson, P. (2015). Caring leadership: A Heideggerian perspective. *Organization Studies*, 36(8), 1013–31.

Tourish, D. (2013). *The Dark Side of Transformational Leadership: A Critical Perspective*. Abingdon: Routledge.

Tronto, J.C. (1993). *Moral Boundaries: A Political Argument for an Ethic of Care*. New York: Routledge.

Tronto, J.C. (2015). *Who Cares? How to Reshape a Democratic Politics*. New York: Cornell University Press.

Van Nistelrooij, A.A.M. (2014). *Sacrifice. A Care-ethical Reappraisal of Sacrifice and Self-sacrifice*. Leuven: Peters Publishers.

PART II

The roots of care: kinship, feelings and bodies

2. Do leaders need to have tender hearts? Emotion and the duty to care

Joanne B. Ciulla

Several years ago, I gave a lecture on ethics and leadership at the University of Fort Hare in South Africa. After it, a student came up to me and told me that he could never be an ethical leader if it meant putting the interests of his followers before those of his family. We had a fascinating discussion about this fundamental conflict of interest between a leader's family and his or her constituents. I pointed out that one of the reasons we have leaders is to take responsibility for, promote, and look after the interests of a group, organization, or country. He said he understood the duties of a leader, which was why he could not be one or be an ethical one. For him, putting the interests of others before his family didn't feel right. He could not imagine caring for a group more than he cared for his family. Our brief conversation illustrates several intertwined questions in this chapter about leadership and care.

The chapter examines a leader's obligation to care for followers, even when that obligation conflicts with their feelings about their followers and/or their obligations to their families and loved ones. I argue that the ethical responsibility to care is a fundamental part of most socially constructed roles of leaders. Hence, feelings of care may not be as important to leaders as acting on their duty as leaders to care. The chapter begins by exploring the meanings of care and their moral implications. It then looks at the subjective and objective nature of care in feminist ethics of care and how it compares with ethics based on justice. Lastly, given the strengths and weaknesses of an ethic of care, I examine the question: Does a leader need a tender heart, or feel care to care?

THE MEANINGS OF CARING AND CURING

Let's start by looking at the meanings of care. When we use care as a noun, it denotes concern or anxiety as in, "She has many cares" or "She has no cares." The verb form of care often means solicitous, paying attention to, taking responsibility for, or even worrying about someone or something, as in "I care about her." Caring about someone may be different from caring for someone. "I care for her" might mean "I take care of her." However, it can also mean,

"I have feelings for her, or I like her." These three related meanings come together in the sentence, "I must care for her because I care about her because she has many cares." Or, "I must attend to her because I have feelings for her, and she has many concerns."

The word "care" comes from the Latin word *cura*, which is also the root of the word "cure." A central part of a leader's job involves curing in the sense of fixing problems, healing disputes, or comforting. Psychologist Erik Erickson (1982) says the human inclination to care is rooted in the impulse to caress someone who is in need or feels helpless and emits signals of despair. This impulse is the same disposition that leads mothers and fathers to pick up and stroke their screaming babies, even when the babies are not hurt or in danger. Writing from the perspective of a psychiatrist, Ronald A. Heifetz tells us, "In times of distress, we turn to an authority." (1994, p. 69). He says when under severe stress, the leader–follower relationship becomes a dependency relationship. In a good dependency relationship, meaning the kind that "cures," leaders help followers learn, adapt, and become empowered. A bad relationship may comfort but not cure the fears of followers, especially if it makes them dependent and willing to give up their freedom in exchange for a leader's protection. Philosopher Baruch Spinoza (1670 [2005], pp. 18–19) makes a similar point in his scathing criticism of tyrants and priests. He says that tyrants and priests "hoodwink their subjects" and mask their fear with the "specious garb of religion." This idea is not unlike Karl Marx, who famously said; "religion is the 'opiate of the masses' that keeps them from questioning or taking control of their lives. Spinoza's tyrants and priests exploit people's fear and 'sad passions' as a means of taking away the freedom of others and establishing their power." (Deleuze, 1988, p. 25, cited in Munro and Thanem, 2018). Hence, both whether and how a leader cares for followers has moral implications. Care that exploits fear cultivates dependency and makes people feel helpless. Such care is not a virtue because it does not bring about excellence. It is not the performance of a duty in the Kantian sense, because this kind of care does not come from a good will, does not show respect for the autonomy of followers or treat followers as ends in themselves (Kant, 1785 [1993]).

THE MYTH OF CURA, THE GOLDEN RULE, AND SLOTH

Besides its emotional, deontic, and curative meanings, care also denotes attentiveness or maintenance, that is, "I take care of him." In *Being and Time*, philosopher Martin Heidegger traces the origins of care to the fable of Care (Cura) by the Roman writer Gaius Julius Hyginus (BC 64–AD 17) (1535 [1976]). According to the fable, when Care was crossing a river, she picked up some mud and shaped it into a human figure. Jupiter happened to come by as she was admiring her creation. Care asked Jupiter if he would give her creation a soul, and Jupiter agreed. Then Care told him that she planned to name the figure after herself, but Jupiter objected and told her that she should name it after him. As the two of them argued, the Earth (Tellus) rose up and said, since Care made the figure from her, it should be named after her. Eventually, the three of them agreed to let Saturn decide who had a claim on the clay figure. Saturn ruled that after the creature died, Jupiter would take back its soul and earth would reclaim its body. However, since Care fashioned the first human being, she would attend to it while it lived (Heidegger, 1996, p. 184). In other words, Care would look after humans.

The myth demonstrates how care literally and figuratively makes us what we are and sustains us as human beings. Heidegger ties the idea of care (*Sorge*) to what it means to be or to exist. He uses the word "*Da-sein*" to mean "being there." Heidegger argues that we not only exist in time, but we exist first and foremost as beings with the capacity to be concerned about our being or self-identity. We are self-reflective in that we make sense of our ability to make sense of the world. However, humans do not exist by themselves. They exist amid a world of other people and things. For Heidegger, care is the uniquely human way of being in this world. It is the experience of care or attentiveness to the world that unifies the self and makes a person into an authentic human being. While Heidegger is looking at the broader philosophical question of "being," it is instructive to use his observations to think about why care is fundamental to what we are as humans, and how we understand our individual and collective morality (Solomon, 2001). Collective morality is vital to the issue at hand concerning leaders. Despite their titles and, in some cases, solipsistic beliefs, leaders are not leaders without followers. However, what sets leaders apart from others is that their role carries the expectation that they will take responsibility for and take care of a group, organization, community, or country. While moral obligations ought to apply to all parties, followers may or may not think that they have an obligation to take care of their leaders, depending on the context and their relationship to each other. The critical difference is that the idea of care, in the sense of attending to others, is implicit in most people's mental model of a leader. For example, it would seem crazy to select someone to be a leader who vowed not to take responsibility for or take care of an organization. (Granted, some leaders do this, but few say so out loud.)

One of the oldest and most pervasive moral principles in a wide variety of human cultures is the golden rule: "Do unto others as you would have others do unto you" or the silver version of it, "do not do unto others as you would not have them do unto you" (Wattles, 1996). The rule draws on empathy to guide moral behavior. It implies that people have similar basic wants and needs – for example, most people do not want others to harm them physically. The golden rule gives us guidance on how to treat people, but it does not capture what it means to care for or about them. Perhaps this is what makes it such a useful principle. Care requires attention, solicitude, and active involvement in a way that the golden rule does not. Unlike the golden rule, which is objective and ostensibly egalitarian, care usually entails having certain dispositions and feelings, and it can be highly subjective and selective.

In the *Bible*, care is so central to morality that the early writers made not caring one of the Seven Deadly Sins. Contrary to widespread usage, the sin of sloth, a loose translation of the Latin *acedia*, not only means lazy, it means apathy or failure to care. Evagrius, an Egyptian monk from the 300s, called sloth "the noonday demon" because it afflicted monks after a big lunch on a warm day, and made them listless when it was time to say their prayers. They sinned when they slothfully prayed to God, meaning they just went through the motions of praying without giving God the attention and enthusiasm that he deserved (Ciulla, 2000, p. 41). In a similar vein, St Thomas Aquinas describes *acedia* as a psychological or spiritual condition that causes morbid inertia and makes humans disdainful of and disinclined to do good works (Aquinas, 1270–74? [1995]). It also entails a kind of self-indulgence that makes people insensitive to the needs of others and apathetic to the obligations of their work. So, as we can see, sloth is the exact opposite of Care's duties in the myth of Cura.

WHO GETS PRIORITY?

We have looked at the meanings of care as a concern, a feeling, and attentiveness, and we touched on the assumption of care that is implicit in the role of a leader. Now let us return to the student from Fort Hare. His concern about being a leader is not about his ability to care, but about who had the first claim on his care. He felt that his moral obligations to his family would and should always come first, and he recognized that this is problematic for someone in a leadership role. We would not have much confidence in a presidential candidate who told us that she would always put her family's interests before those of the country. While we could imagine cases where this would be acceptable – such as canceling a meeting with a foreign dignitary because the president's child had a life-threatening accident – we might nonetheless think differently about the leader if she did this when the country was in the middle of a terrorist attack. These are some of the complex ethical and emotional conflicts of care that a leader could face. It is one of those areas where the moral obligations of leaders are different from those of people who are not in leadership roles.

On the one hand, we would not want leaders who fail to care for their families, while on the other hand, we do want leaders who can judge when caring for their followers ought to take priority over caring for their families. The student's moral commitment to family first may reflect differences in cultural values and traditions of leadership. Throughout history, many, or perhaps most, models of leadership were based on family. Dynasties of kings, emperors, tyrants, and other autocrats somewhat circumvent the conflict between family and country by aligning the family with their work and identity as leaders. In some cases, this has worked well, but democratic leadership and meritocratic organizational leadership both assume that leaders are supposed to put their interests first.

Another way to regard the conflict between caring for family and followers is as a trolley type moral dilemma. The famous trolley problem asks us to imagine that a trolley's brakes have failed, and it cannot stop. You have control of the switch that determines which way the run-away trolley will go. In one direction, there are five people tied to the track, and in the other direction, there is only one person tied to the track. The choice comes down to killing five people or one person (see Cathcart, 2013). At first glance, the utilitarian solution looks like the best option – save five lives and take one life. Like all ethical dilemmas, this is not necessarily a satisfying solution because someone still dies because of your actions. There is a sense in which we would like our leaders to think like utilitarians in such cases – sacrifice one follower to save five followers. This way of thinking may be well and good until the leader discovers that the one person on the track is her daughter. For the South African student, there is moral clarity about the choice. He would save his daughter because his feelings and obligation to care for her are greater than those he has for the five others. What would we think of a leader who did this? We might empathize with the leader's choice. He filled his moral obligation as a father, but did he make the right decision as a leader?

In the 1980s psychologist Carol Gilligan conducted a study about the way that young girls made moral decisions. She discovered that they progressed up Lawrence Kohlberg's scale of moral development more slowly than boys, which meant that it took them longer to engage in moral reasoning that was based on objective moral principles. Her research seemed to imply that girls were less ethical or ethically mature than boys. Unwilling to embrace this conclusion, Gilligan refined her study and found that women and girls thought about ethical problems "in a different voice" than men. Instead of reasoning from moral principles, girls were more concerned with relationships and contexts. When girls examined difficult ethical problems, they were more likely to consider the details of the situation, the relationships of the actors, and how they felt about each other, including whether they cared for each other. Putting aside the differences in Gilligan's and Kohlberg's empirical studies, the conclusions of their research rest on how they constructed their theories of ethics. Most philosophers would agree that moral decision making involves all of these things.

Kohlberg's view of ethics is utilitarian and deontic. John Stuart Mill was very clear about the objectivity of moral principles. In response to critics who said utilitarianism "renders men so cold and un-sympathizing: that it chills their moral feelings towards individuals" (Mill, 1987, p. 278), Mill replied that the minute you start making moral judgments based on who the people in the case are, then you are not making a complaint against utilitarianism but "against having a standard of morality at all" (*ibid.*). Immanuel Kant would agree with Mill for different reasons. According to Kant, ethics is about acting on duties, especially when an action that is demanded by a duty comes into conflict with what you feel inclined to do. So, if your duty as a leader is to save the five people who are your followers and kill your daughter, then you must fight your emotions and inclination to save your daughter and save the others. His categorical imperative also requires a leader to ask, what duty would you want all leaders to act on in this case, the duty to save five followers or the duty to save their daughter?

THE ETHICS OF CARE

Gilligan's findings were controversial because some critics construed them as reinforcing female stereotypes. Moreover, this subjective "female" view of ethics appeared to make women seem less desirable as leaders – that is, would you want to work for someone who made moral judgments based on his or her relationships and feelings for others? However, maybe the problem is not about the way women supposedly think about ethics, but with the way white Western men have socially constructed the dominant idea of leadership and ethics. The ethics of care emerged as a feminist philosophy in the twentieth century. Philosophers saw it as a counterweight to ethical theories that were based on categorical or universal imperatives. Feminist ethics evolved as a way of taking into account the interests of women in the private world, family, community, and relationships. Its emphasis on context, partiality, and responsibility is also a response to the masculine notion of ethics based on rules and impartiality (Jaeger, 1983). One strength of the feminist ethics of care for leadership ethics is that it recognizes that disparities of power influence how one applies moral principles (Ruddick, 1983).

Some of the basic ideas behind the ethics of care, such as the role of emotions, empathy, and sympathy, have deep roots in the history of philosophy. They are not necessarily feminine or masculine, but merely other aspects of moral philosophy. For instance, the Roman philosopher Seneca (1953) observed that rational behavior is only part of morality. He said humans were given reason so that they can achieve the good. They were given the capacity to care so that they can perfect the good. Søren Kierkegaard introduced the notion of care as a means of counteracting the excessive objectivity of philosophy in the early 20th century (Kierkegaard, 1958; Copleston, 1966). But the most essential philosophical background to the ethics of care was formed by the moral sense philosophers.

The moral sense theory is part of meta-ethics, which is concerned with the nature of ethics itself. Moral sense theorists maintain that the way most people distinguish between ethical and unethical behavior is by how they feel about it. Two notable moral sense philosophers are Thomas Hobbes and David Hume. Hobbes thought that people decided what was good and bad based on their appetites and self-interests, whereas David Hume held a more nuanced view about the role of feelings in moral judgment. Hume thought morality was a mixture of emotion (passion) and reason. He said that reason has insight but no agency, while passion has agency but no insight. Hume (1988; 1983) believed that imagination transforms our moral feelings, knowledge, and experiences into a moral obligation to others through sympathy or empathy. In particular, Hume contributes to feminist ethics of care in his discourse on how our love of family and friends influences our moral obligations and behavior. However, Hume's fundamental insight into the ethics of care is that feelings of care and concern are what motivate moral behavior. If this is true, then it might not be enough for leaders to care, in the sense of paying attention to followers and their duties; they may have to have the right sorts of feelings too. It is interesting to note how philosophers such as Hume and Seneca seem to mirror what neuroscientists know about moral reasoning. We use parts of our brains that are responsible for emotions to mediate moral decisions. Hence, in sociopaths, who do not have sympathy or empathy, the emotional parts of the brain do not function properly. Sociopaths know what is right and wrong, but they do not have the moral feelings necessary to act on what is right (see Pujol et al., 2011).

Some care ethicists, such as Nell Noddings, believe that feeling care is the motive for caring, and is central to the ethics of care. She says this motive is preeminent in families and central to the experiences of women (see Noddings, 1986). Others, such as Virginia Held, argue that you do not need to feel the emotion of care to care for someone. Held contrasts the ethics of care with the ethics of justice. She describes an ethic of justice as one that focuses on fairness, equality, individual rights, abstract principles, such as utility and duty, and the consistent application of them. For Held (2006), an ethic of care is about cultivating caring relations, attentiveness, responsiveness to need, and narrative nuance (which includes time and place). She says, "Whereas justice protects equality and freedom, care fosters social bonds and cooperation." (p. 15). These both sound like fundamental aspects of ethics; however, feminist ethics scholars do not agree on whether the ethics of care stands on its own or is a facet of other moral theories. I tend to think it's the latter.

DO LEADERS NEED TO HAVE TENDER HEARTS?

Building social bonds and fostering cooperation seem to be as fundamental to the role of a leader as they are to ethics. Hence, it might not be enough for leaders to care, in the sense of paying attention to followers and their duties; they may have to have the right sorts of feelings as well. But what if a leader does not have these feelings? What if the leader doesn't even like most of her followers? Is her leadership doomed? One could imagine such a leader playing favorites and ignoring the problems of individuals or groups that she finds repugnant. When leaders behave like this, they are unfair, and they lose the confidence of their followers, making it difficult for them to do their jobs well. Fortunately, most people in leadership roles try to care for all of their followers (albeit, sometimes with varying degrees of success). For instance, I sometimes have an obnoxious student that makes me feel like either ignoring him or maybe even punching him in the nose. However, I know that I have to take care of him in the same way that I care for my other students – answering his questions, grading his papers, and so on. In acting this way, I perform a very Kantian duty because I do my duty as a teacher and care for him, even though I do not feel like it. Hence, care is about more than concern for others; it is also about concern for what one does in the role that defines what one is.

We have been looking at the apparent tension between care as an objective moral concept like justice and fairness, and care as something subjective and based on emotion and/or social bonds. Care and morality, in general, seem to require both. This point leads us back to the original question of the chapter – a leader's obligation to care for followers over family or friends, regardless of how they feel about their followers. We want leaders to know what is right and wrong, but should we expect them to have the feelings necessary to care for their followers, when they do not know them, or empathize with them, or like them? What is a reasonable expectation of care from leaders? Maybe the student is right that it is unreasonable, and perhaps unethical, for someone to put the interests of followers over those of his family, but would you want someone who behaves that way to lead your country? These questions open up a can of worms about ethics and our implicit ideas of leadership. The roots of our moral priorities and obligations are both social and personal. Some would argue that even our personal obligations are heavily influenced by society (Wolfe, 1989). Since leadership is a socially defined role, its priorities and obligations are to some extent inscribed in the role. At the same time, leaders' moral priorities usually tend to align with their social priorities. The problem raised by the student is about what to do when these two priorities conflict both morally and emotionally.

It may be unrealistic to expect leaders to have finely honed feelings of care for their followers that would compel them to put followers' interests before those of their loved ones. This is rather like requiring that all leaders have charisma. Nevertheless, leaders have a duty to care for followers, in the sense of attending to their interests and the interests of the organization. Care based on one's duty or care that comes from feelings may both be morally sufficient, but probably not as emotionally gratifying to followers. Consider the difference between how the public perceived care in Princess Diana and Queen Elizabeth II. The Queen conveyed a strong sense of duty to care when she visited hospitals, for example, whereas the public perception of Diana was that she carried out her duties to care because of her feelings about others.

Some of the fundamental moral challenges of leadership involve controlling emotions, having utilitarian rather than personal inclinations, and caring for followers, even when a leader doesn't like them. In the *Republic*, Socrates says a true leader should serve the interests of his subjects, whereas a character in the dialogue named Thrasymachus argues that this kind of "just" leadership is not in the leader's self-interest. He says that a just leader's "private affairs deteriorate because he has to neglect them" and "he's hated by his relatives and acquaintances" for not serving their interests over those of others (Bk I 343-e2) (Plato, 1992, p. 20).

It would be best if leaders cared because of their feelings and sense of duty, but I argue that either motivation may be sufficient for filling their moral obligations and doing their job. Leaders' duties are determined by how to do their work ethically and effectively. As I have argued elsewhere, the ethics of leaders is inextricably tied to and embedded in the skills, knowledge, and competencies of leadership (Ciulla, 1995; see also Ciulla, 2004). Ideally, we want leaders that have feelings of care for other human beings; there is much to recommend in a leader with a strong sense of duty. The duties of leadership can be taught in ways that moral feeling cannot. Leaders may develop feelings of care by proximity to followers and the contexts in which followers live and work. They may also do so by developing relationships and interacting with a wide variety of followers. In short, I have been arguing that care is an objective duty in regard to the leader's role and a subjective one (involving feelings) in regard to various relationships and situations while in that role. So, leaders don't necessarily need to have tender hearts to care, but they do need to possess a strong sense of duty to care for all of their constituents, regardless of how they feel.

REFERENCES

Aquinas, St Thomas. 1995. *On Evil*. Translated by Jean T. Oesterle. Notre Dame, IN: University of Notre Dame Press.

Cathcart, Thomas. 2013. *The Trolley Problem, or Would you Throw the Fat Guy off the Bridge?: A Philosophical Conundrum.* New York: Workman Publishing.

Ciulla, Joanne B. 1995. "Leadership Ethics: Mapping the Territory." *The Business Ethics Quarterly*, **5** (1): 5–28.

Ciulla, Joanne B. 2000. *The Working Life: The Promise and Betrayal of Modern Work.* New York: Crown Business.

Ciulla, Joanne B. 2004. "Ethics and Leadership Effectiveness." in J. Antonakis, A.T. Cianciolo and R.J. Sternberg (eds), *The Nature of Leadership*, Thousand Oaks, CA: Sage Publications, pp. 302–27.

Copleston, Frederick. 1966. *Contemporary Philosophy: Studies of Logical Positivism and Existentialism.* Westminster, MD: Newman.

Deleuze, Gilles. 1988. *Spinoza: Practical Philosophy.* Translated by Robert Hurley. San Francisco, CA: City Lights Books.

Erickson, Erik H. 1982. *The Life Cycle Completed: A Review.* New York: W.W. Norton.

Heidegger, Martin. 1996. *Being and Time.* Translated by Joan Stambaugh. Albany, NY: SUNY Press.

Heifetz, Ronald A. 1994. *Leadership without Easy Answers.* Cambridge, MA: Harvard University Press.

Held, Virginia. 2006. *The Ethics of Care.* New York: Oxford University Press.

Hume, David. 1983. *An Enquiry Concerning the Principles of Morals.* Indianapolis, IN: Hackett.

Hume, David. 1988. *Treatise on Human Nature.* Edited by L.A. Selby-Bigge. Oxford: Clarendon Press.

Hyginus, C. Julius. 1535 [1976]. *Fabularum Liber.* New York: Garland.

Jaeger, Alison M. 1983. *Feminist Politics and Human Nature.* Totowa, NJ: Allanheld.

Kant, Immanuel 1785 [1993]. *Grounding for the Metaphysics of Morals.* Translated by James W. Ellington. Indianapolis, IN: Hackett Publishing Company.

Kierkegaard, Søren. 1958. *Johannes Climacus; or, De Omnibus Dubitandum Est; and A Sermon.* Translated by Thomas Henry Croxall. Paulo Alto, CA: Stanford University Press.

Mill, J.S. 1987. "What Utilitarianism is." In *Utilitarianism and Other Essays* edited by A. Ryan (pp. 272–338). New York: Penguin Books.

Munro, Iain and Thanem, Torkild. 2018. "The Ethics of Affective Leadership: Organizing Good Encounters Without Leaders." *Business Ethics Quarterly*, **28** (1): 53–69.

Noddings, Nel. 1986. *Caring: A Feminine Approach to Ethics and Moral Education.* Berkeley, CA: University of California Press.

Plato. 1992. *Republic.* Edited and translated by G.M.A. Grube.

Pujol, J., Batalla, I., Contreras-Rodríguez, O., Harrison, B.J., Pera, V., Hernández-Ribas, R., Real, E. et al. 2011. "Breakdown in the Brain Network Subserving Moral Judgment in Criminal Psychopathy." *Social Cognitive and Affective Neuroscience*, **7** (8): 917–23.

Ruddick, Sarah. 1983. "Maternal Thinking." In *Mothering: Essays in Feminist Theory.* Edited by J. Trebilcot. Totowa, NJ: Allanheld, pp. 213–30.

Seneca. 1953. *Seneca ad Lucilium Epistulae. Vol. 3 of Epistulae Morales.* Translated by Richard M. Gummere. Cambridge, MA: Harvard University Press.

Solomon, Robert C. 2001. *From Rationalism to Existentialism.* Lanham, MD: Rowman & Littlefield.

Spinoza, Baruch. 1670 [2005]. *Theological-Political Treatise*, Part I. Translated by R.H.M. Elwes. Project Gutenberg E-Book #989, Preface (18–19).

Wattles, Jeffrey. 1996. *The Golden Rule*. Oxford: Oxford University Press.

Wolfe, Alan. 1989. *Whose Keeper? Social Science and Moral Obligation*. Berkeley, CA: University of California Press.

3. The caring leader: an exploration of family archetypes

Yiannis Gabriel

Few issues have proven as enduring and contested as the moral standing of leaders – an issue that preoccupied some of the greatest political minds in history, from Plato to Machiavelli, and from Gandhi to Martin Luther King. The thorny question of whether leadership is essentially a moral concept remains highly contested. Can a successful leader be a morally flawed or even an amoral person? And if a leader is to be judged in the first instance as a moral agent, what Archimedean point of morality can act as the basis for such judgements?

In this chapter, I discuss the moral standing of leaders not from any particular philosophical or political vantage point, but rather from that of the followers. Followers, I will argue, expect leaders to be competent, just as they expect competence from other professionals. They expect them to be knowledgeable, to have visions, to build strong teams and so forth. Beyond these expectations, however, followers also expect their leaders to provide 'moral' leadership. Followers frequently judge leaders by standards of morality that are considerably harsher than those by which they judge other people, yet, paradoxically, followers may also forgive a leader's failings and sins that they would not forgive in others. As a result, leaders are often cast in black and white, viewed as either saints or devils. The chapter will demonstrate that the criteria used to judge leaders are rooted in fantasy and myth, as well as early life experiences that leave lasting residues. These elemental criteria are 'archetypes' (Jung, 1968), of which an especially significant one is that of the 'caring leader', epitomized in images like that of Christ as a good shepherd. Leaders, I argue, will always be judged by their followers against their ability *to demonstrate that they care.*

In light of this, the moral standing of leaders can be linked to the ethics of care, a perspective that has assumed increased currency in philosophy, psychology and politics, but not leadership studies. An ethics of care emphasizes the interrelatedness of human beings and highlights the importance of attentiveness, empathy, responsiveness and responsibility for others. Being cared-for is a fundamental aspect of every human's early life experience when

40

they are dependent on others for their survival and well-being and one that, in the view of care ethicists, later sets the moral compass for many people. I will conclude the chapter by highlighting how a responsibility to care for their followers leaves leaders with several fundamental dilemmas, including whether all followers should be treated equally or each should be treated according to their need.

GOOD LEADERS, BAD LEADERS

The distinction between good and bad leaders reveals a fundamental experiential dichotomy that sets leaders apart from other individuals or groups, like plumbers, therapists, or even managers. They, too, can be described as good and bad, but such distinctions are based on their professional competence, skills and abilities. Good leaders, on the other hand, are set apart from bad leaders not merely in terms of competence but in terms of their success or failure to live up to certain standards that are often unspoken and uncodified, different from those by which we would judge most other people. Thus, a deception, a change of mind or even a lie may be excusable in most people as temporary aberrations, but taint a leader's reputation for life. A leader's substantial achievements may be nullified by a single instance of unethical behaviour, calling into question his/her integrity and character.

If leaders are judged by stricter moral standards than other people, it is partly because their moral failings can easily translate into group and organizational failures. Authoritarian leaders who lack the courage to change course when circumstances change may cause major military or political disasters. Likewise, narcissistic leaders preoccupied with their image can precipitate organizational decay and death (Schwartz, 1990). All the same, it seems to me that our readiness to judge leaders from an ethical vantage point, the severity and even inconsistency of our judgements of leaders, and our feelings of betrayal and outrage when leaders are judged to have done wrong, point to something deeper and more fundamental. A leader may occupy a *position*, but this position is not only *an external one* at the head of a group or an organization; it is also an *internal* position in our minds, which demands to be occupied and whose occupant becomes the carrier of numerous powerful and unconscious fantasies. A leader embodies one of the cast of archetypes that populate our minds; someone who may be a saint in some plotlines, a devil in others, a devious schemer in others, and a sacrificial lamb in yet others. This is how we encounter the leader in myths, stories, fairy-tales and other narratives that give expression to collective fantasies. Archetypes, as Jung (1968) argued, are elements of humanity's great stream of ideas and images, surfacing from time to time in dreams, images, fantasies, ecstatic and other experiences.

Inspired by Jung, Moxnes (1999) argues that the characters of organizational narratives enact deep unconscious roles drawn from a relatively small cast of twelve archetypal figures whose origins lie in the essential family – father, mother, son and daughter. These deep roles recur regularly in organizational mythology and real individuals come to occupy these roles in specific narratives, thereby drawing on the symbolic power of the original archetype. A leader can then be experienced, after the father archetype, as benevolent god-like father or, alternatively, as devil. Under different circumstances, a leader may be experienced and narratively cast as prince (whether hero or clown). These archetypal light and dark sides of leadership have resurfaced recently in work by Kociatkiewicz and Kostera (2012), who demonstrate that the concept of a 'good manager' is inevitably drawn toward the shadow of tragedy. My own work (Gabriel, 1997) has explored narratives in which followers' encounters with leaders trigger powerful unconscious fantasies wherein leaders feature as larger-than-life characters. I identified four clusters of follower fantasies, each entailing an axis with a positive and a negative pole:

1. The leader is *omnipotent*, unafraid and capable of miracles. Omnipotence extends to omniscience, an ability to read the minds of his/her subordinates and predict the future. Conversely, the leader is *weak*, externally driven, afraid and fallible.
2. The leader has a *legitimate claim to power*, whether based on expertise, achievement or the procedure followed for his/her appointment. Conversely, the leader is an *impostor* who usurped power fraudulently.
3. The leader *cares* for his/her subordinates, offering recognition and support. He/she also cares for the organization and is capable of sacrificing his/her personal interest or even his/her life for the collective good. Conversely the leader is *selfish*, indifferent to his/her subordinates and only cares for him/herself, his/her career and power.
4. The leader is *accessible* and can be seen and heard when needed, even if these appearances constitute special occasions. Conversely, the leader is *invisible*, liable to disappear, abandoning and betraying his/her followers, especially in times of difficulty.

These bipolarities surface in organizational narratives, but can also be found in numerous religious, mythological and other narratives. Importantly, actual leaders cannot be located somewhere along a continuum represented by each axis – they are placed in one pole or the other. Thus, a leader is not judged to be 'quite powerful', enjoying a 'fair degree of legitimacy', being 'reasonably caring' or 'fairly accessible'. Instead, s/he is all-powerful or all-weak, all-legitimate or a total impostor.

LEADERS JUDGED AGAINST ARCHETYPAL FANTASIES

A leader is liable to be judged according to whether s/he lives up to archetypal fantasies rather than in a more nuanced manner. Taking the first two fantasies first, followers expect the power, wisdom and courage of their leaders to be used to promote collective ends, rather than the leader's own agenda. In particular, the leader's power must be deployed to protect followers from collective foes. Leaders who use their talents to enhance their own careers or enrich themselves – a perception inexorably linked to many CEOs, bankers and political leaders – are experienced as morally flawed, for such selfish uses of power undermine a leader's claim to legitimacy. Leaders have a legitimate claim to rule by virtue of qualities (wisdom, courage, etc.) which, in the minds of followers, set them apart, as long as these are used to promote collective ends. A leader's legitimacy collapses if s/he fails to demonstrate these qualities consistently, or if they are put to selfish ends. The collapse of leader legitimacy is a crucial and spectacular political phenomenon, seeming to afflict numerous political leaders, including, for different reasons, several of Britain's recent prime ministers. I would argue that the moral expectations that issue from these first two fantasies are consistent with the idea of *heroic leadership*, one that continues to dominate public discourses and be presented as the panacea for various social and other ills.

Numerous authors have critiqued heroic leadership and its dysfunctional ramifications for groups and organizations. In spite of its now well-recognized dysfunctions, however, attempts to replace heroic leadership with other models – distributive, collective, and so on – have not generally been successful. As Grint (2010, p. 103) argues, 'post-heroic alternatives remain unviable (except in organizations that are very small scale or short term) because they would undermine the sacred nature of leadership and that, in turn, would destabilize the ability of an organization to function'. Whilst the heroic leader archetypes have received extensive attention from both advocates and critics, far less attention has been paid to the archetype that stems from the other two fantasies noted above – those that cast the leader as a caring, accessible figure. It is to these fantasies that the remainder of this chapter is devoted.

THE CARING LEADER AND ETHICS OF CARE

The caring leader has, in my view, received inadequate attention from scholars (for a rare exception, see Simola et al., 2010). Yet its importance can hardly be exaggerated, whether talking about military leaders like Nelson, political leaders like Mandela, religious leaders like Christ or the Dalai Lama or even business leaders. A dominant theme in narratives of such leaders is the various good turns they do for their followers, frequently *going beyond the call of duty*. The metaphor of the good shepherd captures precisely the archetype of the caring leader. This is found in the parable of Christ as the shepherd who abandons 99 sheep in order to search for the lost one (John 10:11–18; Luke 15:3–7). Caring leaders are compassionate, giving and concerned for followers' well-being. If *power* is the dominant feature of heroic leaders, *love* is the foundation of caring leaders. Caring leaders share a deep emotional bond with their followers, which Freud (1921) had no difficulty in interpreting as a desexualized erotic one, in which libido becomes sublimated into powerful feelings of empathy, compassion and solidarity, which unite followers through a common experience of being loved by the leader.

Caring leaders are also accessible and visible, especially in times of stress and crisis. An inaccessible leader, one who is not there when needed, is readily cast as one deserting their flock and betraying their duty of care. 'My leader has abandoned me. I am standing in utter darkness. I cannot take another step alone. Help me.' says the protagonist of Hermann Hesse's Demian (1920 [1969], p. 122), a cry of the heart, common in moments of confusion and doubt. A leader who is absent triggers fantasies of abandonment and betrayal, reinforcing the feeling that he/she does not genuinely care for his/her followers.

At the level of archetypes, the caring leader may be even more significant than the heroic leader. A leader who is experienced as uncaring can hardly be viewed as a 'true leader', care outweighing any other consideration regarding the moral obligations of leaders in the eyes of followers. A leader may be strong and competent but, if s/he is seen as uncaring, s/he will be viewed as a failing leader. Given the power of this archetype, it seems surprising that it has not attracted more scholarly attention. This is especially so, given the rise in the field of philosophy of the ethics of care, following the publication of Gilligan's (1982) book *In a Different Voice*, which sought to reclaim a moral voice that had not been heard previously, by challenging her mentor Kohlberg's (1981) account of children's moral development. According to Kohlberg, the destination of moral development for all humans is a concept of justice revolving around abstract principles that apply equally and imperson-ally to all. On the basis of her own field work with children, Gilligan argued that this ideal of morality is deaf to a different moral voice, one much more in evidence in young girls, which revolves around caring for those close to them. Kohlberg's predominantly male conception of morality, Gilligan argues, fails to honour the distinctly female voice on moral matters, one that is personal, immediate and direct, based on ongoing relationships rather than abstract ethical considerations. Care ethics grows out of people behaving not as sov-ereign individual actors, but as members of communities and networks that require constant effort and nurturing to sustain.[1]

Gilligan's pioneering work opened up a new way of studying care in philosophy, psychology and politics, mostly but not exclusively by feminist theorists (e.g., Held, 2006; Noddings, 1986; Tronto, 1993). In contrast to the 'ethics of justice', care ethicists argue for a system of morality that does not rely on claims of universality, absolute judgements of right and wrong, and perfect virtues. Instead, they identify a practical morality that grows out of a recognition that all people are embedded in webs of social relations, being dependent on others for their survival and well-being and capable of supporting others in their moments of need and helplessness. Care is not a scripted emotional performance, but involves a wide range of actions, concerns, and feelings that grow out of sensitivity and attentiveness to the needs of those close to us. Thus, a fundamental aspect of the ethics of care is that those close to us and in direct contact with us are experienced as entitled to more care and attention than those distant and unknown.

While there are various tensions within the care ethics discourse, there is widespread acceptance of certain underlying themes that set it apart from other ethics traditions. Care is not an attitude or a virtue but a *practice*, 'a species activity that includes everything we do to maintain, continue, and repair our "world" so that we may live in it as well as possible' (Tronto, 1993, p. 103). Caring is relational and there are limits to how much it can be depersonalized; machines may facilitate care work but cannot replace it (Sevenhuijsen, 1998). Caring for another person is individualized work, relying on face-to-face interaction, resisting bureaucratization and formalization. Caring evokes complex emotions in both carer and cared-for, including both positive and negative emotions, such as love, gratitude, envy, fear and anxiety, which are liable to entail ambivalence. Finally, caring and being cared-for are vitally important, if problematic, aspects of individuals' identities (Meyers, 2002).

In spite of its importance, caring work in Western societies is systematically devalued, underpaid, and disproportionately occupied by marginalized and underprivileged groups. Care work (in old people's homes, schools, hospitals, etc.) is heavily gendered and racialized, as is domestic labour (looking after children, older and disabled individuals at home). Despite the considerable aptitudes and talents it demands, care work is widely viewed as low skill and low cost. In a culture that lionizes the sovereign individual who earns and spends money, the person dependent on the care of others cuts a dejected figure. Being cared-for implies being a burden to others, but the carer is also tarnished by having his/her freedom diminished. In a prototypical way, both caring mother and cared-for child are seen as enmeshed in dependency relations inferior to those of 'independent' men who enjoy infinitely greater freedom (Meyers, 2002). Caring for others creates a secondary dependency (Kittay, 1999), a fetter holding back careers and restricting freedom. Yet, despite such negative associations, a caring orientation to others retains elements of being a valued quality, even in our highly narcissistic and individualistic culture. A 'caring person' may not be the most common self-description in today's inflated résumés, but remains the description of a valued and valuable person. And it is these caring qualities that are seen as essential for leaders.

There have been numerous criticisms of the care ethics discourse. Many of these have focused on dyadic relations between the carer and the cared-for which can breed excessive dependency. Attempts to develop a politics and political institutions based on the ethics of care have been disappointing (Engster, 2004). All the same, what is beyond doubt is that followers generally expect their leaders to act consistently in a caring manner. For this reason, a useful distinction may be made between the ethics (plural) of care as a philo-sophical body of argument which is as yet underdeveloped in connection with political theory and an ethic (singular) of care as a set of values and practices that guide social relations. The ethic of care, then, can be conceptualized by analogy to the Protestant ethic as a set of values and practices that inform and guide judgements and actions, providing an important vantage point from which the actions of leaders are assessed.

LEADERS AND THE ETHIC OF CARE

What then are the qualities of a leader when judged from an ethic of care per-spective? Leaders who care must be *visible*, able to connect with their follow-ers (Gabriel, 1997); they must be willing to give generously their time, advice, recognition and support and demonstrate that they are genuinely concerned for the realization of a mission or a project. They must treat their followers with consideration and respect, rather than as pawns on a chessboard. Caring leaders do not merely respect their followers' desires, but display watchful-ness over their changing needs and aspirations, just like watchful teachers or parents. Empathy is a very significant characteristic of caring leaders, as is the ability to offer constructive but objective feedback and act as toxic sponges to protect followers from excessive anxieties.

Caring leaders are relational; yet caring leaders, like leaders in general, remain *separate* from their followers (Grint, 2010) in an asymmetric relation-ship. Although caring is consistent with an altruistic orientation, caring leaders are not averse to conflict, nor are they necessarily 'nice' or 'soft'. On the contrary, the real test comes when they have to fight to defend those for whom they care, rather than opt for convenient compromises (Gabriel, 2008). Far from being a universally mild attitude, caring means taking responsibility for others and being prepared to take personal risks in fighting for their well-being. Nor would a caring leader always seek to please her followers, if doing so would risk their welfare. For this reason, a caring leader listens to followers, aware that what they demand is not always consistent with group interests.

The two most persistent requirements that set care clearly apart from other ethical vantage points are that leaders' relations to their followers are *personal* and that they should be seen to go *beyond the call of duty* in discharging their responsibilities. An ethic of care thus eschews the principle of equality in the most blatant manner (Held, 2006). A leader will discriminate in favour of his/her followers just as a mother will discriminate in favour of her child, with modest concern for the implications of this for others. In a similar manner, a caring leader may seek to address the needs of the follower who has special needs and vulnerabilities (the 'lost sheep'), even if this means offering preferential treatment to that person. In every instance, caring leaders will opt to serve the needs of their own followers rather than the interests of abstract justice or those of anonymous others.

ILLUSTRATION

The qualities of a caring leader came into sharp relief in a piece of field research into hospital leadership in which I participated. Hospital leadership offers a critical space in which to observe the ethic of care in its application, not only in relations between leaders (clinical as well as administrative) and their followers, but more widely in relations between clinical staff and patients. No other environment exacerbates anxieties over issues of life and death as that of a healthcare system, anxieties that affect not only patients but also staff at nearly all levels (Lökman et al., 2011); and no other environment places such heavy responsibilities in the hands of people who almost invariably do not know each other personally.

When asked to illustrate good leadership and good quality patient-care, nearly all the clinicians in our study offered examples of *personalized care that went beyond what was seen as the call of duty*. The illustrative example below is a story told by a male junior doctor during a focus group discussion. The story was enthusiastically endorsed by other participants as an excellent example of good leadership and good patient-care.

> A pregnant woman came in through A&E [Accident and Emergency]. She was having problems with her pregnancy. I asked the registrar [senior clinician] what to do. They decided that the best thing to do was get the woman scanned to find the problem. However, being a night shift there were no porters to be seen and the scanning units were closed. I felt that the anxious woman could not stay in A&E surrounded by drunks and druggies as it was inappropriate. Instead of calling for porters, which would have taken time, I and the registrar moved the pregnant lady to the maternity ward ourselves where we opened up a scanning unit to find out what was wrong with the lady's pregnancy. I was proud of the leadership that I had received from my registrar; not every registrar would have done this but he solved the problem and delivered good patient-care in the process. The problems were resolved within an hour with only skeletal night staff.

It is striking to note the contrast between the individualized care for the woman in trouble, who becomes a 'lady' in the course of the narrative, and the indifference towards the plight of the anonymous 'drunks and druggies', whose treatment was negatively affected by the preferential treatment offered to the pregnant woman. On the one hand, there is the deserving patient with a human face, the individual with unique needs who evokes empathy. On the other hand, there is the impersonal patient, cast as undeserving and parasitical who provokes resentment and anger. It is also interesting how the narrative stays quiet about the nature of the problems that afflicted the woman, as if these are irrelevant to the story. What is relevant is her distress over the possibility of losing her baby. It is telling to note the expression of 'pride' in the 'leadership' displayed by the registrar who acted, in effect, as a porter transporting the deserving patient and throwing the hospital's procedures out of the window in offering urgent and personal treatment. In this way, the clinical senior was seen as someone caring for his junior personally, going beyond the call of duty to support *him* in what he felt was his own (as well as the patient's) moment of acute vulnerability. This theme of the senior being present and available when a junior is confronted with a possible crisis was one that surfaced throughout the field research.

CONCLUSIONS

An ethic of care does not only apply to leaders but also to other social groups, notably those with a duty to care for needy or disabled people. Paradoxically, people whom we expect to care are among the lowest in the status hierarchies *as well as* the highest – CEOs, Prime Ministers, and so on. This paradox brings leaders very close to servants – a suggestion which lies at the heart of 'servant leadership' developed by Greenleaf (1977), based on an idea that Greenleaf himself traced to Hesse's (1932 [1972]) novel, *The Journey to the East*. The novel describes a spiritual journey undertaken by members of a League, narrated by one of the characters who, along with others, loses faith in the mission when one of the servants, Leo, goes missing. Leo is the 'perfect servant', described as always prompt, gentle, simple and unobtrusive, anticipating the needs of the League's other members. Following Leo's disappearance, the League disintegrates morally and spiritually and never reaches its destination. Later, we learn that Leo was, in fact, the leader of the League, and his disappearance was meant to test the members' faith in the mission. The story demonstrates how Leo switches from a caring leader to a testing leader, with devastating consequences for his followers. It can, therefore, be viewed as an allegory *against* the dependence that excessive reliance on a caring leader creates, an interpretation that is at odds with Greenleaf's.

This offers a clear warning against idealizing the caring leader. Caring leaders, like heroic ones, can have a paralysing effect on others. As every caring parent knows, excessive caring can seriously inhibit the autonomy of followers, instilling dependence and inertia. Care ethicists would claim that caring for somebody is based on a recognition of their needs which *include* a need for autonomy. But at what point does caring turn into overprotection and cosseting? In line with Winnicott's (1980) notion of the 'good enough mother', a caring leader must try to strike a balance between containing followers' anxieties without eliminating them to the point where followers lapse into dependence and inaction.

Equally importantly, when taken to extreme, an ethic of care can become a recipe for discrimination and nepotism. Some of the worst cases of nepotism are undertaken in well-intended efforts to help and support those closest to the leader. Again, the dilemma is not dissimilar to that of a parent who may be tempted to discriminate against the healthy and strong child in order to support the troubled and vulnerable one. This dilemma constantly confronts those with a duty of care, and sets it in opposition to the ethic of justice that requires equal treatment for all.

Living and acting consistently with an ethic of care is not easy for leaders (or indeed others). Care is frequently opposed by formidable forces. First, care is costly in terms of time, energy and effort, and can easily be overwhelmed in the maelstrom of ceaseless activity and crisis management. Second, an ethic of care is frequently opposed by an ethic of justice. The former dictates privileged treatment for those who need it and those who are close to the leader; the latter dictates equal treatment for all. A leader can then easily find herself with no safe moral options. Third, an ethic of care is often at odds with itself, dictating conflicting courses of action. How much extra care should a leader dedicate to the missing sheep without endangering the survival and growth of the remaining ones? Finally, an ethic of care is at odds with the fundamental impersonality, individualism and insecurity of our times. When loyalty and long-term commitments seem in short supply in every aspect of social life, when freedom, choice and independence are elevated above all moral values, what chance for an ethic of care that values relationship, dedication, gentleness, humility and duty?

In spite of such difficulties, an ethic of care maintains its vigour and vibrancy when followers judge their leaders. This is what accords the caring leader archetypal qualities, which endure across changing social and political circumstances. This is why leaders who fail to demonstrate that they care for their followers, no matter what other qualities they possess, are unlikely to be viewed as moral leaders or command people's trust, affection and respect.

ACKNOWLEDGEMENTS

A previous version of this chapter appeared as: Gabriel, Y. (2015). The caring leader – What followers expect of their leaders and why? *Leadership*, **11**(3), 316–34.

We are grateful to SAGE for permission to include this abridged version here.

NOTE

1. The question of whether boys' moral reasoning is different from that of girls is highly contested. A meta-analysis by Jaffee and Shibley-Hyde (2000) found little support for the claim that the care orientation is used predominantly by women and the justice orientation predominantly by men. This is not an issue I address in this chapter, although the concentration of women (and minority groups) in the caring occupations is crucial for the latter part of the argument presented here.

REFERENCES

Engster, D. (2004), 'Care ethics and natural law theory: Toward an institutional political theory of caring', *Journal of Politics*, **66**, 113–35.

Freud, S. (1921), *Group Psychology and the Analysis of the Ego*, London: Hogarth Press.

Gabriel, Y. (1997), 'Meeting God: When organizational members come face to face with the supreme leader', *Human Relations*, 50, 315–42.

Gabriel, Y. (2008), 'Latte capitalism and late capitalism: Reflections on fantasy and care as part of the service triangle', in M. Korczynski and C. MacDonald (eds), *Service Work: Critical Perspectives*, London: Routledge, pp. 175–90.

Gilligan, C. (1982), *In a Different Voice: Psychological Theory and Women's Development*, Cambridge, MA: Harvard University Press.

Greenleaf, R.K. (1977), *Servant Leadership: A Journey into the Nature of Legitimate Power and Greatness*, New York: Paulist Press.

Grint, K. (2010), 'The sacred in leadership: Separation, sacrifice and silence', *Organization Studies*, **31**, 89–107.

Held, V. (2006), *The Ethics of Care: Personal, Political, and Global*, Oxford: Oxford University Press.

Hesse, H. (1920 [1969]), *Demian, the Story of a Youth*, London: Panther Books.

Hesse, H. (1932 [1972]), *The Journey to the East*, St Albans: Panther/Granada.

Jaffee, S. and J. Shibley-Hyde (2000), 'Gender differences in moral orientation: A meta-analysis', *Psychological Bulletin*, **126**, 703–26.

Jung, C.G. (1968), *The Archetypes and the Collective Unconscious*, London: Routledge.

Kittay, E.F. (1999), *Love's Labor: Essays on Women, Equality, and Dependency*, New York: Routledge.

Kociatkiewicz, J. and M. Kostera (2012), 'The good manager: An archetypical quest for morally sustainable leadership', *Organization Studies*, **33**, 861–78.

Kohlberg, L. (1981), *The Philosophy of Moral Development: Moral Stages and the Idea of Justice*, San Francisco, CA: Harper & Row.

Lökman, P., Y. Gabriel and P. Nicolson (2011), 'Hospital doctors' anxieties at work: Patient care as intersubjective relationship and/or as system output', *International Journal of Organizational Analysis*, **19**, 29–48.

Meyers, D.T. (2002), *Gender in the Mirror: Cultural Imagery and Women's Agency*, Oxford: Oxford University Press.

Moxnes, P. (1999), 'Deep roles: Twelve primordial roles of mind and organization', *Human Relations*, **52**, 1427–44.

Noddings, N. (1986), *Caring: A Feminine Approach to Ethics & Moral Education*, Berkeley, CA: University of California Press.

Schwartz, H.S. (1990), *Narcissistic Process and Corporate Decay*, New York: NYU Press.

Sevenhuijsen, S. (1998), *Citizenship and the Ethics of Care: Feminist Considerations on Justice, Morality, and Politics*, London: Routledge.

Simola, S.K., J. Barling and N. Turner (2010), 'Transformational leadership and leader moral orientation: Contrasting an ethic of justice and an ethic of care', *Leadership Quarterly*, **21**, 179–88.

Tronto, J.C. (1993), *Moral Boundaries: A Political Argument for an Ethic of Care*, New York: Routledge.

Winnicott, D.W. (1980), *Playing and Reality*, Harmondsworth: Penguin.

4. Magically horrific: caring leadership and the paradoxical evolution of parenthood

Gerardo Abreu Pederzini

No matter how old we get, deep down inside we keep always longing for our caring leaders, who will protect us and take care of things for us. Caring leaders are supposed to be 'compassionate, giving and concerned for the well-being of' their followers (Gabriel, 2015, p. 321). The caring leadership bond is usually so powerful, because it provides followers with 'someone to protect them or to blame if things go wrong' (Abreu Pederzini, 2019, p. 1). Yet caring leadership cannot be understood by itself, but should be conceived as overdetermined in time. Particularly, caring leadership represents (sometimes) simply how childhood relationships are transferred into adulthood. Just as the parent, the caring leader, is supposed to be a pastor that guides while protecting. Thus, parenthood forms, in many ways, the archetype for caring leadership relationships, and therefore, any exploration of the paradoxes of caring leadership should include a careful analysis of how parenting works. In humans, parental caring is as essential (and more) than in most other species, because humans are born still largely underdeveloped, and hence, incapable of surviving on their own. For instance, a foal – a baby horse – will be walking and running within a few hours after birth. A human baby, by contrast, relies completely for months (or years) on his/her parents (caregivers), making, as such, the parental relationship and its caring one of the most powerful traits of human behaviour.

Many ways exist to study parenthood, but one of the most important is through the lens of evolution. In this chapter, I will explore the biology of parenthood, particularly in terms of why and how it might have evolved as a caring leadership relationship. Through the lens of evolution, two paradoxes of caring leadership in parenting will emerge. *Paradox 1* is about why caring from parents might take place in evolution, which is a process that is supposed to be about competition. *Paradox 2* is about how caring in the archetypal caring leadership relationship (i.e., parenthood) looks different if we look at it from a systemic evolutionary point of view than if we look at it from a subjective one. These evolutionary paradoxes of parental care are essential to understand caring leadership, as they will teach us two important things. First, that evolutionarily, caring might not exist as such, but that it is simply a successful strategy that has endured because it can, not because it is right or wonderful. Second, that caring, thus, might only exist in the subjective experience of human beings, as evolution has transduced human beings' perception of what has biologically actually happened.

Let us begin by talking about evolution.

AN ODYSSEY OF EVOLUTION

Within the many powerful ideas that have emanated from science, perhaps the most powerful is the theory of evolution through natural selection. Inspired by previous works, Charles Darwin's genius was to suggest not only a theory regarding our past connections, but most importantly a mechanism regarding how life develops. The theory of evolution refers to how life shares a common origin, and how as time has passed it has resulted, through natural selection, in various forms of living beings. Particularly, the term 'evolution' is related to the idea of 'descent with modification' (Garson, 2015, p. 18), meaning that all life is connected but that as time goes by it changes. Natural selection, thus, would be the mechanism through which life changes and results in new expressions.

In natural selection, we have at least three essential processes: variation, selection and retention (Blackmore, 1999). The first one, variation, is about how at some point we have living forms with different traits. Each of those traits might bestow varying degrees of fitness (i.e., survival that results in successful reproduction). Those traits that provide an advantage to endure, hence, will enable the holders to pass on the traits to their offspring (retention). If such traits remain strategic, they, therefore, will continue being spread throughout the population. However, for those traits that are not strategic, their presence within the population will start dwindling. Eventually, traits that provide a disadvantage might disappear, while those that are advantageous might become dominant (selection). It is because of this that, if we wait long enough, eventually it will look as if organisms that populate the ecosystem have been designed. Interestingly, within those traits that evolution selects we find behaviours, which are genetically coded, and by being potentially strategic, become robust. A parent's (that is, the primordial caring leader's) disposition towards devoted caring of his/her offspring is probably one of those behavioural traits that were selected due to their strategic endowment.

Before taking this topic any further, there is an inescapable evolutionary conundrum that should be mentioned. Human behaviour is not only biologically determined. By contrast, humans distinguish themselves by their (significant) plasticity, which enables them to develop new routines as they interact with environments, including through socialization. However, regarding social influences on caring leadership a lot has already been said. Thus, I will not touch on that here. I will focus on the potential biological genesis of parental caring, and possible paradoxes on caring leadership that emerge from this.

Let us, therefore, now talk about what caring means in an evolutionary perspective: altruism.

BIOLOGICAL CARING AND *PARADOX 1*

When the second offspring of a Nazca booby (a type of seabird in the Sulidae family) hatches, it faces an immediate and dramatic challenge to its survival, as the first offspring – its sibling – will indulge in the unexpected pleasure of trying to expel it, sometimes even murdering it by starvation. Siblicide, as it is known, is sadly (sometimes) strategic, as it emanates from the desperation to become the object of more parental investment (i.e., more parental/leadership caring), which in the case of the Nazca booby is essential, as usually there are conditions to enable the survival of only one offspring. Thus, it could be assumed that it might (sometimes) pay off to get rid of your siblings, because siblicide could represent, in certain circumstances, an evolved stable behaviour to face the constraints of existence.

Historically, hence, cooperation represents one of the juiciest debates within evolutionary theory, as evolution for a long time was supposed to be mainly about competition, such as the brutalist competition expressed in Nazca booby seabirds. The relevance of competition emerges due to Darwinian theory being (originally) based on the Malthusian concept of the struggle for existence. Malthus famously suggested that since populations might grow faster than resources available for their survival, organisms would fight a struggle to survive, *the struggle for existence*. Thus, competition is presumably the quintessential ethos of Darwinism. If we think about it, we will see that competition is precisely what variation, selection and retention are all about: alleged winners and losers.

It is here that *Paradox 1* looms, because if it is all about competition, how could we explain cooperation in nature? For example, how could we explain something like the calling of Vervet monkeys? Vervet monkeys have three different calls to indicate to others that either a snake, an eagle or a leopard has been spotted. This is not a unique behaviour of Vervet monkeys, as in other species calls are also strategic for groups to prevent attacks. However, calling as a behaviour goes (partly) against the logic of competition, because the one doing the calling is actually sacrificing itself for others, as potential predators will more easily identify it. Similarly, countless accounts of cooperation among humans would go against the ferocious competitive interpretation of evolution, including repeated expressions of human siblings, who unlike the Nazca booby, actually help each other and make sacrifices for each other. Officially, these devoted acts to help others are called, in biology, altruism; where an 'altruistic act is one that looks, superficially, as if it must tend to make the altruist more likely (however slightly) to die, and the recipient more likely to survive' (Dawkins, 2006, p. 4). For the purposes of this chapter, we could simply think of altruism – sacrificing yourself for others – as the biological definition of caring. In the end, of course, the question is: if it is all about competition, why would an individual put its welfare at stake, for instance, to help a child or a sibling? Why would we have, for example, caring leaders – such as parents – who are willing to risk their lives to protect their own?

The Gene

One of the reasons why biological caring sometimes happens in nature has to do with genes. In short, certain human relationships (not all) are partly genetically determined to be caring, because caring has sometimes been naturally selected as a strategic behaviour. The relationship that best expresses a biological bias towards caring for others is of course the parenting relationship, which eventually forms an archetype of how a caring leader is supposed to be. Thus, if we wish to understand caring leadership, we need to understand biological parental caring, and for parental caring we need to understand genes.

Genes are segments of DNA (that double helix macro molecule we learned about in high school), and they are encharged with coding proteins, which eventually result in certain observable traits of an organism, including some of its behaviours (Wagner, 2014). Now, some of those traits, as previously explained, might be strategic, enabling their hosts (their vehicles, such as a human) to survive and reproduce more successfully. Thus, the genes responsible for such traits are more likely to be passed on to the next generation and endure. Because of this, then, for some (not all) traditions in evolutionary theory, what natural selection *selects* are genes (or configurations of them). This is why genes are so important in evolutionary theory.

The question is: which genes are more likely to endure through history? To understand this, let us go to the legendary riverbank of JBS Haldane, which is a *just-so-story* that Haldane used to explain caring among people within the same family. I am not going to discuss Haldane's story *per se* (for the original story, see Wilson, 2014, p. 65), but I will twist it a bit, to make my point on how biological caring in parents – that is, primordial caring leaders – might evolve. So, imagine you are standing on a riverbank, and you see some people in the river drowning. When you look closer, it turns out that it is your son and daughter. Incidentally, because of your specific genetic make-up, you have a behavioural trait that pushes you to behave like a hero – that is, like great caring leaders do – by jumping into the river and saving your kids. Thus, you jump into the freezing river, despite knowing that you might well die, as you are not a good swimmer. Now, imagine that this is a very calamitous river, and that another person is standing on the opposite extreme of the riverbank, and sees her own son and daughter drowning too. This mother, however, does not have a genetic makeup that has hardwired in her a trait to save her kids (that is, she is not hardwired to want to be the hero, she is selfish). Thus, she lets them drown in the river.

Let us think about the consequences of this twisted melodrama. It turns out that in your case, perhaps you died when you jumped into the river to save your kids, yet as your son and daughter carry a significant number of your genes, some of your genes survive in/through them, including those programming people to behave as caring parents. As time goes by, your also parentally heroic and caring kids keep successfully reproducing, constantly protecting their kids, and hence transmitting those caring genes. In the case of the dreadful selfish mother, her kids have died. She still carries her genes of selfishness; however, when she dies, her genes of selfishness might (partly) die with her. In the grand scale of things, what would happen is that, therefore, genes that got together and produced the behaviour of caring for your kids might have higher chances of surviving and being passed on to the next generation, while the ones that were not caring might disappear. This encapsulates, in simple terms, how evolution works, so that eventually we have a world where most humans look like caring parents. Yet this has nothing to do with them. This is not about what they decide to do; there is no intentionality here. This is simply about lengthy systemic processes of evolution and the genes that make it – that endure – through them.

It is important to emphasize that there is also no moral judgement in evolution. Genes (and their vehicles) that survive and become dominant, do not survive because they are *'better'*. Genes that survive, survive because they can, and because they can, they keep surviving and replicating: that is it. Furthermore, it turns out that genes that develop parental caring might be precisely of the *'kind'* that survive and replicate fairly successfully. This is what we could call overall *biological parental caring*: because of blind and unintended evolutionary processes 'a creature behaves in such a way as to increase the fitness of others at its own expense' (Garson, 2015, p. 29). Like this, parental caring – which will eventually form the archetype for caring leadership – endures, but it endures because it can, not because it is a winner or because it is better or because it was planned. We must remember that in the end, as Whitehead once said, 'Nature is a dull affair, soundless, scentless, colourless; merely the hurrying of material, endlessly, meaninglessly' (1967, p. 54). Thus, in biological parental caring there is apparently no romance or grandiose movie with the mother or father hero. There are only genes that were selected, including some that drive us to cooperate with our genetically related offspring. Thus, in terms of *Paradox 1*, we could say that there is cooperation and caring in evolution, but it is just a blind product of systemic processes of natural selection.

Finally, what I have described so far regarding biological (parental) caring is just one form of cooperation in nature; there are many others (see Nowak, 2012), including cooperation among individuals that, unlike parents and off-spring, are not necessarily genetically related. Yet these other types are not relevant for parental caring, and would require a full chapter for themselves. So, I will not mention them. Instead, let us now think about what psychological parental caring is.

PSYCHOLOGICAL CARING AND *PARADOX 2*

As some genes partly survive and become dominant through vehicles that are caring towards their offspring, the interesting conundrum now is how those vehicles (gene hosts) perceive this process internally, while becoming moti-vated towards such actions. For instance, is a parent – the proverbial caring leader – thinking: I must jump into the river because saving my children will allow me to propagate my genetic material? Or is a parent thinking: I have genes that programmed me to jump into the river so I must do it? Hmmm, I do not think so. This, then, is the question that *psychological (parental) caring* considers: which desires/motivations move parents internally to feel that they should care for their children? As we all know, those desires are complicated. The conventional debate centres on whether or not those desires are egotistical (Garson, 2015). For instance, if a father helping a son feels satisfaction or real-ization when doing it, then we might say that there is something in it for him by being a caring father. It is highly likely that indeed evolution has shaped our psychology so that we have some ultimate desires that are (probably) self-regarding: all about us.

However, many authors claim nowadays that it is perhaps more likely that psychologically we have (some) ultimate desires that are other-regarding (Tomasello, 2013): we are hardwired genuinely to care about others, including most especially our own (e.g., our children). For instance, the fears that often move a mother to protect her child seem usually focused on the child. Hence, given the sacrifices that we see parents, overall, making for their children, there might be ultimate desires that fuel caring and that are other-regarding. Because it would be hard, for instance, to think about a hedonistic reward for a parent that in a matter of seconds jumps onto the tracks to save his kid while dying almost instantly after being hit by a train.

This romance of psychological caring is paradoxical when juxtaposed against cold-hearted biological caring in parents. Thus, this is *Paradox 2*, on how an inert and emotionless process of parental caring surviving simply because it is an evolutionary stable strategy, is turned into an emotional and passionate act of love in the psychology of those who feel it. Therefore, this apparent paradox indicates, in a way, that for those broader evolutionary processes to function, nature has to transduce itself and create in the vehicles of those genes, desires that although rejecting and denying what is happening at the level of the system and history, motivate organisms towards the necessary actions. To explain this transducing process, I will now make an insolent turn towards the arts, so that this is more digestible.

Magical Realism and a Transducing Process

So, there seems to be a transducing process in nature, where the emotionless reality of genes – including those that programme parental caring – propagating through time, is transmuted in our psychologies into a dynamite experience of romantic emotions that move the necessary actors. From a purely scientific approach, this apparent paradox does not exist, as this is simply how nature works to make evolution function, and the paradox emerges only from the biased ways – subjective gazes – through which we see the world as humans. If we saw things objectively, scientists would claim, we would see that there is no paradox. However, for most people this explanation still leaves us lacking. We need a more human type of explanation that allows us to express what we feel when processing caring as a by-product of blind, unintended and emotionless evolution. The arts, historically, have been the most powerful mechanism for humans to express themselves. Thus, let us look for an arts way to express and explain *Paradox 2*. In this section, I will suggest, particularly, the art of magical realism as a tool to enable us to express, in a human way, what *Paradox 2* makes us feel and how it might be solved.

Let me begin by introducing what magical realism is. Franz Roh coined the term 'magical realism' to denote a painting style during the Weimar Republic in Germany, where elements of a crude and carefully depicted reality were juxtaposed against subtle (yet fantastical) elements of magic (Bowers, 2004). Eventually, magical realism became the voice of the Latin American novel, as its ethos captured in many ways the passions and realities behind the perpetually romantic Latino, living, nevertheless, surrounded by a harsh reality. Yet, beyond the Cuban conception of Alejo Carpentier and his marvellous realism (1949), where the ethos of magical realism is supposed to be something exclusive to Latin America, 'magical realism has [actually] become a global phenomenon, which encompasses any effort to disguise the magic of fantasizing as a matter-of-fact that is somehow blindly accepted as part of our reality' (Abreu Pederzini, 2018, pp. 327–8).

Gabriel García Márquez (Gabo) took magical realism to a whole new level, where its power was not only the juxtaposition of the magical and the mundane, but their complete fusion to a point that it was impossible to distinguish them. Gabo built many fictional worlds, like his *One Hundred Years of Solitude*, where the distinction between the imaginary and the real was erased, so that the magical elements were unconsciously perceived as part of the real. Similar efforts in film consecrated magical realism as a powerful tool to express human experience. For instance, in Guillermo del Toro's *Pan's Labyrinth* (2006), a young Ofelia finds herself entrapped in a crude reality of a civil war, a war whose villain is about to become her stepfather. Surrounded by such monstrous expressions of the cruelties of the world, Ofelia finds a labyrinth, which seems dead. Yet, in it, if you look close enough, you will find a faun. This magical creature, emerging as part of such a crude reality and fused with it, sets Ofelia onto a journey for salvation; her salvation and the salvation of her baby brother. So a crude reality has been turned into authentic magic.

Now, if we go back to our conundrum of explaining the transducing process that seems to have happened in nature, between biological and psychological caring, we could express how it humanly makes us feel, by portraying it precisely as magical realism. In a word, we could conceptualize the psychology of parental caring as magically realist for us, because it transforms mundane evolutionary trends that for us seem empty and meaningless, into magical passions and emotions that for us seem like true love and caring. This transmutation, thus, results in a human subjectivity, where far from parental caring being an inert tool that exists because it is evolutionarily strategic, it exists for us as a romance of authentic devotion for our own people.

In sum, in parenthood – the primordial expression of caring leadership – it seems, first, as if the caring parent is only an evolutionary patsy that sacrifices his/her desire for that of others, because according to biological caring (the realist part of this equation) that is what evolution has produced. Yet, in terms of psychological caring (the magical part of this equation), the parent, by caring and sacrificing himself/herself for others, actually feels himself/herself as an authentic loving and grandiose hero, because human subjectivity – our gaze of the world – transduces nature to show it to us in a way that is, metaphorically, convenient for it and not necessarily accurate.

INESCAPABLE PARADOXES: MAGICALLY HORRIFIC

If parental caring is to be the archetype of caring leadership, we need to acknowledge that it is not only about parents, but about offspring (followers) as well. Thus, as much as parents' psychologies have been shaped by evolution, so have children's too. Particularly, the mind of, for instance, a human baby has been shaped to be ready, from the outset, to seek the parent and

rejoice in his/her caring. The latter is a disposition that although usually ful-
filled through our parents during childhood, could easily be transferred into
other authority figures later on, to create further caring leadership bonds that
mimic those of parenting.

During childhood, one of the most powerful mechanisms for that disposition
of children to long for their carers is called imprinting. Imprinting represents
the absorptive developmental period, where certain things make long-lasting
impact on who we are and the behavioural preferences that we will develop.
This disposition to be affected is strategic if young animals – including humans
– are affected/imprinted by figures from whom they can learn some valuable
lessons. The power of imprinting goes far beyond humans. For instance,
goslings – baby geese – have an extraordinary capacity to form a preference
for their mothers, which pushes them to follow them and learn from them.
Overall, we could say that because young animals, including human babies,
are open through imprinting (among other mechanisms), to be influenced by
their parents, a romance grows, through which children *'magicalize'* too the
mundane reality of a parent that crossed their way, forming a bond that pushes
them to eagerly keep longing for their heroic and idealized parents. Eventually,
as we grow up, people might keep on doing this, but now with other potential
caring leaders.

In sum, parental caring functions because both parents' and offspring's
psychologies have been shaped through evolution to behave in ways through
which one is open to be caring, while the other one is open to receive care.
Having said that, this is where we need to remember that if we want to express
how we feel about something as complex as caring in evolution, then using
the metaphor of magical realism will always be imperfect, incomplete and
biased. Thus, at some point, our metaphor will keep producing more paradoxes because, in the end, it is not all about the subjective magic that we feel
caring entails. It is not all about magical worlds of love and devotion despite
the crudeness of evolution. As much as cooperation through caring might be
a necessary process of evolution, which we feel through strong subjective
emotions, nothing deletes completely the vestiges of competition in our own
evolved minds. Thus, in our intricate and impossible-to-capture psychologies,
intertwined with our magical dispositions to support parental caring, there are
also sordid dispositions to protect processes of competition. In a word, caring
leaders – including caring parents – sometimes, from a human perspective, will
not be so caring or magical, but simply horrific. Again, for evolution there is
no horror; parents simply are how they evolved to be, and that is it. Yet, for us,
through our biased subjective gazes of the world, they can look purely horrific
sometimes.

The conventional caring versus bearing debate would be a nice example of
this. For evolution, sometimes parents whose inner desires move them to care

for their offspring – i.e., to be a caring leader – is strategic. Yet, other times it is not. Because other times, perhaps, what is strategic would be to bear another child, and another, and another. This is not something new, as it is well known that in many poor societies people have many children. As they cannot care for them and guarantee their survival, the best they can do is to have as many as possible. As sombre as this might sound, the strategy works, because in the end it usually allows a decent number of children to survive to carry the parent's genes forward. In the end, therefore, what we need to remember is that there is no romance, there is no magic. The magic only exists within our gaze and our desperation to express artistically – from human bias – a process that might simply be inconceivable for us. We certainly see this in the parental relationship (i.e., the archetype of caring leadership), where many times conflicting interests between parents and children lead parents to abuse their children or even abandon them. Where is the magic then? And, is there real horror? There is not; it is just a human interpretation.

To conclude, if caring leadership is modelled on the caring parent, who is a product of intricate evolutionary processes, paradoxes might be perpetually inescapable for us humans and our subjective gazes. Perhaps the best example that could capture the inescapable paradoxes of parental caring is that of the praying mantis. Mantises are carnivorous insects, and when copulating it is not unusual that as the male craftily mounts the female mantis, the female bites the male's head off. Losing the head does not necessarily end the act of copulation, actually some inhibitory nerve centres reside in the head, so the male mantis provides an even better performance during the final acts of copulation. This, in a way, could be seen, from a human perspective, as baffling (unconceivable) caring by the female mantis, as she could potentially be increasing the chances of successful reproduction. Additionally, the energy she gets from eating the male's head will probably make her stronger for the purposes of reproduction. However, in the end, within all of this paradoxical (unconceivable) caring, there is inevitably an element of this is just how things are; the male was there, it was an easy prey, and she took advantage. That was it. In other words, we cannot simply pretend that we can objectively express caring leadership as magical realism. The metaphor, as humanly biased as it is, eventually ends up failing. In the case of mantises, for example, there was not much magic. It was simply nature blindly working its way to endure, while producing paradoxes in us because of our desire to conceptualize the world in human terms. Thus, the magic seems to be only ours, dwelling in our gaze. Yet, as delusional as it might be, it is who we are, it evolved in us as well for a reason, and hence, who we are we cannot deny. Our caring might seem falsely magically realist for us, but it moves us, it gives us meaning, it makes us love, it makes us feel with purpose. Is it not amazing that an apparently blind/unintended process – evolution – created, from nothing, caring leaders, such as parents, for whom the world is, even if perpetually paradoxical, a magically realist attempt to devote your life to others?

ACKNOWLEDGEMENTS

I would like to thank Enrique Galindo Fentanes and Enrique Reynaud Garza for their kind advice on previous versions of this manuscript, as well as Leah Tomkins for her support and guidance.

REFERENCES

Abreu Pederzini, G.D. (2018), 'Leaders, power, and the paradoxical position', *Journal of Management Inquiry*, **28** (3), 325–38.
Abreu Pederzini, G.D. (2019), 'Realistic egocentrism: Caring leadership through an evolutionary lens', *Culture and Organization*, 1–16. DOI: 10.1080/14759551.2019.163787510.1080/14759551.2019.1637875.
Blackmore, S. (1999), *The Meme Machine*, Oxford: Oxford University Press.
Bowers, M.A. (2004), *Magic(al) Realism*, London: Routledge.
Carpentier, A. (1949), *Prologue to The Kingdom of This World*, Ontario: The University of Western Ontario.
Dawkins, R. (2006), *The Selfish Gene*, 30th anniversary edn, Oxford: Oxford University Press.
del Toro, G. (2006), *Pan's Labyrinth*, Spain and Mexico: Picture House.
Gabriel, Y. (2015), 'The caring leader – What followers expect of their leaders and why?', *Leadership*, **11** (3), 316–34.
Garson, J. (2015), *The Biological Mind*, London, UK and New York, USA: Routledge.
Nowak, M. (2012), 'Evolving cooperation', *Journal of Theoretical Biology*, **299**, 1–8.
Tomasello, M. (2013), 'Origins of human cooperation and morality', *Annual Review of Psychology*, **64** (1), 231–65.
Wagner, A. (2014), *Arrival of the Fittest*, New York: Penguin Books.
Whitehead, A. (1967), *Science and the Modern World*, New York: The Free Press.
Wilson, E. (2014), *The Meaning of Human Existence*, New York: Liveright Publishing Corporation.

5.   Leading with embodied care

Amanda Sinclair and Donna Ladkin

It's definitely the most difficult part of my job; trying to figure out which mother and baby situation is the most critical; who most needs the hospital bed. I became a midwife because I care about new mums particularly – I remember how overwhelming birth and the first days of having a newborn can be. It breaks my heart when lack of resource means I need to discharge a poorly baby before he or she is really ready to go. It can affect me quite badly sometimes... (Fiona Kelly, Manager of a Neonatal Unit in the UK's National Health Service).

This quote highlights the central concern of this chapter: how might we understand – and instate – the significance of embodied care and self-care in leadership? How do leaders tap into the wisdom of their bodies to make decisions and choices which 'pull on their heartstrings' or 'churn their gut'? What dilemmas and costs do leaders face, especially women leaders, seeking to practise care as part of effective, ethical leadership?

Our view is that bodies play a central role in caring, and caring is central to leadership. Our bodies alert us to what and who is important *to* care for, guide us in sensing vulnerabilities and help us discern between competing calls on our care. Importantly, our bodies speak to us of our own physical and emotional limits, telling us when we ourselves are in need of care (should we choose to listen!). Yet such arguments are controversial. Traditionally, most leadership and ethical theories have held bodies and being open to caring as disruptive, not conducive, to effective leadership.

Each of us has come to an interest in embodied care in leadership from our different personal and professional histories. For example, drawing on cases such as that of former Victorian Chief Commissioner of Police, Christine Nixon, and Australian Indigenous school principal, Chris Sarra, Amanda has argued bodies and physical presence are often crucial ingredients of leaders effectively supporting followers (Sinclair, 2005). Donna has explored how practices of bodily dwelling and aesthetic sensibility can enhance ethical perception and awareness (Ladkin, 2015). For both of us, many years as MBA and leadership teachers have given us a passion for teaching differently and practising care in how we work with students. If we started out in our careers thinking that teaching and leadership were projects of the mind, we've learned that neither can – should – be done in a disembodied way.

To emphasise care and bodies in leadership is not just a compelling interest for us. It is a political and ideological stance. We are seeking to disrupt conventional wisdom which lionises disembodied logic and 'mental mastery' in leaders, an approach which also often deems self-care in leaders contemptible. We also want to engage with critics who regard a concern with embodied care as 'soft' or as betraying important ethical values of truth or transparency for special conditions. It is precisely this leadership territory of navigating the tensions and ethical trade-offs in practising care – for others and oneself – that we explore here.

To elucidate these complexities, our chapter interweaves vignettes of leaders and our own experiences with theoretical material, including the extensive feminist scholarship on care that has been largely ignored in leadership studies. Our aim is to build – and elicit in you – pictures of the kinds of practices in which a leader who embodies care might engage.

VIGNETTE 1: AMANDA'S STORY OF TEACHING MBA ETHICS

When I fell into teaching Management and Ethics as an MBA subject, I spent a lot of time scouring 'Business Ethics' texts. Most were/are weighty tomes with extended case studies seeking to corral students briskly through a quick tutorial in utilitarianism and deontology with some cultural relativism thrown in. Philosophical theories were tilted at and turned into decision trees and tools for resolving ethical dilemmas: 'If encountering a culture where bribes are accepted and offered a substantial gift then a. consider the consequences b. evaluate the significance of the ethical norms to that culture....' and so on.

Even though the students appeared to have an appetite for these models, I had none. They extolled calculation and cognitive notions of virtue and good. They lacked any recognition of the viscerality experienced by leaders and managers of being in the middle of an ethical dilemma. They ignored the push and pull, the tug of conscience versus the seduction of going with the flow. The inadequacy of what was on offer led me to women philosophers and feminist theorists. My first point of call was Carol Gilligan's work (1982) and Belenky et al.'s *Women's Ways of Knowing* (1986), both of which I was reading in recognition of the ways MBA culture, curriculum and pedagogy was gendered. These women researchers showed how women's approaches to learning were assigned a lower order in traditional models of moral reasoning.

I developed several classes and provoked discussion offering a critique of business ethics, its grounding in conventional philosophical models, and the possibility of adding calculations of care and context, employing criteria of preserving relationships and reducing particular suffering as legitimate considerations in moral deliberation and ethical decision-making. These ideas became key and helpful tensions guiding my students and my own learning beyond the immediate subjects I was teaching. I noticed that it was women and particularly feminist scholars who articulated courageous critiques of the sacred postulates of ethics. Their scholarship offered a different way not just of thinking but of living and being for me, putting an overarching value on relationships and tending the spaces and connections between people. Thus it began to percolate into my research of leaders and leadership.

As Amanda found when researching ethics, traditional models have devalued women's moral experiences and the ways in which they develop ethical judgements (Gilligan, 1982). Indeed a key prompt for Carol Gilligan and others' work in the 1980s was the unproblematised use of male populations to codify levels of moral development, for example in the influential studies by psychologist, Lawrence Kohlberg. One result of Kohlberg's oft-cited study (1971) – in which Gilligan was acting as a research assistant – was the creation of a framework of moral development that categorised the moral thinking of girls as inferior to that of boys when they put a higher value on caring for and preserving particular relationships, rather than applying universal principles. When young girls lied in order not to hurt a friend's feelings, this was considered a lower form of moral development compared to those boys who would tell the truth but risk harming the friendship.

As Australian philosopher Rosalyn Diprose shows, '(i)n Gilligan's revision of stages of moral development the ability to consider context, the details of relationships and the viewpoint of the particular other is seen not as moral failure but as essential to moral maturity' (1994: 11). Diprose goes on to argue, along with other feminist philosophers, that long-cherished societal moral codes have clear and demonstrable downsides for women. Inherited thinking about what matters in ethics is all too often a colonising and patriarchal moral order which 'is at the expense of justice for women and ... the usual approaches to ethics perpetuate and/or remain blind to such miscarriages of justice' (Diprose, 1994: vi).

Feminist ethics thus highlights that identities, moral and otherwise, can't be understood independently of bodies. A remedy according to Diprose is 'corporeal generosity'. Differentiating herself from those who see generosity as an individual mental virtue, Diprose says our bodies and affective sensibilities are integral in offering generosity and care. She puts a spotlight on the gendered norms of conventional thinking which memorialise the generosity of the privileged, while not registering or devaluing the generosity of others. Her intent is to promote justice and 'ways to foster social relations that generate rather than close off sexual, cultural and stylistic differences' (2002: 15). Central to such formulations is the requirement for dialogue, a true exchange between engaged parties imbued with respect and care for one another. The aim is to give moral urgency to addressing systemic, and often gendered, inequalities and suffering, and to provide ways of living together in open, generous and respectful ways.

Ethics, then, cannot be understood as a disembodied individual property or a virtue earned independently of relationships. Feeling pain, distress or discomfort in our own bodies provides the bridge for empathetically relating to others. Without our own embodied experience, it would be virtually impossible to appreciate how others might be affected by our actions. Ethical relations are always produced in relationship where the value and rights of sexed bodies are assumed and being constituted. As Donna has argued, it is the quality of relations and the space between people, rather than characteristics of a person, that are the measure of ethics (Ladkin, 2015).

Tensions in Practising Embodied Care

The notions described above of how bodies and care might be central to ethics and leadership have been controversial, including among some feminists who argue that linking the notion of care to the way women 'naturally are' fortifies unhelpful stereotypes. In this section we explore key tensions in pursuing embodied care in leadership:

- the dominant view that caring is the antithesis of the toughness required in leadership;
- how not to drown in caring for others, rather finding simultaneous self-care and authenticity;
- how care sits in relation to competing ethical values such as the need for truth and transparency; and
- scrutiny and marginalising women's caring as not leadership.

Care is often portrayed as the opposite of what leaders need: the capacity to stand up and make difficult decisions, to oppose or arbitrate popular opinion, with wartime leaders such as Winston Churchill offered as examples. Yet this view perpetuates a false dichotomy. Studies of effective leaders – as opposed to those who are driven by personal power and the need to dominate – overwhelmingly reveal intentions to advance the interests and welfare of communities. Exemplars such as Martin Luther King and Nelson Mandela show that empathy, care and a deep concern to relieve suffering are not evidence of sentimentalism but motivational for transformational leadership of nations.

When researching the interrelations between mindfulness and leadership, Amanda remembers coming across the Dalai Lama's Buddhist teachings on the role of love in leadership (Sinclair, 2016). Love is understood as the wish for another to be happy. Compassion is the wish for another to avoid suffering. No 'airy fairy' or idealised sentiment, love and care can be cultivated practically without necessarily liking others or sharing their point of view. Indeed, when Amanda looked for these approaches in leadership, she came across many leaders practising love and care in diverse and unlikely contexts – from football teams to those working against family violence. Feeling cared about was pivotal to team success – in conventional senses but also in wider terms of people finding fulfilment, meaning and connection in work and life. As argued by philosopher Martha Nussbaum (2013), love should be advocated by leaders because it is a strong motivating force for free and fair societies, occurring alongside and even supporting difficult decisions and courageous stands.

A second tension is how to practise care for others in leadership while not burning yourself out. Indeed it was a key dilemma for the leader in health care in our opening quote. Attending to one's self is a particular form of care that is typically devalued in leadership theorising which characterises leading as a hyper-masculine pursuit requiring toughness, endurance and rejection of bodily weakness. Self-care has also been critiqued as a concept that neglects structural and societal causes of suffering, putting the onus on individuals (those with the means to do so) to look after themselves.

It is part of leadership to make sure we understand and put first what matters. The growing body of work around resilience and mindfulness in leadership as well as the costs of psychopathology and illness, highlights the imperative for leaders to tend to their own well-being in order to fulfil their roles. In the following vignette, the NHS manager quoted at the start reflects on the importance of self-care.

VIGNETTE 2: CARE WITHIN THE UK'S NATIONAL HEALTH SERVICE

Fiona Kelly (a pseudonym) is a senior midwife and manager within the UK's National Health Service. The service has come under increasing pressure to cut costs over the last twenty years, and Fiona constantly finds herself making difficult trade-offs between the needs of patients and their babies. For instance, because of lack of space within neo-natal units, she is often placed under pressure to discharge babies before they are fully ready, in order to free up their space for newborns with serious health issues. How does she go about making such tough choices?

First of all, she says that she tries not to frame the situation in such a binary form. Although it is easy to jump to the view that a baby needs to leave in order to make room for another, she tries to imagine a more fluid way of thinking of the situation. This requires her to have an up-to-the-minute appreciation of resource flows within the larger NHS structure and her own hospital in particular. She is often able to call on support from other areas because of the care and attention she puts into developing relationships throughout the hospital, not just within her own unit. She also says she tries to hold the care for all of the patients at the heart of everything she does while attending to each as an individual. She stresses that each family situation and resourcefulness is different – it is by really knowing each patient and the kind of support structures that they do or don't have that leads to the best solutions. This sometimes means going against 'guidelines' – but she stresses that guidelines are for general situations and each case she deals with is unique. It requires caring about the uniqueness of each patient.

She also stresses that working with the high levels of relational attention that she expends would not be possible without the support and care of her family and friends. After experiencing a period of 'burn out', she now makes it a priority to provide herself with adequate down time. Unless she does that, she knows that she will not be able to provide the high level of care which makes her job enjoyable and sustainable in the long term.

The vignette raises a number of tensions inherent to leading with a care-based orientation. What happens to guidelines which indeed may be in place for very good reasons, when a caring response requires the leader to discard them? Here the wisdom of discretion comes into play. Fiona seems to be indicating not that guidelines should be discarded in a wanton fashion, but that the needs of the particular moment should also inform a leader's response. Additionally her vignette reveals the need to find creative and novel approaches which may not completely break the guidelines, but which take into account the fact that some problems may be outside the guidelines' remit.

Fiona's story also offers the insight that foregrounding care, on the one hand, and understanding the structural causes of oppression, on the other, are not mutually exclusive. Sara Ahmed argues, drawing on poet Audre Lord's *A Burst of Light*, that self-care may not be self-indulgence. 'As feminism teaches us: talking about personal feelings is not necessarily about deflecting attention from structures'. Self-care that involves speaking out about individual suffering, about 'histories that hurt, histories that get to the bone, how we are affected by what we come up against' is critical to changing structures (Ahmed, 2014).

A third tension in embodying care in leadership is how to personify care and maintain ethical values such as transparency and honesty, while under intense public scrutiny. The challenges of this are particularly apparent in the next two stories of women leaders who we perceive as undertaking their roles with care: Jacinda Ardern, New Zealand's Prime Minister, and Christine Nixon, in her role as Chair of Bushfire Reconstruction after the devastating 2009 Victorian bushfires. In each case there are also tensions between caring for others and for themselves in situations of duress. As women, both have had their caring approach (including in Ardern's care for her baby) portrayed as evidence that they are unfit to lead and should remove themselves from office.

VIGNETTE 3: LEADING A COUNTRY WITH CARE: JACINDA ARDERN, NEW ZEALAND PRIME MINISTER

Jacinda Ardern was elected Prime Minister in a 'cliff-edge' 2017 New Zealand election. Her actions and style of leading embody care at a series of levels: policy, political and ambassadorial, interpersonal and personal. While undoubtedly there are colleagues and constituents who have not experienced her leadership in this way, we identify some themes of care that have led to Ardern experiencing an international profile and reputation as a principled NZ Prime Minister.[1]

New Zealand governments have almost always worked by coalition. Unlike in Australia or the United Kingdom – where minor parties such as the Greens are regarded as enemies who need to be trounced – Ardern kept talking in the days immediately after the election, exhibiting genuine openness to building governing relationships. She found common ground with the conservative New Zealand First Party and made its leader, Winston Peter, her deputy. He has acted as PM in her periods of leave, including while she had her baby in 2018. 'She kept both parties in the tent and talking', observed a colleague.

The policies on which Ardern initiated immediate action were tackling child poverty, increasing housing availability and affordability, making the first year of tertiary education free and lifting the minimum wage. Interviewers and economic doubters challenged these initiatives with 'how can you afford it?' She responded courteously but briskly, saying that they had done the numbers and could afford it. They were also not proceeding with the tax cuts that her opponents had promised. Actions to fund, for example, an $890 million families package, were taken without fuss.

Ardern's own body has been highly visible and commented on. She announced that she was pregnant in early 2018 and gave birth to a baby girl in late June 2018. Shortly after the birth she posted photos of herself – looking tired and like she'd just given birth – with husband Clarke and baby Neve on social media. She thanked all the people who'd sent gifts and congratulations. There was a tenderness, vulnerability and openness that she offered at this time which few leaders allow.

Attending a Commonwealth meeting of heads of government in London in April 2018, Ardern was asked to wear and was loaned a Maori coat, beautifully decorated with feathers and a recognised symbol of her status. The symbolism spoke especially about respecting and celebrating Maori culture.

Observers are invited to feel Ardern's leadership and its ups and downs in a grounded and material way, including the pressures on her and the need for care and self-care. Her partner Clarke Gayford says it's his job to make sure she's eaten and hasn't got lipstick on her teeth. He said – before baby arrived – 'there's three of us in the relationship now. Me, her and the cabinet papers'.

As evident from these examples, Ardern expresses an ethos of leadership care with humour and lightness. She is comfortable in her body and willing to be with others in ways that are not stage-managed, but are spontaneous instead. For instance, in various interviews she has made comments such as:

- 'I'm sorry I've given you a nectarine hand (shake)'
- 'I value being able to do normal things, like driving myself and going to the department store to buy some maternity jeans … I was stopped by an older man in the lingerie department wanting to do a selfie with me. It's not something you'd want really, being photographed with the underwear…'

- 'I'll be sitting in a meeting and working hard on something, then I'll get a kick. That's the beauty of children. It's easy to think the moment you're in is the most important but there is life beyond it'
- 'People come up and say to me "Can I hug you?" I say "of course you can."'

Perhaps most remarkably, Ardern seems unbothered by doubters, critics and spin doctors who, no doubt, advise her to manage her image. She is disarming and gives a lot away about herself, her life, her experiences. She responds candidly to tricky questions (for example what she thinks of Donald Trump). She trusts interviewers to respond in kind to her authenticity.

Christine Nixon, who is the focus of our final vignette, has found herself under similar public scrutiny to that which Ardern encounters. Here we examine how the care which is central to her leadership approach informed the way in which she engaged with the reconstruction and recovery effort in the wake of the 2009 bushfires in Victoria.

VIGNETTE 4: CHRISTINE NIXON, CHAIR OF BUSHFIRE RECONSTRUCTION AND RECOVERY

There are many impactful examples across history and generations of what happens when women leaders voice and embody their differences on public stages (Nixon and Sinclair, 2017). Amanda's colleague Christine Nixon did just that in her swearing-in ceremony as Victoria's Police Commissioner in 2002. She publicly declared that being a woman, a partner and a daughter, would influence how she went about her job – and it did. She was never intimidated into not being a determined advocate for women and for greater equality.

The particular example of leading with embodied care we focus on here is how Christine went about her subsequent role as Chair of the Victorian Bushfire Reconstruction and Recovery Authority (VBRRA). Christine had announced her retirement as Chief Commissioner when the devastating February 2009 Victorian bushfires occurred. The Victorian Premier asked if she would lead the reconstruction and recovery effort.

It was daunting. Many lives and families had been lost. Huge tracts of land were burnt black with terrible consequences for the natural environment, the community and economy. The state and the country were traumatised. Where does one start? Christine says:

> I was not angling for the job, but I knew that the political instinct in these situations was to install a military commander at the helm, and my gut told me this would just not be right for the enormous task ahead. To be given the best chance to rebuild their futures, people needed to be asked what they wanted, consulted and engaged with – not told what to do. Recovery would not merely be a matter of infrastructure

and logistics; it would turn on matters of heart and soul. It was about reconnecting not just roads and power, but people with each other (Nixon, 2011: 314).

The task of leading the recovery effort thus involved Christine's physical presence over many months (and is still ongoing 10 years later), in many visits and meetings with desperate and grieving individuals. Often she could offer no solution. Instead her presence simply ensured that experiences, personal situations and needs for help were heard. She lost her own voice after a particularly lengthy round of community meetings. Christine also knew that people who'd lost families, homes and businesses had to be supported to make tough decisions, such as whether they'd start again in the area. No bureaucrat could make this decision for them. There were also local self-appointed leaders who claimed to know 'what's best for this community'. For those affected, Christine had to navigate the traumatised communities and the politics of emergency services. Most importantly she needed to embody a sense of care and build trust that she would ensure the right things were done, such as providing assistance with practical demolition, support services and housing, ensuring financial compensation was offered, as well as memorialising the losses for those affected.

Research on emergencies and disasters shows that leaders, especially those working on the ground of disaster, pay a high price. One of the ways some defend against the trauma and the difficulty of the task they are entrusted with is to 'parachute in', to retreat to procedures or to apply generic templates. It is much harder to offer 'corporeal *interdependence*' (Diprose, 2013), to be present to the devastation and loss, to listen and then to set about empowering those affected through one's confidence in the human spirit. This is what Christine did.

As the example of Nixon's leadership after the Victorian bushfires indicates, care of others and self-care need not be exclusive but are two sides of the same leadership coin. They are interdependent and each vitally important. Nixon's partner accompanied her on many visits and the long drives around affected, often remote, areas. Nixon made deep enduring friendships with members of affected communities and in the authority she led. She eventually took time out with lots of beach walks with a neighbour's dog, an eternally keen and undemanding companion. In order to respond to the exacting demands of caring, it is essential that leaders find such sanctuaries of care and attention for themselves.

CHALLENGES AND PROSPECTS FOR LEADING WITH EMBODIED CARE AND SELF-CARE

Perhaps one of the most demanding aspects of being a leader who approaches their role with care is that doing so is often accompanied by a heightened awareness of the suffering of others, much of which may be beyond the leader's capacity to change. At such times it is especially important to remember that leadership is not located in one, individual leader. It occurs in the relational spaces between and around people. When leadership is conceived in this way, the possibility of care being given and received becomes clearer. It is this kind of mutual reciprocity which makes for truly caring leadership spaces.

At the same time it is important to remember that those very spaces are also underpinned by deeper structural relations of power, class, gender and race. As discussed earlier, the notions of care and embodied care have acquired gendered meanings. Women are more likely to be expected to offer selfless devotion to a greater cause and to be typecast as weak when they do so. Men negotiate different, also damaging, minefields when their care or self-care is read as evidence of 'not having what it takes' to lead. As we have sought to show, innovative and engaged leadership demands we challenge these disembodied templates. Leaders practising embodied care and self-care create a radically different, potentially rich and satisfying space for their followers, including a sense of being supported and held.

Towards the end of one of our many Skype/Zoom conversations (we live on opposite sides of the globe), we were chatting about our yoga practice. For each of us yoga is both balm and fortifier, enabling us to keep perspective, do the (often taxing) teaching work we do and still look after ourselves. We turned to talking about our own yoga teachers. Amanda was admitting how lovely it felt to put herself in the hands of a teacher, being guided to find whatever was needed that particular day: a stretch in tired muscles, a letting go of a worry, a release into the simplicity of the breath or choosing peace. Donna was similarly sharing the profundity of giving herself over to the familiar embodied voice and rhythms of a trusted teacher, and how her own body – without her thoughts mediating – responds to the care with which he creates a peaceful and soothing space.

Many good teachers and leaders create this feeling for followers of being seen and held. It is the reason they are able to inspire and enthuse others to feel restored, to go to new places or to let go of self-doubts that haunt them. Our own experiences of being acknowledged by teachers and then supported – literally and physically – but more often emotionally and psychologically, have led us both to teach and lead differently ourselves. These experiences have prompted us in our research, our broader academic practice and our lives to know that bodies, caring and allowing ourselves to be cared for, are indispensable ingredients of ethical leadership.

NOTE

1. This chapter was written before the Christchurch massacre in March 2019. In relation to what we are writing here, it is important to note how Jacinda Ardern's response of care and compassion was internationally praised as an outstanding model of moral leadership. When Donald Trump called Ardern and asked her what support NZ needed she responded 'sympathy and love for all Muslim communities'. Furthermore, as a direct response to her leadership, within weeks of the atrocity gun laws in New Zealand were also radically reformed.

REFERENCES

Ahmed, S. (2014). 'Selfcare as warfare', *feministkilljoys*. Available at https://feministkilljoys.com/2014/08/25/selfcare-as-warfare/.

Belenky, M.F., Clinchy, B.M., Goldberger, N.R. and Tarule, J.M. (1986). *Women's Ways of Knowing: The Development of Self, Voice, and Mind*. New York: Basic Books.

Diprose, R. (1994). *The Bodies of Women: Ethics, Embodiment and Sexual Difference*. London: Routledge.

Diprose, R. (2002). *Corporeal Generosity: On Giving with Nietzsche, Merleau-Ponty and Levinas*. New York: State University of New York Press.

Diprose, R. (2013). 'Corporeal interdependence: From vulnerability to dwelling in ethical community', *SubStance* **42**(3), issue 132, 185–204.

Gilligan, C. (1982). *In a Different Voice*. Boston, MA: Harvard University Press.

Kohlberg, L. (1971). 'Stages of moral development', *Moral Education*, **1**(51), 23–92.

Ladkin, D. (2015). *Mastering the Ethical Dimension of Organizations*. Cheltenham, UK and Northampton, MA, USA: Edward Elgar Publishing.

Nixon, C. with Chandler, J. (2011). *Fair Cop*. Carlton: Melbourne University Publishing.

Nixon, C. and Sinclair, A. (2017). *Women Leading*. Carlton: Melbourne University Press.

Nussbaum, M. (2013). *Political Emotions: Why Love Matters for Justice*. Cambridge, MA: Belknap Press.

Sinclair, A. (2005). 'Body possibilities in leadership', *Leadership*, **1**(4), 387–406.

Sinclair, A. (2016). *Leading Mindfully*. Crow's Nest: Allen & Unwin.

PART III

The risks of care: dependency, exploitation and vulnerability

6. The shepherd king and his flock: paradoxes of leadership and care in classical Greek philosophy

Carol Atack

We bore in mind that, for example, cowherds are the rulers of their cattle, that grooms are the rulers of horses, and that all those who are called herdsmen might reasonably be considered to be rulers of the animals they manage.

(Xenophon, *Cyropaedia*, 1.1.2)

When Xenophon, the fourth-century BCE Athenian soldier and writer, and once one of Socrates' students, tried to explain the nature of leadership, in his extended case study and biography of Cyrus the Great, king of Persia in the sixth century BCE and founder of its empire, his *Cyropaedia*, he turned to a familiar image, that of the king or leader as shepherd.[1] For Xenophon, Cyrus provided a model of how to lead and inspire troops, and how, after the campaign was over, to set up a stable government in the conquered territory. Xenophon explores what qualities enabled Cyrus to rule more successfully than others. But when he invokes the image of the king as shepherd, Xenophon opens a set of questions about the consequences of the unequal and asymmetric relationship between leaders and those they lead, as well as emphasising the centrality of care to ideas of what constituted good leadership. Like other thinkers of his time, the image of the ruler as shepherd enables a debate on the paradoxes of leadership and care (Brock, 2013: 43–52).

Among the questions were: does being led somehow dehumanise the led, or deprive them of agency? Does it imply a duty of care for the leader? Is this duty different when leading creatures of the same type (other humans) or different (animals)? What qualities in the ruler, such as intelligence and knowledge, might persuade subjects to obey him? Or could all humans be treated as if they were of the same status as the leader, dissolving the hierarchy implied by the power relationship of shepherding? Because a principal goal of ancient politics was to secure a happy or 'flourishing' existence (Aristotle's concept of *eudaimonia*, or living well), individuals' surrender of political agency could be seen to create obligations for the ruler to whom they had assigned their claim to political participation. The image of the shepherd king provided a means of exploring this problem from the perspectives of both rulers and ruled.

Xenophon's introduction focuses on the ruler himself and avoids direct confrontation with the paradox set up by the analogy between ruling humans and shepherding animals. But his language shows the presence of that hierarchy: cowherds are 'rulers' (*archontes*, the word used in democratic Athens and elsewhere to describe the magistrates who administered civic government) and 'manage' (*epistatōsi*, more literally 'are set over') their flocks. Xenophon wants to demonstrate the special qualities of Cyrus, which led his subjects to surrender their political agency and the self-directed pursuit of their own well-being to him. Unlike the care of animals, Xenophon observed, ruling humans is difficult: 'it is easier to rule over any and all other creatures than to rule over men' (*Cyr.* 1.1.3). For Xenophon, Cyrus maintained his rule because his subjects were willing to obey him, and this came down to his intelligent style of leadership.

The possibility of the notionally equal citizens of a Greek polis surrendering to similar rule is much explored by Greek thinkers: Plato, in the *Republic*, envisages philosopher-kings with unparalleled knowledge or wisdom, while Aristotle imagines citizens making a conscious decision to put themselves in the hands of an absolute ruler, the *pambasileus* ('total king'), because of his outstanding excellence.[2] Despite the democratic context of Athens, questions of individual leadership dominated the discussions of Athens' political thinkers in the mid-fourth century BCE. During this period Athens gave greater individual responsibility to some of its magistrates, created new financial management roles, and also saw the rise of strong monarchs elsewhere, such as Philip II of Macedon, whose ability to command his forces without engaging in collective decision-making processes appeared to offer him a competitive advantage over the Athenians, with their endless debates and tendency to prosecute their unsuccessful generals.

This paradox of leadership and care was fundamental to ancient literature and thought, appearing in the literature of the Ancient Near East from its earliest beginnings. It is connected to ideas in which the care of human rulers for their subjects mirrored the care of gods – or God – for the cosmos as a whole. Michel Foucault observed that: 'The association between God and King is easily made, since both assume the same role: the flock they watch over is the same; the shepherd king is entrusted with the great divine shepherd's creatures.' (Foucault, 1981: 228).

Such a reading is central to the image's appearance in Hebrew texts such as the Book of Psalms: Psalm 23 evokes it to represent divine care for humans as an act of shepherding.

The shepherd king image appears in other Near Eastern cultures; the Babylonian epic *Gilgamesh*, originating in the fourth millennium BCE, informs the Greek use of the idea of the shepherd king (Haubold, 2015). Gilgamesh is identified as 'shepherd of Uruk the sheepfold', but his behaviour at the start of his story seems to fall short of a divine ideal, displaying arrogance towards his people, in contrast with his shepherding role (*Gilgamesh* I.86–87). The gods hear his people's complaints, and Gilgamesh endures chastening adventures until he returns home to rule in a more considerate fashion.

Agamemnon, the leader of the Greek forces in the Trojan War, also has lessons to learn about the importance of care. Homer's *Iliad*, the epic poem which is the foundational work of ancient Greek culture, dating in its written form to the seventh century BCE, opens with Agamemnon facing a crisis that challenges his reputation as 'shepherd of the people' (*Iliad* 1.263, and repeatedly thereafter).[3] Although Agamemnon has kept together a complex Greek coalition through nine years of battle, his greed in taking back a captive woman distributed to Achilles disrupts the stable order of his forces, provokes the gods, and threatens the campaign. The tension between Agamemnon's desire to fulfil his own desires, and his societal function ensuring the maintenance of order and satisfaction of the gods, is opened up, with the recurrent epithet reminding us of his role. While Xenophon's Cyrus listens to his troops and rewards their efforts, and also protects captive women from sexual aggressors, Agamemnon acts autocratically in pursuing his own desires even when a plague makes the gods' displeasure clear.

But the leader's duty of care is not absent from the Homeric world. Odysseus exemplifies a different style of leadership, in which risk-taking and trickery is balanced by care and concern. Odysseus risks his men's lives by lingering in the cave of the Cyclops (himself a shepherd) but uses his cunning to extricate the survivors. Some episodes begin with lapses in his concern, as at the final stage of their journey; Odysseus relaxes with home in sight and falls asleep, at which point his men ransack his belongings for secret treasure. They open a bag which turns out to contain all the winds, sending them far away from home again. In failing to share information with his men, Odysseus had created a risk that became critical when his attention failed: does the shepherding image imply a distrust in the ruled? His men, in turn, demonstrated that they needed a watchful leader to take care of them, perhaps one whose intelligence, like that of Odysseus, was marked through acts of cunning. The idea of leaders having a special status, differentiating them from those they led and linked to special responsibilities for them, was foundational in the epic poems revered by the Greeks, but episodes such as these show that it provided opportunities for analysis and debate of the qualities of both leaders and those they led.

THE RETURN OF THE SHEPHERD KING

While the idea of the shepherd king clearly had a place in the aristocratic societies of the distant past featured in Homer's epic poems, Michel Foucault argued that the egalitarianism of historical Greek cities made it less relevant to their citizens (Foucault, 1981: 5). Foucault claimed that these citizens regarded themselves as conceptual and practical equals, and that the sharply differenti- ated hierarchy of the shepherd king model should have no purchase for them. But Foucault fails to explain its continuing presence in Greek literature, which suggests that even democratic citizens (or perhaps critics of the difficulties of democratic practice) found it useful.

The egalitarian setting of the Greek city-state sharpened the paradox of the traditional image, because it revealed what was at stake in treating a ruler as the equivalent of a shepherd, particularly the implications of loss of autonomy and self-direction, valued aspects of citizenship, were citizens to submit to such a ruler. One could object that even in the democratic Greek city, most residents did not participate in decision-making; with women, children, the enslaved, and immigrant workers excluded from participation in political deliberation, every citizen male effectively exercised the power of the shep- herd king over his own household. When it came to deciding his own interests, however, would he choose to submit himself to the rule of a shepherd king rather than participate in decision-making for himself?

There was one context, military service, in which Athenian citizens did submit willingly to expert leadership. As examples from Homer's Agamemnon to Xenophon's Cyrus suggest, military leadership was one area in which caring oversight (*epimeleia*) in the context of command was expected. The context of war was significant; war was always seen as an occasion for decisive and skilled individual leadership, in which a general's experience and knowledge granted him an authoritative status, ability to decide when to act, and what to do. Such situations required obedience from citizen soldiers. But even so, during the period Xenophon documents in his history and writes, the Athenians as citizens frequently prosecuted the military leaders they had previously elected for their battlefield performance, particularly when there had been heavy losses.

Plato and Xenophon used the shepherd king image to refresh this debate, making a new case for strong leadership which might result in civic stabil- ity and the flourishing of the citizens, and often harking back to Homeric examples. While we already saw Xenophon use the image in the context of Persian monarchy, he also uses it in the texts in which he imagined the phi- losopher Socrates in discussion with a range of Athenians. Xenophon draws on his own military experience in his historical and philosophical writing;

his depiction of Socrates reveals much about conventional discussions of leadership in fourth-century Athens. His personal experiences of military action and leadership, as well as of philosophical education and debate, inform a series of dialogues in which Socrates and a series of Athenians discuss how to be an effective general and political leader. The brief opening discussion (*Memorabilia* 3.2) invokes Agamemnon to frame the debate in terms of the shepherd king:

> Once [Socrates] happened to meet someone who had been chosen to be a general. 'For what reason,' he said, 'do you think that Homer addresses Agamemnon as "shepherd of the people"?' Is it because the shepherd should take care (*epimeleist-hai*) that the sheep are safe and have the things they need, and that the purpose for which they are reared comes about, and a general too should take care that his soldiers are safe and have the things they need, and that the purpose for which they serve in the army comes about? And they serve in the army, so that when they win, they can be happier (*eudaimonesteroi*). (*Memorabilia* 3.2.1)

Some of the difficulties of the image emerge from this passage. The emphasis on the choice or election (the Greeks use the same word for both) of general or ruler does not transfer to both sides of the analogy. In democratic Athens, citizen-soldiers were led on campaign by leaders they had chosen, in pursuit of the goals decided in the city's democratic assembly. But this does not apply when sheep rather than humans are the objects of the leader's care; sheep do not elect their shepherds, or give them orders. The work of those being led is not the same. Sheep 'are reared (*trephontai*)', a true passive verb, while soldiers 'serve in the army (*strateuontai*)'; although the Greek verb endings are identical, and imply a parallel, the second verb is not a true passive, but indicates the soldiers taking an action which affects them personally. Even in this short passage, the difference between the sheep and soldiers is evident. While the soldiers can decide and communicate their goals, and choose a leader to help them achieve them, the sheep do not choose, and the shepherd must assume that the sheep will be content with what he feels will cause them to flourish.

However, the image works better from the perspective of leadership. Socrates goes on to argue that a king is 'chosen (*haireitai*) not to take care of himself well, but so that those who chose (*helomenoi*) him might do well through him' (3.2.3); generals have similar responsibilities to achieve the goals of those who have appointed them. The language of care runs through the whole conversation; the Greek concept *epimeleia* includes ideas of oversight, concern and caring.

In the end, Xenophon has Socrates conclude, the real concern of the leader is 'making those he leads flourish (*eudaimonas*)' (3.2.4), picking up the claim from the start of the passage that this is the aim of those who appoint the general. The benefit of the activity of leading, in this example, accrues to the led. In a democracy, this might be realised through the identity of leader and led; an Athenian general is also a citizen and benefits as a citizen from his military successes. But the shepherd king image also intimates a distinction between leaders and led. This was most plainly characterised by Plato as a distinction in the quality of knowledge possessed and used by each group; philosopher kings can use knowledge not available to those they rule, who only have access to shadowy and unstable opinion. The Greeks also thought that some kings (especially those of far-away places) claimed a special connection to the divine, whether through a special relationship with the gods, or actually being of divine status themselves.

Xenophon attempts to defuse the paradox inherent in the shepherd king analogy with a surprising claim. In the opening of the *Cyropaedia*, he claims that the flocks have consented to being led, and to the shepherd benefiting from his care for them:

> For the herds go wherever their keeper directs them and graze in those places to which he leads them and keep out of those from which he excludes them. They allow their keeper, moreover, to enjoy, just as he will, the profits that accrue from them. And then again, we have never known of a herd conspiring against its keeper, either to refuse obedience to him or to deny him the privilege of enjoying the profits that accrue. (*Cyropaedia* 1.1.3)

Xenophon's fullest illustration of the shepherd king in action is given by the mature Cyrus, ruling a new empire, and claiming a position distinct from that of his subjects:

> He said that the work of a good shepherd and a good king were about the same: for he said that a shepherd should make his flocks flourish while making use of them, if there is well-being (*eudaimonia*) for sheep, and the king in the same way should make cities and people flourish while making use of them. (*Cyropaedia* 8.2.14)

The alignment of the interests of rulers and ruled offers a way to defuse the paradox even in a case where the difference between them is assumed. Given that rule in the collective interest was a standard Greek definition of good government, whether a monarchy or democracy, this alignment suggests that the implications of surrendering to an absolute ruler need not be troubling. But Xenophon hints at doubts; he suggests that we do not know what *eudaimonia* might be for sheep, or even if the concept is applicable to them.

THE SOPHIST AND THE SHEPHERD

Not everyone in classical Athens agreed with Xenophon's ideas about the ethics of leadership, or saw leaders as benevolent shepherds concerned with meeting the needs of their flocks rather than themselves. Another perspective, often associated with educators in rhetoric known as sophists, emphasised individual gain, the satisfaction of ambition in competition with others and the pursuit of personal interest, narrowly defined. Such views are demonstrated in the 'Melian dialogue', an episode from Thucydides' history of the Peloponnesian War in which the historian imagines the people of Melos seeking mercy and justice from the Athenians, after the latter had defeated them, but are rebuffed with the claim that by necessity 'wherever anyone is stronger, they rule' (Thucydides *History of the Peloponnesian War* 5.105.2).

In his *Republic*, Plato introduces a character, Thrasymachus, based on a historical sophist and orator of that name, who expresses these views in argument with Socrates. He represents a 'realist' position in which the ethics of care, so central to the model of the shepherd king established by Xenophon, are dismissed as an irrelevance; his shepherd is a *homo economicus*, motivated only by the profit to be made from his use of the sheep. The welfare of the ruled becomes an instrument to the pursuit of the leader's own ends, not an end in itself.

Plato's critical analysis makes the strengths and limitations of the shepherd king model, which we saw Xenophon avoiding in the *Memorabilia*, explicit. In the course of a long argument in which both parties resort to some dubious sophistic moves, Thrasymachus and Socrates debate the attitude of the leader to those he leads (at this point in the *Republic*, the ruler is envisaged as a male, conventionally enough for the ancient world, although Socrates' later depiction of an ideal society imagines both male and female leaders operating as equals). Thrasymachus asserts the sophistic view that 'justice is nothing other than the advantage of the stronger' (*Republic* 1.338c), a view that clearly points back to Thucydides' Athenians. In this view, the powerful – whether they are many, as in a democracy, or few, or even a single monarch – rule in their own interest.

Earlier Greek thinkers had established a typology of regimes, organised by the number of rulers: one, few, or many (Herodotus 3.80–82). But this was refined (there is some debate as to when this happened, but the distinction was well-established by Plato's time) into a dual typology. In this revised model, each form of rule had a 'good' form, in which the rulers ruled in the interests of all citizens and the common good of the community, and a 'bad' form, in which the rulers ruled only in their own interest. The contrast between the idea of the good king, ruling for the benefit of the citizens, and the bad tyrant, extracting the resources of a society for personal benefit, typifies this opposition. In this typology, democracy was a problem case, because if all citizens ruled in their collective interest, the distinction collapses.[4] But the development of this typology provides another angle on the problems of the shepherd king analogy; can the shepherd king be said to be ruling in his own interest, or that of the herd he protects? If the former, as Thrasymachus suggests, that rules out any ethics of care beyond any extent to which the welfare of the ruled is congruent with the interests of the ruler. But Socrates (and Xenophon) disagree.

Unfortunately for Thrasymachus, his introduction of the ruler as an example enables Socrates to shift the argument to a consideration of the fallibility of craftspeople, using his principle of specialisation in which any craft only has a single aim and purpose – a doctor might misdiagnose their patients, and in the same way a ruler might issue a command which won't produce the desired result when their subjects obey it. Socrates uses the analogy of the doctor and the navigator to shift the question from the perspective of the ruler to the perspective of the craft itself, to argue that the craft seeks not what is advantageous to itself, but what is advantageous to its objects, the health of patients and the safe arrival of ships and passengers.[5] We can see in this argument the possibility of an ethics of care, in that the correct performance of a craft is necessarily beneficial to those on whom it acts, but Socrates does not foreground it. What he does do is argue for the advantage of those who are ruled as the proper object of the ruler's attention:

> No one in any position of rule, insofar as he is a ruler, seeks or orders what is advantageous to himself, but what is advantageous to his subjects; the ones of whom he himself is the craftsman. It is to his subjects and what is advantageous and proper to them that he looks, and everything he says and does he says and does for them. (*Republic* 1.342e, translation Grube)

This is the point at which Thrasymachus introduces the shepherding analogy, as he suggests that Socrates has improperly failed to account for the self-interest of rulers. Thrasymachus has already expressed impatience with the ideas being put forward by Socrates, and has argued with him about the motivation of the rulers of cities.

> You think that shepherds and cowherds seek the good of their sheep and cattle, and fatten them and take care of them, looking to something other than their master's good and their own. Moreover, you believe that rulers in cities – true rulers, that is – think about their subjects differently than one does about sheep, and that night and day they think of something besides their own advantage. (*Republic* 1.343b, translation Grube)

Socrates' response is to use his principle of specialisation to restrict the scope of what constitutes shepherding to the care of sheep. First, he outlines Thrasymachus' position: 'You think that, insofar as he's a shepherd, he fattens sheep, not looking to what is best for the sheep but to a banquet, like a guest about to be entertained at a feast, or to a future sale, like a money-maker rather than a shepherd' (*Republic* 1.345c).

Thrasymachus' error, he argues, is to assume that these functions are part of shepherding itself, but, for Socrates, shepherding is strictly the nurturing of sheep; selling them for profit is the province of an entirely different craft. This enables him to conclude that: 'Every kind of rule, insofar as it rules, doesn't seek anything other than what is best for the things it rules (*archomenōi*) and cares for (*therapeuomenōi*), and this is true both of public and private kinds of rule.' (*Republic* 1.345e).

For Thrasymachus, the shepherd king analogy is useful, because his 'realist' model does not differentiate between the ruled or sheep. Rulers seek only to extract whatever profit they can from those in their charge, regardless of kind. If they appear to be caring for them, as shepherds do when they fatten their flocks, it is simply that they are seeking to add value and maximise their future profits. Animal welfare is only a concern in that it supports the shepherd's goal of maximising his investment in the flock. For Socrates, on the other hand, the limitations of the analogy can be surmounted by an appeal to specialisation. The true work of the shepherd is in caring for the sheep; not just oversight, but nurture and care. Socrates' argument for this narrowed definition of the role has been much criticised, and Plato appears not to have been satisfied with it, returning to the theme again in later dialogues.

THE ABSURDITY OF THE HUMANS' SHEPHERD

In one of Plato's later works of political theory, the *Statesman*, Plato depicts his characters once more attempting to identify the elusive skill which makes one leader a good politician who is beneficial to the citizens and another not. The shepherding analogy enters again, first in a fantastically convoluted and complicated exercise in definition, and then in a powerful but grandiose myth. Both will show it to give an inadequate account of what is at stake when one human organises the lives of others.

The dialogue's main speakers, the Eleatic Visitor, a philosopher from Elea in southern Italy visiting Athens, and Young Socrates, a student Socrates chooses to take part in the discussion because of his shared name, attempt to produce a definition of the political leader or statesman by isolating the skills and features that distinguish being a statesman (*politikos*) from other endeavours. The first stage is to agree that it involves the care of living creatures, looked after in groups: farmers of horses and cattle are a better analogy than grooms taking care of individual horses (*Statesman* 261e). The next step is to differentiate the statesman from others who care for herds. Young Socrates suggests, using a word used for rearing children as well as livestock: 'I think there's a difference between the maintenance (*trophē*) of human beings and the maintenance of beasts' (*Statesman* 262a, translation Waterfield).

The Eleatic Visitor grandly rejects this straightforward opposition of human and animal as objects of care, developing a fantastically complex framework within which the 'collective maintenance of human beings' (267e) does not differ from that of animals. Plato does not emphasise the implication of the typology, but this model provides a mechanism through which it might be possible to treat some humans as non-equals. He then turns to delivering a myth in which this typology is realised, in a long-past age in which humans and animals received the same kind of care from the divine spirits who herded them: 'a different divine spirit was assigned to every species and every flock, to act as its herdsman, so to speak. Each spirit had sole responsibility for supplying all the needs of the creatures in his charge.' (271d)

While Plato's description of the idyllic life of these early humans draws on other Greek depictions of a golden age – the spontaneous availability of sufficient food, the lack of need for clothes or bedding – this version is distinctive because it suggests a possibility that these humans lack opportunities available to humans living now in the Age of Zeus, the possibility of autonomous participation in the political and social life of the city.

Another vision of life under a shepherd king is provided by Xenophon, in his description of the mature Cyrus' rule over his empire, and particularly over his extensive royal household. The preparations for a royal hunting expedition provide an image of the organisation of society as a whole. Cyrus distinguishes between the participants; the nobles taking part must follow aristocratic conventions about refraining from eating while in the field, but the slaves accompanying them are looked after in the same way as the horses the nobles ride. When the animals are given a rest break and led to water or given food, so are the enslaved workers (*Cyropaedia* 8.1.44). In return, those taken care of address him as 'father'. Cyrus' slaves are managed in the same way as the flocks of Plato's divine spirits; the hierarchy operates between groups of humans classified with different statuses.

From the perspective of the ruled, living under a shepherd ruler might result in a less fulfilling life for a human flock, because the automatic satisfaction of their physical needs would reduce the opportunities for the exercise of distinctively human characteristics in the pursuit of human goals, the use of the capacity to reason, the exercise of agency, in activities such as the organisation of political communities. Plato's model of the practice of the *politikos*, developed to replace the definition and the myth, avoids the cosmology and transposes the hierarchy to the practices and craft of the ruler rather than the ruler himself. His characters identify a distinctive and superior 'political' or 'kingly knowledge' (*Statesman* 292e) which supervises the practice of other crafts, ensuring that they combine in a productive way. Plato does not envisage many humans demonstrating the necessary qualities.

CONCLUSION

The image of the shepherd king provided a fruitful space for the ancient Greeks in considering the ethical obligations of leaders to those they led, in political and military contexts, and paradoxes arising from the conflict between the advantages of clear leadership and the loss of individual agency and autonomy in submitting to such rule. It enabled ancient theorists of leadership to conceptualise relationships between leaders and those they led, to consider how and why there might be a question of care in this relationship, and on what basis such power relations might be justified. While it originated in a context of rulers characterised by special access to the divine, the possession of skill and intelligence emerged as a prime justification for granting a ruler the status of a shepherd king, enabling leaders to extricate the led from difficult military and political situations. Throughout Greek literature, Homer's contrasting models of leadership, represented by flawed characters such as Agamemnon and Odysseus, were used to illustrate the complex and often paradoxical ethics of care the model imposed on leaders.

NOTES

1. Wayne Ambler's edition of the *Cyropaedia* offers an up-to-date translation and a glossary of Greek philosophical terminology used by Xenophon (Ambler, 2001).
2. Plato *Republic* books 5–7; Aristotle *Politics* 3.14–17 (1285b20–1288a32).
3. Variants of 'shepherd of the people' occur 56 times in Homer (Haubold, 2000: 197).
4. Greek thinkers tended to assume that democracy resulted in a tyranny of the majority, with the poor ruling in their own interest and against the interest of the wealthy.
5. Plato's argumentation in this passage has been much criticised; see Nawar (2018).

REFERENCES

Ambler, W. (2001), *Xenophon: The Education of Cyrus*, Ithaca, NY: Cornell University Press.

Brock, R. (2013), *Greek Political Imagery from Homer to Aristotle*, London: Bloomsbury.

Foucault, M. (1981), '*Omnes et Singulatim*: Towards a Criticism of "Political Reason"', *Tanner Lectures on Human Values*, 223–54. Accessed 9 January 2019 at https://tannerlectures.utah.edu/_documents/a-to-z/f/foucault81.pdf.

Grube, G.M.A. and Reeve, C.D.C. (1992), *Plato: Republic*, Indianapolis, IN: Hackett Publishing.

Haubold, J. (2000), *Homer's People: Epic Poetry and Social Formation*, Cambridge: Cambridge University Press.

Haubold, J. (2015), '"Shepherds of the People": Greek and Mesopotamian Perspectives', in R. Rollinger and E. van Dongen (eds), *Mesopotamia in the Ancient World: Impact, Continuities, Parallels*, Münster: Ugarit-Verlag, pp. 245–54.

Nawar, T. (2018), 'Thrasymachus' unerring skill and the arguments of *Republic 1*', *Phronesis*, **63** (4), 359–91.

7. Leadership and the fiduciary: addressing asymmetrical power by caring well

Helen Mussell

Studying juridical concepts in their historical context opens up new perspectives on institutional change and contributes to our understanding of social reality.[1]

INTRODUCTION

The legal concept of fiduciary, from the Latin *fiducia* meaning trust, plays a fundamental role in all financial and business organisations, as well as governing other professional relationships including medical care.[2] It acts as a moral safeguard of the relationship between trustee and beneficiary, ensuring that the beneficiaries' best interests are met. It is often referred to as a duty of care. Originally formulated within English common (familial) law to protect property put into Trust while the rightful (male) owner of the property was absent, for example fighting Crusades, beneficiaries were women and children, allocated passive and subordinated roles. As the lawyer Benjamin Richardson writes; "Historically, trusts arose in England primarily to protect family wealth and to provide for the wife and children, who were socially constructed as passive and dependent. Modern investment law transplanted these arrangements for the private trust into a very different context" (Richardson, 2011, p. 6).

With this in mind, the fiduciary arrangement – referred to as both relationship and duty – could be said to have been devised as a substitute for a familial relationship, one supposedly underpinned by care, and taking place within the private sphere. In this way, the fiduciary, and its associated body of fiduciary law constituting part of tort law, is concerned with managing this substitute relationship in all its complexity, a point also made by Paul Miller who notes that; "Fiduciary law, more than any other field, undergirds the increasingly complex fabric of relationships of interdependence in and through which people come to rely on one another in the pursuit of valued interests" (Miller, 2018, p. 1).

However, what must be made clear alongside this acknowledgement of fiduciary and interdependence, is that the distribution of power within this relationship is not egalitarian. Indeed, the relationship is *premised* on an unequal distribution of power, of the trustee having power (and subsequent authority) over the beneficiary, with the trustee leading on decision making (economic or otherwise). So it can be safely concluded that this substitute caring relationship has a *prerequisite of a power mechanism*, of an assumed responsibility of the trustee, with the trustee leading the relationship.

With this in mind, this chapter not only treats the trustee as leader and the beneficiary as follower, but also seeks crucially to draw attention to the rationale behind this power imbalance, to deduce why this power mechanism plays such an integral role in the fiduciary. This can arguably be done by fleshing out some of the presuppositions regarding the beneficiaries' agential capabilities, presuppositions which underpin the social construction of passivity and dependency which Richardson draws attention to – specifically that women (and children) were deemed to be without full reasoning capability, and so incapable of economic agency. They were allocated, as has been well-argued by feminist philosophers[3], the role of being the "emotional gender", whilst males were deemed capable of reason, and a result of this particularly dangerous and damaging gender divide has ultimately been the subservience highlighted by Richardson in the context of the fiduciary.

The assumed capabilities of this subservient role are now embedded in the fiduciary in the corporate context, and as Richardson writes,

> Rather than treating beneficiaries as self-governing and responsible owners of assets, the trust provides a legal fiction whereby ownership and control become separated, with the owners (beneficiaries) assuming a subservient role while control is vested in trustees to act on their behalf (Watt, 2006). Trustees, unlike an agent who is subject to control of his or her principal, are not legally obliged to consult with beneficiaries. They only need to act in their "best interests", yet they need not enquire what those best interests are. (Richardson, 2011, p. 6)

Richardson added later that "the notion that investors are expected to be largely passive has become well entrenched as a matter of law and business practice" (*ibid.*)

GENDER STEREOTYPES AND POWER

The above brief introduction to the fiduciary, including its evolution as a juridical concept, along with the central role that power and care play in the relationship between trustee/leader and beneficiary/follower, highlights a number of central conceptual characteristics requiring further attention. First, the foundations of the asymmetrical power at the core of the fiduciary, when read in light of this gendered relational dynamic, are revealed to be implicitly rooted in gender stereotypes. Power differentials are open to abuse. Indeed, the assumed inequity of power between trustee and beneficiary is precisely why the fiduciary duty exists: it is there to safeguard against the trustee using their power to gain advantage – economic or otherwise – over the beneficiary.

Secondly, the (original familial) fiduciary also requires examination for its assumptions regarding the agency and capabilities of the beneficiary/follower. In short, the fiduciary is premised on a fiction regarding the (ir)rationality and limited decision-making capabilities of the (female) beneficiary. This is clearly a false gender stereotype, steeped in assumptions about the supposed *nature* of females and their agency. And what is more, there is another damaging gender stereotype also playing a part in the fiduciary, this time steeped in assumptions about (male) trustees having rational and self-interested natures, mirroring the fallacious claims made regarding rational economic man, also known as *homo economicus*, who is, by contrast to the supposedly selfless and emotional beneficiary, a self-interested rational agent. It is of course this supposedly self-interested nature which must be fettered via the fiduciary, to ensure against abuse of the position of trust the trustee is placed in. In summary then, the fiduciary is premised on a number of gendered stereotypes which rely on warped caricatures of the supposed natures of males and females, stereotypes which have been shown to be erroneous and outright damaging – and neither males nor females emerge from the portrayals in a particularly pleasant or desirable light.

With all this in mind, and whilst acknowledging there are a wide range of interesting angles from which to investigate the fiduciary, the objective of the remainder of this chapter is as follows: (1) to determine how fiduciaries are currently identified by judiciary, and through doing so explore the gendered asymmetrical power dynamic embedded in the fiduciary and related legal theory; and (2) to offer some thoughts on what these investigations concerning exposed power structures, including the lived experience of them, can suggest about how the fiduciary relationship can be re-thought for future use.

IDENTIFYING THE FIDUCIARY AND EXPLORING THE GENDER AGENDA

In his chapter focusing on how fiduciary relationships can be identified, Miller provides a helpful account of the multitude of ways in which fiduciary relationships are determined and recognised by judiciary. Miller's objective is to lay out the process of identification, highlighting key characteristics that judiciary look for in determining if a fiduciary relationship existed. This is important because, as we shall come to see, the social process of legal identification both reinforces and (re)constructs the power asymmetry and continues to embed the implicit stereotypes already highlighted.

Noting the predominant use of two methods of identification – status-based and fact-based reasoning – Miller starts by outlining the "default" position of status-based reasoning, drawing attention to the importance placed on social positions and occupations of trustees, occupations characterised by their underpinning by, and predominant use of reason. He writes:

> The prevalence of status reasoning is reflected in conventional wisdom about fiduciary law: one tends to think of fiduciary principles as attaching to persons by virtue of the legal or social role or position they occupy. Thus, we say that trustees, directors, agents, lawyers, and doctors are fiduciaries, and so too, by implication, we attach a fiduciary characterization to the relationships in which these persons perform their roles. We – and by "we" I mean here to include lawmakers – usually say these things unreflectively. As we will see, habitual reliance on status is encouraged by black letter law. Over time, fiduciary laws come to encompass an increasing number of kinds of relationship to which authoritative attributions of fiduciary status have been made. One searching for a principle of growth – i.e., clear public justification for the extension of status – will find it elusive. (Miller, 2018, pp. 7–8)

There is a lot to draw out of this statement, particularly if we use a lens of gender theory, along with aspects of feminist philosophy, to address and correct the lack of reflectivity (and thereby implicit presuppositions) which Miller so honestly and graciously highlights. What is crucial to note here, and to explicitly link back to the aforementioned allocations of the gendered emotional (f) and reasonable (m), is that until relatively recently, the identified professional roles – the roles of lawyers, doctors, directors – were out of reach of females. And what is also crucial to note is that these occupations afford participants the requisite *status* used by judiciary to identify fiduciary, with status implicitly imposing "hierarchy", and with those with status having power or benefits over those without.

It will be useful here to refer to a classic text which explores the emotion/reason hierarchy and its gendered history. Genevieve Lloyd's *The Man of Reason* (1993) was central in highlighting elements of this male bias and has since inspired generations of feminist theorists. In her book, Lloyd extensively reviews the way in which central figures in Western philosophy have set out the role of reason, of what it is, of how to achieve it, and what its purpose is. She examines how these central figures constructed reason within the context of gender, and how this maps onto wider social structure. By examining the work of Descartes, Rousseau, Kant, Hegel, Hume, Sartre and De Beauvoir, Lloyd demonstrates how reason has developed as an ideal, an ideal constructed *through the image of maleness*. An ideal which constitutes femininity as that from which transcendence, via rationality, can be obtained; the flight from the feminine and a *quest for separation.*

The result of the maleness through which this ideal has been constructed and the femaleness against which it has been contrasted, an ideal which can be said to have determined the course of philosophical and scientific method, is a philosophical history riddled with value-laden hierarchical dichotomies: of reason/ emotion, male/female, rationality/nature, public/private. As Lloyd writes:

> What is valued – whether it be odd as against even numbers, "aggressive" as against "nurturing" skills and capacities, or Reason as against emotion – has been readily identified with maleness. Within the context of this association of maleness with preferred traits, it is not just incidental to the feminine that female traits have been construed as inferior – or, more subtly, as "complementary" – to male norms of human excellence. Rationality has been conceived as transcendence of the feminine; and the "feminine" itself has been partly constituted by its occurrence within this structure. (Lloyd, 1993, p. 104)

The existence of such dichotomies is not, however, as Lloyd is keen to point out, evidence of intentional construction, noting that "The exclusion of the feminine has not resulted from a conspiracy by male philosophers." (*ibid.,* p. 109). However, exposing and identifying these dichotomies is crucial, for these are not harmless relics of the past. Such dichotomies are still very much active and effective in present day thinking. They underpin social structures and block progress. They continue to limit individual's potential, and they narrow thinking:

> Contemporary consciousness, male or female, reflects past philosophical ideals as well as past differences in the social organization of the lives of men and women. Such differences do not have to be taken as norms; and understanding them can be a source of richness and diversity in a human life whose full range of possibilities and experience is freely accessible to both men and women. (*ibid.,* p. 107)

One need not look too far to identify how "past philosophical ideals" regarding reason play out in gendered vocations listed by Miller. Indeed, I would argue that any search for "a principle of growth – i.e., clear public justification for the extension of status" might do well to start with an examination of such philosophical ideals. And it is important to note the stickiness of such past philosophical ideals and the normative function they fulfil. Again, without having to expend too much energy in the search for examples, we see that those academic disciplines regarded as requiring advanced reasoning skills – including mathematics, philosophy, and law, and associated disciplines such as engineering and economics – are still widely dominated by male participants. It is then no coincidence that those careers which are dependent on the attainment and use of these disciplines, which are often seen as the pinnacle of reason, are also highly remunerated and afforded the high social status that "qualifies" them to be identified as fiduciaries.

By contrast, examples abound of the low remuneration and poorer social status often afforded to those occupations on "the other side" of the gendered dichotomy, such as caring roles including nursing and childcare, which whilst recognised for their crucial contribution to society, are caught in a valued/ devalued "care paradox"[4], of being systematically morally elevated whilst being poorly remunerated.

But how does all of the above assist in exploring the gendered asymmetrical power dynamic embedded in the fiduciary, of the trustee/leader and benefi-ciary/follower? How does it draw out the *paradox of care* in the fiduciary, or help in explaining the *experience of asymmetry* in the relationship, both of which are important in the context of this collection? It is worth turning again to Miller's helpful paper in this regard, and to the second most dominant method judiciary use to identify fiduciary *in the absence* of clear and evident "status-based" reasoning; namely that of "fact-based" reasoning, or the identi-fication of "the necessary and sufficient properties of a fiduciary relationship" (Miller, 2018, p. 11). It is here, in this second identificatory process – which to recall is important because it both reinforces and (re)constructs the power asymmetry – that perceived issues of vulnerability, of trust, and the role of power imbalance and associated issues of authority really come to the fore. In short, when the implicit role of power hidden in "socially accepted" positions of status is removed, we get a clearer view of the experience of asymmetry in the fiduciary relationship. Noting that the identified range of necessary and sufficient properties is broad and often vague, Miller does however provide the following summary:

> Fiduciary relationships are variably said to implicate: *the possession and exercise of legal authority and/or power by one person relative to another; an inequality in material position, power, strength or influence; the dependence and/or vulnerability of one person upon another*; a more specific susceptibility to harm, as where one's assets or person is placed at risk of conversion or exploitation; the exchange of confidential or private information; a repose of trust and/or confidence; *the legal or actual incapacity of a party and/or a complete or situational inability to engage in monitoring, reporting, or other form of self-protection; the reliance of one person upon another*; or, one person's expectation of goodwill, altruism, loyalty or compe-tent or considered advice or judgment from another. (*ibid.*, p. 12 – *emphasis added*)

It is in this list of characteristic properties, used by judiciary for fact-based identification of fiduciary, that the clear asymmetry of power embedded in the fiduciary relationship is starkly revealed, where leader/follower relations become clearer. The disempowerment, legal and otherwise, of the beneficiary/ follower comes sharply into focus. By extension, it is also here that we see the degree of importance which the trustee – placed in such a position of power as "protector" over the beneficiary (who, as we must recall, in the original familial context had limited choice regarding such dependency when the legal doctrine of coverture is also taken into account, with married women legally obliged to sign over all property to their husbands) – must consider this great moral responsibility and learn to *care well*. This moral responsibility being framed as one of caring is a point taken up by Goldstone et al. (2013) in their special report on fiduciary professions entitled "The moral core of trusteeship: How to develop fiduciary character".

Situating their discussions squarely within the financial/Trusts context, and contemporising their example with the Trustee being female, they advise the following:

> But the trustee isn't pure minded. As Aristotle indicates, character shapes the passions. The equitable tradition (not to mention modern litigation) suggests that the first passion of this character is acquisitiveness. The trustee must develop a settled habit of choosing well with regard to taking and not taking for herself. Further, the tradition points to the importance of the passion of care. *The trustee has to develop a settled habit of caring well, both for the grantor (or her wishes) and for the beneficiary. Only by developing this active condition can a trustee hope to avoid the twofold pitfall of paternalism and infantilization.* (Goldstone et al., 2013, p. 51, *emphasis added*)

So according to Goldstone et al. the fiduciary relationship – or as they describe it "good Trusteeship" (*ibid.*, p. 50), requires the Trustee/leader to develop "a fiduciary character" (*ibid.*), one which fundamentally involves learning how to *care-well*. But what does this entail? And how will it help avoid paternalism and infantilisation (which can be interpreted as another articulation of over-caring and its associated issues of infringement of an individual's autonomy)?

Goldstone et al. present a suggestion for how to develop the "fiduciary character", and crucially – particularly within the context of ethics – they frame it in the language of "the particular", as opposed to "the universal", noting that, "what's crucial to good trusteeship isn't primarily a set of rules, but the development of a type of character" (*ibid.*), adding later that, "Developing character involves shaping the vision of the good through attention to particular examples. We call this work exercising 'moral imagination'" (*ibid.*, p. 51).

It is at this point that a reflection on the Ethics of Care, or Care Ethics, will be beneficial, in order to consider what "caring-well" could look like, and to further unpack the suggestion of how fiduciary relates to care, or more specifically, how fiduciary can be theorised using Care Ethics. Care Ethics is a contemporary body of ethical theory originating from the work of Carol Gilligan, initially undertaken within the discipline of moral developmental psychology, but later developed within philosophy and political science, and widely accepted to have stemmed from the publication of her book *In a Different Voice* (1982). Responding to the work of her supervisor Lawrence Kohlberg, whose Kantian influenced theory of moral development suggested that females appeared to "stall" at the level of "conventional morality" – characterised by Kohlberg as being hampered by a preoccupation with the maintenance of relationships and social order, rather than considering and using universal principles and rights in the reasoning process – Gilligan instead identified a *different* moral orientation, expressed via a *different voice*. Summarising the process of moral reasoning she had identified, Gilligan notes:

> In this conception, the moral problem arises from *conflicting responsibilities rather than from competing rights* and requires for its resolution a mode of thinking that is *contextual and narrative rather than formal and abstract*. This conception of morality as concerned with the activity of care centers moral development around the understanding of responsibility and relationships, just as the conception of morality as fairness ties moral development to the understanding of rights and rules. (Gilligan, 2003, p. 19, *emphasis added*)

Gilligan's work was celebrated for its identification and validation of a moral perspective which has always been in existence, but which had become lost behind Western ethical theory that values individualist, rights and principle centred ethics (i.e., certain interpretations of Kant) – theory which had influenced Kohlberg's work. Returning to this chapter's context, the importance of Care Ethics for theorising how the Trustee/leader can develop a fiduciary character – including learning how to care-well – is two-fold. First, Care Ethics has a strong focus on the contextual/particular as opposed to universal rules, and secondly, and relatedly, the use of moral imagination, centring on responsibility towards an individual (beneficiary) and an understanding of their particular needs and best interests, is paramount.

Taking Care Ethics into the realm of practice, by helpfully developing some normative guidance, Virginia Held builds on Gilligan's work in her 2014 paper, "The ethics of care as normative guidance: Comment on Gilligan". She writes:

> Practices of care call for sensitivity, empathy, trust and especially responsiveness to need. They cultivate the development of trust and mutual consideration. Care relies on the insights and motivations of the emotions as well as on reason. It values especially caring relations, not simply the dispositions of individual persons. In contrast with the model of the "liberal individual" of the dominant moral and political theories, it conceptualizes persons as relational. It especially understands how the whole framework of self *versus* other, of egoism *versus* altruism, is misplaced for much of human life already, and how it could and should be reduced rather than expanded in applicability. (Held, 2014, p. 111)

But Held's work goes a step further in helping outline how Care Ethics can provide the requisite ethical framework needed by Goldstone et al. for the development of their "fiduciary character". She directly confronts the issue that "A common objection to the ethics of care is the supposition that it encourages paternalism. Instead of the rugged individual of contract theory, what is conjured up is the domineering mother. Not only is this a mistake, but on the contrary, the ethics of care may be unusually helpful in avoiding paternalism" (*ibid.*). She continues by outlining an example of avoiding paternalism in development work, where there is a concern that caregivers can confuse their desires by projecting them onto the individuals they wish to help, resulting in a sort of unconscious paternalism. Held's conviction is that:

> Caregivers need to *learn* how to avoid doing so, need to *cultivate* the ability to distinguish their own needs and desires from those of the recipients of their care. The ethics of care directs them to do so and shows them how. It aims to enable people to provide and receive *good* care, not merely the minimal care required for life to continue, and to do so in morally admirable caring relations. (*ibid.*, p. 112, *emphasis in original*)

This emphasis on needing to *learn* how to care-well – that caring-well is something that must be developed – clearly mirrors the suggestion of Goldstone et al., who, to recall, emphasise that "Developing character involves shaping the vision of the good through attention to particular examples. We call this work exercising 'moral imagination'", and who, to reiterate, are also keen to underscore that, "The trustee has to *develop* a settled habit of caring well". This is then a learning process indeed. And one which, as we may recall from the status-based reasoning used by the judiciary of earlier – which *still* unreflectively elevates reason over emotion, and *still* sees reason as best detached from emotion – will potentially be resisted by "fiduciary professions" who may view this form and subject of education as "out of place", due to its confliction with still strongly imbued past-philosophical ideals.

A FUTURE-FIT FIDUCIARY, WITH REALIST UNDERPINNINGS

I have of course promised to deliver on a second point: to reflect on how the above investigations – exposing implicit gendered power structures and the care paradox they present – can help in thinking through a future-fit fiduciary, one in which gendered caricatures no longer run riot through the underpinnings of an appropriated legal concept harbouring past philosophical ideals.

Where to begin? Thankfully, much work has already been done in uncovering the damaging emotion/female and reason/male dichotomy on which some of the core tenets of Western philosophy were premised, and some of that work has been highlighted (again, see Lloyd, 1993 and Prokhovnik, 2002, amongst many others). But the application of that work to feminist jurisprudence – or the philosophy of law – is still rather scant and requires focus. There has also been considerable work undertaken in exposing the caricature of rational economic man, or *homo economicus*, within the context of economic (and relatedly finance) theory (for recent contributions see Mussell, 2018 and Nelson, 2016). However, the track record of weakening *homo economicus'* hold on economic theory is not strong, despite robust, rigorous and repeated arguments against. Why? Without laying out chapter and verse on the issue, I believe this has already been rather neatly summarised within the context of organisational and management studies – "Culture eats strategy for breakfast"[5] – and culture, which is performed and reinforced by people, and which includes the judicial identification process investigated here, acutely retains unconscious bias, protects vested interests, and may be highly resistant to change.

Out of theory and into practice, there is however arguable evidence of push-back against the fiduciary premise that the trustee knows best, and therefore need not consult with beneficiaries regarding their best interests. One example is shareholder activism. This can take the role of increasing demands on investment managers to communicate investment decisions in the context of socially responsible investments. But shareholder activism also includes push-back against company directors, not only questioning remuneration packages, but also demanding information on corporate social responsibility or sustainability strategies. The era of the silent shareholder, passive in their asset ownership, appears to be shifting towards a more vocal beneficiary, one who no longer accepts a purely subordinated position, but who instead demands details of the rationale behind the trustees' decision making and calls into question their performance. A beneficiary who, it can be argued, demands a more balanced caring relationship, one in which practices of caring-well include "sensitivity, empathy, trust and especially responsiveness to need" and one which "cultivate[s] the development of trust and mutual consideration" (Held, 2014, p. 111). In the context of shareholder activism, it appears that beneficiaries are increasingly resistant to following the trustee's lead.

FINAL THOUGHTS

The trustee – positioned as having power over the beneficiary – necessitates them being the leader in the fiduciary relationship, thus assuming a position of responsibility. The history of the fiduciary, including the premises regarding beneficiaries' agency and reasoning capabilities, are outdated and fallacious. They were – and still are – founded in dubious gender politics, upheld by now outdated laws including coverture. Yet these presuppositions and the past philosophical ideals on which they are founded are still clearly evident in present-day fiduciary relationships. So much so that judiciary unreflectively default to, and so perpetuate and reinforce, the supposed core characteristics by which a fiduciary can be determined. By emphasising and elevating reason in their reliance on status-based reasoning, and by seeking evidence of the characteristics of inequality, dependence, reliance and authority in fiduciary relationships, the inequity of power in the relationship is enforced as a key determinant.

The fiduciary relationship is at core a *moral* relationship. But the sort of ethical theory we can use to understand what *sort of moral nature* it is need not be limited to only that of justice, rules and rights. Calls for a more sophisticated and nuanced appreciation of the fiduciary relationship, including that of the development of a "fiduciary character", call for the trustee to care-well, highlighting that "good trusteeship isn't primarily a set of rules, but the development of a type of character".

Care ethics can add something to the fiduciary conversation. With fiduciary and trusts having their roots in familial law – in the domestic/private sphere where care has historically been relegated (although it must be noted that numerous care ethicists seek to contest and dissolve the public/private boundaries that confine caring to the private) – fiduciary has past dealings with care. Appropriated into corporate law as a way of placing assets into trusts, and of keeping company directors in check against acting in self-interest, the fiduciary relationship has morphed into more of a "detached duty". Indeed, that the language of deontological duty has become commonplace as fiduciary moves into the corporate/public realm from the familial/private may be of no coincidence. And on detached duty, it is worth highlighting that pension fund managers often do not know who their investors are, and likewise investors have no name or face to put to them. Just exactly who is leading and who is following has become lost due to many degrees of separation in global financial institutions. But there is increasing interest and concern about investment decision-making, with both institutional and individual investors demanding details of investment decisions, as well as demanding that fiduciaries "empathize with investors' needs" and "respond to the[ir] unique needs".[6] The catalyst for change in development of "fiduciary character", of leaders who care-well, could then be caused via agitation of their beneficiaries addressing the power asymmetry, or in other-speak, by increasing market demands.

NOTES

1. Simon Deakin (2015, p. 1).
2. Paul B. Miller (2018, p. 1).

3. See Genevieve Lloyd, *The Man of Reason: "Male" and "Female" in Western Philosophy* (1986) and Raia Prokhovnik, *Rational Woman: A Feminist Critique of Dichotomy* (2002), amongst many others.
4. See Vinca Bigo (2010).
5. See Andrew Cave's 2017 article in which he notes the phrase was attributed to Peter Drucker by Mark Fields in 2006.
6. Black Rock Chairman's letter (2017).

REFERENCES

Bigo, Vinca (2010). "The Care Paradox: Devaluing and Idealising Care, the Mother, and Mother Nature", *International Journal of Green Economics*, **4** (2), 117–33.

BlackRock (2017). "Chairman's letter", available at https://www.blackrock.com/corporate/investor-relations/larry-fink-chairmans-letter.

Cave, Andrew (2017). "Culture Eats Strategy for Breakfast. So What's for Lunch?" Accessed 7 November 2019 at https://www.forbes.com/sites/andrewcave/2017/11/09/culture-eats-strategy-for-breakfast-so-whats-for-lunch/#182961a77e0f.

Deakin, Simon (2015). "Juridical Ontology: The Evolution of Legal Form", *Historical Social Research*, **40** (1), 170–84.

Gilligan, Carol (1982). *In a Different Voice: Psychological Theory and Women's Development*, Cambridge, MA: Harvard University Press.

Gilligan, Carol (2003). *In a Different Voice: Psychological Theory and Women's Development*, 38th printing, Cambridge, MA, USA and London, UK: Harvard University Press.

Goldstone, Hartley, McLennan, Rev. Scotty and Whitaker, Keith (2013). "The Moral Core of Trusteeship: How to Develop Fiduciary Character", *Trusts & Estates*, May, pp. 49–52.

Held, Virginia (2014). "The Ethics of Care as Normative Guidance: Comment on Gilligan", *Journal of Social Philosophy*, **45** (1), 107–15.

Lloyd, Genevieve (1993). *The Man of Reason: "Male" & "Female" in Western Philosophy*, London: Routledge.

Miller, Paul (2018). "The Identification of Fiduciary Relationships", in Evan J. Criddle, Paul B. Miller and Robert H. Sitkoff (eds), *The Oxford Handbook of Fiduciary Law*, New York: Oxford University Press.

Mussell, Helen (2018). "Who Dares to Care? (In the World of Finance)", *Feminist Economics*, **24** (3), 113–35.

Nelson, Julie A. (2016). "Husbandry: A (Feminist) Reclamation of Masculine Responsibility for Care", *Cambridge Journal of Economics*, **40** (1), 1–15.

Prokhovnik, Raia (2002). *Rational Woman: A Feminist Critique of Dichotomy*, Manchester, UK and New York, USA: Manchester University Press.

Richardson, Benjamin J. (2011). "From Fiduciary Duties to Fiduciary Relationships for Socially Responsible Investing: Responding to the Will of Beneficiaries", *Journal of Sustainable Finance and Investment*, **1** (1), 5–19.

8. Leadership in the ancient and modern military: carelessness and moral injury

Liz Sawyer and Ben Sawyer

LIZ

I've been thinking about how military leaders in ancient Greek myth expressed their love for their own troops, families, or their social status. To what extent did love and care feature in your time as a leader in the Army? Which aspects of Army leadership training do you find transfer most directly to civilian work?

BEN

Leadership styles in the British Army generally vary greatly with the situation, the nature of the leader, and the nature of the led. For example, my style of leadership when commanding a small team of bomb disposal experts was very different to my style of leadership when commanding a large team of 180 soldiers. Likewise, my leadership style when leading my bomb disposal team in barracks was very different to leading them in combat situations. This situational approach to varying leadership style is embedded in the operational Army and is taught at all levels of Army leadership training, combined with elements of transformational and transactional leadership theories and leadership lessons from previous conflicts. A common thread throughout all these styles is caring for the team. For officers, the first 11 months in the British Army is training to be a leader at the Royal Military Academy Sandhurst (RMAS), the Army's 200-year-old leadership school. At RMAS, the overriding need to care for soldiers is emphasised at every opportunity. RMAS' motto has been 'Serve to Lead' since 1947. This paradoxical motto is central to almost everything an officer cadet does during the 11-month leadership course.

Caring for team members is a constant theme in British Army leadership doctrine as well. In September 2015, the British Army published a 32-page guide to their new leadership code. The head of the Army at the time wrote in his introduction to the guide: 'This requires leaders to know those they lead, to understand them, and to place the care of their subordinates at the forefront of all that they do.' (Centre for Army Leadership, 2015, p. 2). This is a common theme in other modern Western militaries as well. The Non-Commissioned Officer (NCO) creed for the US Army includes the lines: 'my two basic responsibilities will always be uppermost in mind – accomplishment of my mission and the welfare of my soldiers. . . I know my soldiers and I will always place their needs above my own' (US Army NCO Creed, 1974). The US Army leadership development doctrine uses 'Demonstrates Care for Follower Well-being' (Department of the Army, 2015, Table 7-31) as a leadership competency indicator and includes a table with assessment criteria and advice for how to improve that competency.

When an officer reaches their first regiment, a very clear, if trivial, indication of the priority given to caring for the team is the unwritten rule that 'leaders eat last', and in reverse order of seniority. If the team run out of food or time to eat, the officers and NCOs should go hungry, not the soldiers. Caring for the members of the team obviously involves more than just making sure that they are fed. It is far ranging and will vary from person to person. Care is likely to include having empathy for their personal situation, developing them in their professional career and as a person, and looking after their welfare. Caring for the team will also include disciplining soldiers when required, preferably in a way that helps them develop in the future.

The paradox for the caring leader in the Army is that they have to build an intimate and honest relationship with their soldiers in order to lead them in combat. The team have to have absolute trust in the leader if they are to follow the leader, and to be effective in a potentially lethal situation. However, the caring leader's job is often to order the same team members to their possible deaths by risking their lives to fulfil the mission. Until mid-WW2, the junior combat leader could use personal example to lead their soldiers, with the ageless cry of 'follow me'. With the development of a new battle drill that put the officer in a safer location in the middle of the team to coordinate the battle, junior officers were faced with having to inspire their soldiers to risk their lives whilst remaining comparatively safe themselves. This change in role puts more emphasis on the leader's moral courage over their physical courage.

Since leaving the Army, I've realised how much easier it is for a leader in the Field Army (the bulk of the Army that deploys on operations around the world) to know and empathise with their team than for a leader in a civilian business to know and empathise with their team. This is largely due to the level and depth of interaction between the leaders and their team.

Unlike many civilian organisations, most unmarried members of a regiment will all live together in barracks. Most married members of a regiment live next door to each other on Army estates. Work social events are frequent, and often with partners and families. This means that the identity of the team isn't limited to the soldiers. In regimental life, to some extent, it historically extends to the family. This situation is becoming more obscured as many officers and soldiers are starting to commute daily or weekly. This has been influenced by an increase in spouses maintaining their careers, which was always difficult to do if being posted from Army base to Army base every few years, and changes to the Army employment model that encourage members to buy their own house. These changes have been driven by both a recognition that moving around the country wasn't working for many military families and a cost-cutting measure after selling all of the Army housing stock to a third party. This is quite a new trend and only time will tell how it affects team cohesion and combat effectiveness.

When teams go on operations, they live and work together 24/7 in very confined conditions for half a year at a time. Intimate living conditions, shared experiences of deprivation, and frequent shared exposure to danger lead to a very high level of empathy within the team and many very honest conversations. As a leader on operations, asking one of the team how their family is doing is not just making polite conversation around the kettle. It is normally a genuine concern driven by deep-seated empathy and the knowledge that if the team member's family isn't in a good place, the team member might be distracted and potentially a weak link in the team – which could be fatal on operations. In particularly cynical conversations, laced with the very dark humour that can be critical in order to mentally survive warzones, it was sometimes suggested that a leader had to know about their soldiers' personal lives, likes and dislikes so that they could write a nice letter to the soldier's family if they are killed – one of the hardest things a military leader will ever have to do.

LIZ

Interestingly, in ancient Greek myth the care that leaders have for their soldiers and other dependents is a clear indication of their moral worth. We see Prince Hector, Troy's future king and greatest fighter, talking kindly with his mother, wife and son, and learn how the motivation behind all his military decisions is to protect them and Troy. The Greeks, however, have only their own lives, and their personal status, to fight for, because their families are far away, back in Greece. We see a great variation in the ways that the Greek warriors care for each other, or fail to do so. Greek epic (such as Homer's *Iliad* and *Odyssey*) and tragedy seem preoccupied with how leaders make their decisions, and often put them in stark terms. In contrast to Hector, Agamemnon is leader of all the Greek contingents, and he is at Troy to reclaim Helen for his brother, her former husband Menelaus. Greek mythology almost always portrays him as an authority figure making poor decisions in difficult circumstances that then have serious and long-lasting effects on others. For instance, before the war even starts, the fleet assembles on Greece's Eastern shores to sail to Troy.

But the gods hold back favourable winds, on condition that Agamemnon first sacrifice his own daughter, Iphigeneia. Agamemnon faces the same choice as many people today – career or family? – but in the harshest of terms. In order to maintain his position as leader, he must destroy his family, or he can protect them and retire. He chooses to sacrifice the girl, but it is not forgotten: when he returns home 10 years later, Iphigeneia's mother and his own wife, Clytemnestra, kills him for his act of betrayal. Agamemnon and Hector are polar opposites in their decision-making styles, even though they are both heads of armies.

Most importantly, Agamemnon causes a huge rift between himself and the Greeks' most powerful fighter, Achilles, which triggers the *Iliad's* entire plot. Not a natural diplomat, Agamemnon confiscates a prize of honour (the woman Briseis) awarded to Achilles, to compensate for losing one of his own (called Chryseis) after a ransom request from Chryseis' father. This has been compared to a modern officer taking a Medal of Honour from one of his soldiers and pinning it onto his own uniform; a similar civilian comparison might be a CEO reclaiming his employees' bonuses for himself, to make up for tax that he has been forced to pay on his own bonus. The sense of indignation and outrage that Agamemnon's decision inspires in Achilles causes the warrior to withdraw from the fight with his entire contingent, and as a result the Trojans rally and many Greek lives are lost.

Agamemnon is not just an uncaring leader, but he is driven by prestige, greed, and often anger, rather than a sense of caring or responsibility. He is easily swayed by others, since he lacks the moral backbone to enact what he knows is the right way to behave. Achilles is equally hot-tempered and self-centred, but also cares passionately for others, which leads him to make better decisions: he initially convenes the assembly of generals (where Agamemnon insults and abuses him), because he sees that the troops are suffering from a debilitating plague and he wants to take action to protect them. He recognises that his withdrawal from battle hurts others, and is anguished, unlike Agamemnon who takes little personal responsibility for the impact of his decisions. Achilles' relationship with his cousin and dearest friend Patroclus is often reinterpreted in later antiquity as a homosexual one, but in the *Iliad* itself it is most closely compared to that between a mother and child, demonstrating the incredible care and closeness between these comrades-in-arms.

While Agamemnon is a straightforwardly poor leader, Odysseus is one of the most ambiguous leaders in Greek myth. Admired for his ingenuity (the Trojan Horse was his idea), loyalty to Agamemnon (his commander-in-chief), and dedication to return to his homeland and wife Penelope, he is also a liar, a cheat, and someone who will sacrifice others to achieve his own goals. While Agamemnon is portrayed as too stupid (or lazy) to think through the consequences of his actions, Odysseus is the other extreme: a consummate political mover, manipulating the reactions of others for his own benefit. He knows what is morally right and wrong, but, unlike those with grand 'heroic' temperaments such as Ajax and Achilles, whose sense of personal honour forbids them from carrying out morally reprehensible acts (such as lying), Odysseus is prepared to do the morally wrong thing to achieve his desired outcome. As a result, he manages to conclude a ten-year war (through a trick) and, after a decade's travel through the Mediterranean, reach home to his wife and son and evict the upstart suitors lodged in his house. However, he loses all his men (and his ship) along the way, partly because he cannot inspire their loyalty and trust when they realise that he cares far less for them than for his own self and goals. In the *Odyssey*, Odysseus receives a bag of winds from the god Aeolus, who also provides a helpful Westerly breeze. Within sight of Ithaca, Odysseus falls asleep – and his crew are so suspicious of him that they tear open the bag (thinking it must contain secret treasure) and the escaping winds blow them far from home once more.

As so often in Greek literature, we hear abstract quandaries put into concrete and memorable story form, such as Odysseus' choice of facing Scylla or Charybdis. In order to lead his men through this lethal strait between Sicily and Italy, Odysseus chooses to give them only limited information to achieve the necessary end. After telling his helmsman to hug the rocks to avoid Charybdis' whirlpool:

> I did not mention the inescapable horror of Scylla, fearing that in their panic my men might stop rowing and huddle below decks. But now I allowed myself to forget Circe's irksome instruction not to arm myself in any way. I put my famous armour on. . . The rocks re-echoed to her [Charybdis'] fearful roar, and the dark blue sands of the sea-bed were exposed. My men turned pale with terror; and now, while all eyes were on Charybdis as the quarter from which we looked for disaster, Scylla snatched out of the ship the six strongest and ablest men. Glancing towards my ship, looking for my comrades, I saw their arms and legs dangling high in the air above my head. 'Odysseus!' they called out to me in their anguish.[1]

What other decision could Odysseus make? He seemingly cares for his men, but his arming himself could equally be interpreted as self-defence rather than defence of the whole ship. Privy to secret information (a forewarning from the witch Circe), he does not divulge it to his crew, deciding to sacrifice a few for the potential homecoming of the rest. Is this the act of a 'caring leader', however, or would even the most caring leader, facing this impossible dilemma, make the same choice? The consequence is a growing resentment among Odysseus' crew, who listen more often subsequently to the mutinous Eurylochus, Odysseus' second-in-command. Later, when they are severely tested by being stuck on an island with dwindling food supplies and tasty-looking but sacred local cattle, Odysseus cannot restrain them, and their sacrilegious act of slaughter results in all their deaths. Odysseus' ambiguous character blurs the extent to which he cared for his men, or whether he quashed his sense of responsibility towards them in order to achieve the bottom line: saving his own skin.

While literature such as the *Iliad* and the *Odyssey* cannot 'prove' anything, it does show situations from which we, by empathising with these fictional but realistic and believable figures, might learn about how to make our own decisions. By exploring these scenarios from multiple viewpoints, and considering what factors influenced their decisions and what consequences followed, we can develop vocabulary for examining our own decision-making capabilities as leaders.

This is partly why these myths are re-read and reinterpreted by generation after generation, and why each reader identifies with the characters differently. One of the most influential 'new' lights cast on the *Iliad* is that by Jonathan Shay, a psychiatrist working in Cambridge, MA, with Vietnam War veterans with post-traumatic stress disorder (PTSD). He realised that in the *Iliad* the character of Achilles had endured remarkably similar experiences to those of his most severely traumatised patients, to the extent that he used the figure of Achilles to train psychiatric nurses to identify those at risk of the most profound PTSD. He developed his work into a ground-breaking book, *Achilles in Vietnam* (published in 1994), which juxtaposed the ancient myth with modern veterans' stories, to illustrate that one of the most damaging aspects of veterans' experiences was that of 'moral injury'. Shay's primary example of this is the treatment I described above of Achilles by Agamemnon: where 'what's right' is violated by a figure in authority in a situation where the consequences are serious. The consequences of moral injury, as Shay describes it, are serious and long-lasting: withdrawal from personal relationships and an inability to trust. . .

BEN

I hadn't really considered what I could learn about leadership from the classics until you gave me a copy of *Achilles in Vietnam* (Shay, 1994). I had just got back from my fourth operational tour in Iraq and I found some of the case studies in the book hugely moving and disturbingly familiar. I was fascinated by the concept of moral injury. The Army had taught me about the basics of PTSD and what to watch for in my team members. The Army had also introduced a programme called Trauma Risk Management (TRiM) that helped leaders and peers to assess mental trauma experienced by soldiers with the aim of getting them the appropriate help early if they needed it. TRiM was dependent on the subject being honest and open. This can be problematic for soldiers, who pride themselves on their toughness, to openly discuss their feelings, especially given the stigma that some still attach to mental health problems. However, this was very much focused on the mental trauma of being personally involved in distressing, and stressful, situations that could create the lasting fear or anxiety based response that is PTSD. I'd never been taught, and hadn't considered, the separate concept of moral injury that is concerned with shame, guilt and self-condemnation. Litz et al. (2009) broaden Shay's morally injurious experiences to include: 'Perpetrating, failing to prevent, bearing witness to, or learning about acts that transgress deeply held moral beliefs and expectations.' (Litz et al., 2009, p. 700).

From my experiences, I'd hypothesise that the nature of the wars in Iraq and Afghanistan made them particularly ripe for causing moral injury in soldiers. Both wars largely consisted of fighting against insurgents in amongst the civilian population. Action by either side often resulted in civilian casualties, and insurgents' tactics – including improvised explosive devices and ambushes – often inflicted casualties on soldiers without warning and without a chance for the soldiers to respond. This idea is mentioned by several authors, including Litz et al. (2009, p. 696). I'd also suggest that because both wars were fought for ambiguous reasons and with movable ambiguous objectives that defied a chance to celebrate victory and the completion of the task, the potential for moral injury could be exacerbated. After the UK withdrawal from Afghanistan, I certainly feel emotionally conflicted over Taleban victories that have left them in control of territory that cost so many UK, US and Afghan soldiers' lives to take and hold.

Given that moral injury is a hazard that caring leaders will have to try to protect their teams from, what can they do? There doesn't appear to be much empirical evidence for preventative measures yet, but there is a great deal of expert opinion that largely seems to agree that good leadership is essential. Leaders can prepare their teams to be more resilient to moral injury. Lachman (2016, p. 121) writes about this in the context of nursing as 'moral resilience'. Matthews (2018), following Shay, mentions that social cohesion in military units may also be psychologically protective. He found that elite units, which tend to have higher levels of camaraderie, esprit de corps, and better leadership than regular combat units, typically experience half the PTSD rates of regular combat units, despite normally deploying on more frequent tours and being involved in more combat than many other units (Matthews, 2018).

Leaders can also prepare their teams in other ways. In the British Army, all personnel have to complete Mandatory Annual Training Tests. Of the nine annual tests, one is on Values and Standards (Soldier's Values and Standards, n.d.), which includes a heavy moral element, and another is on Operational Law, including Rules of Engagement (ROE). This mandatory training is repeated, and expanded on, before any operational deployment. The Army's main concern is that a breach of the ROE, or other laws of war, could have a detrimental effect on the operation. However, the training has the complementary benefit that it helps reduce the chance of soldiers transgressing their values and exposing themselves to the risk of moral injury. In combat itself, there is much the leader can do to minimise damaging situations for their team. Combat will often involve killing enemy combatants (which in itself can lead to moral injury), and sometimes non-combatants will be killed accidentally, but strong leadership can ensure that the ROE are enforced, the Laws of War are obeyed and atrocities largely avoided.

Actions that a leader can take following operational deployment are less clear. It is recognised that a slower return to normality results in lower rates of PTSD. In conflicts prior to Vietnam it could take weeks, or even months, for soldiers to return home from conflicts by ship. In modern conflicts a soldier can fly home in hours. From personal experience I found this quite distressing on at least one occasion. In a matter of 12 hours I had gone from conducting a mission in Baghdad to being in a supermarket in the UK – I had to leave the supermarket abruptly. To counteract this dislocation, the Army sent formed units of soldiers returning from Afghanistan or Iraq to a camp in Cyprus to 'decompress' before returning to the UK. This would give them time to calm down, talk through their experiences together, talk to a counsellor, receive a mental health briefing and be eased back into normality. The US Air Force had a similar programme based in Ramstein (Germany). However, Schell et al. (2017) concluded that this decompression programme did not have any effect on long-term mental health. This doesn't necessarily mean that the decompression period wasn't worth doing, because, as they acknowledge, it does have other benefits, especially in the short term.

Since leaving the Army, I've been managing behavioural and process changes in a civilian organisation. One of the almost inevitable aspects of any change is resistance to a change from some employees. Listening to people talk about changes they have gone through, and reading case studies of particularly difficult changes, reminded me of conversations with people who had suffered moral injuries in the Army and some of the interviews in *Achilles in Vietnam*. Some of the descriptions of how they perceived that their leaders, or the organisation, had treated them in the change did resemble minor moral injuries. What if the same end result arises from many breaches of not so deeply held beliefs? Perhaps a series of moral papercuts? We could see this as a moral disaffection that changes the subject's moral outlook, as a moral injury does.

LIZ

I think that there are also plenty of situations outside the military where people risk incurring severe moral injury or inflicting it. Increased interest in Shay's concept has already percolated into the fields of medicine and the emergency services, whose staff must make life-and-death decisions regularly, sometimes endangering their own lives and their colleagues' too. Many businesses deal, directly or indirectly, with high-stakes situations, such as companies that supply the military or the vocations mentioned above. At the most basic level, there is a 'high-stakes' situation wherever anyone's body is at risk through their work, as writers such as Matthew Beard have identified (Beard, 2018). Serious workplace accidents can cause moral injury if there is a continual, or repeated, betrayal of trust by those in authority that leads to the accident, or it is not properly investigated. Sexual assault and bullying are further examples, especially if the perpetrator is in a position of power or the relevant authorities take no action to ensure justice for the victim. For example, Nestlé's practices regarding sales of baby milk to impoverished mothers are notorious, as is the boycott of Nestlé in the 1970s. But even in the 1990s, its practices were still causing profound moral injury for some employees. One sales representative in Pakistan, Syed Aamir Raza Hussain, abruptly resigned in 1997 after just three years, citing the following event:

> I was on a routine visit to a doctor in a hospital in Sialkot. While I was there a crit-ically ill infant was brought into the clinic with chronic diarrhea [*sic*] and severe dehydration. The doctor I was visiting rushed off to begin emergency treatment. But the baby died. The detailed medical revealed that this four-month-old baby had been breastfed for his first month but was then started on formula milk by a local doctor. The mother had been assured that formula milk would help the baby to gain weight and become healthier and chubbier. She was also directed to stop breastfeeding and was told that her milk was not suitable for her baby. The baby was being fed formula milk with a feeding bottle and had been having episodes of diarrhea for the last two months. The doctor I had been visiting and who attended the baby is trained as a pre-ventive paediatrician who in his practice actively promotes breastfeeding. Over my next several visits he explained to me how formula feeding was affecting the lives of thousands of children in Pakistan. I, a father at that time expecting my second child, understood the role I was playing in this crime and decided to leave my job.[2]

In terms of moral injury, it is clear that what Hussain experienced made him feel extremely guilty and damaged his core beliefs about his work and his employer's values. His injury caused him to campaign to expose these prac-tices. This is one example of whistle-blowing, in just one company; but for every whistle-blower, there are many employees who see the same practices being carried out and understand their consequences, but who stay silent and do not act. Although whistle-blowers can begin to ease their own conscience by speaking out about transgressions, for the silent majority the daily habit of carrying out actions that contravene their own beliefs could well result in the kind of 'moral disaffection' that we have suggested above. Those people who become disaffected morally from their employers would find it hard to trust others within their organisation, would expect poor treatment such as betrayal and exploitation (and perpetrate it themselves), and could lose the ability to be sensible decision-makers. Clearly this dovetails with corporate social responsibility, although that lies outside the scope of this conversation.

To conclude, one of the primary responsibilities of a caring leader should be to reduce the likelihood of carelessly inflicting moral injury on their workforce. Also, if someone has experienced moral injury, the caring leader must help them recover by ensuring justice takes place and is seen to take place, so that the organisation's culture neither tolerates nor perpetuates morally injurious behaviour. How can leaders achieve this, however? First, leaders should receive explicit training in what moral injury is, what causes it (such as lying, betrayal and exploitation), and why it is a serious threat to everyone involved. There will always be occasional bad luck causing someone to experience moral injury (such as being involved in a terrorist event that exposes the sheer depravity of a very small proportion of people). But perhaps the frequency of cases where the leader must make 'impossible' decisions, such as Odysseus' choice between Scylla and Charybdis, might reduce if the leader is experienced at making morally responsible decisions (i.e., being a caring leader) more often? Deeply idealistic, I know, but perhaps it is good to have something to aim towards. . .

NOTES

1.　*Odyssey* 12.223–228, 240–250 in Homer (2003).
2.　Association for Rational Use of Medication in Pakistan (ARUMP) (1999, p. 8).

REFERENCES

Association for Rational Use of Medication in Pakistan (ARUMP) (1999). *Milking Profits: How Nestlé Puts Sales Ahead of Infant Health*. Islamabad: The Network.

Beard, M. (2018). Moral injury is a new test for employers. The Ethics Centre, accessed 29 January 2019 at www.ethics.org.au.

Center for Army Leadership (2015). *The Army Leadership Code: An Introductory Guide*. RMA Sandhurst: British Army.

Department of the Army (2015). *FM 6-22 Leader Development*. Washington, DC: Department of the Army.

Homer (2003). *The Odyssey*, trans. E.V. Rieu. London: Penguin.

Lachman, V. (2016). Moral resilience: Managing and preventing moral distress and moral residue. *MEDSURG Nursing*, **25**, 121.

Litz, B.T., Stein, N., Delaney, E., Lebowitz, L., Nash, W.P., Silva, C. and Maguen, S. (2009). Moral injury and moral repair in war veterans: A preliminary model and intervention strategy. *Clinical Psychology Review*, **29**, 695–706.

Matthews, M. (2018). Moral injury. *Psychology Today*, 10 March, accessed 8 February 2019 at www.psychologytoday.com.

Schell, T.L., Farris, C. and Scharf, D.M. (2017). The Air Force Deployment Transition Center. *Rand Health Quarterly*, **7**(1), 7.

Shay, J. (1994). *Achilles in Vietnam: Combat Trauma and the Undoing of Character*. New York: Simon and Schuster.

Shay, J. (2014). Moral Injury. *Psychoanalytic Psychology*, **31**(2), 182–91.

Soldier's Values and Standards (n.d.). *Army – Who We Are*, accessed 27 January 2019 at www.army.mod.uk/who-we-are/our-people/a-soldiers-values-and-standards.

US Army NCO Creed (1974). *US Army Values*, accessed 27 January 2019 at www.army.mil/values/nco.html.

9. A metamorphosis for leaders: caring in good faith

Jen Jones

INTRODUCTION

Through the lenses of Kafka's (1883–1924) *The Metamorphosis* (1915) and Hazel Barnes's (1915–2008) Existentialism, this chapter offers an alternative understanding of care for leadership studies. Hazel E. Barnes is most frequently noted as the translator of Sartre's *Being and Nothingness* (1943). However, her own ideas in existentialist ethics, which have largely been ignored by scholars, have a great deal to offer for understanding human conditions and living in good faith. Barnes's existentialist ethics calls leaders to be responsible and accountable for their free choices while aiding the liberation of others' ability to choose their own destinies. Barnes is the best choice for examining the ethical question, 'what does it mean for a leader to care', because she explores intimate human relationships between self and other that are so vital to leadership. Furthermore, Barnes observes a parallel of Feminism with Existentialism, and her work precedes feminine theorist Nel Noddings (1984) and feminist theorist Carol Gilligan (1995) who articulate an ethic of care. Barnes, because of her sex, was largely overlooked by the academy. Fortunately, because of her fortitude to forge her way in spite of this, her perspective may lend unique insight to disrupt traditional notions of caring, and the resulting conception of caring in good faith.

Barnes studied myths to help her wrestle with existential questions, which include the Ancient playwriters and the 20th-century existentialists. Her article, 'Myth and Human Experience' (1955), examines Kafka's existential philosophy in *The Metamorphosis*. While many different meanings may be derived from this work, relevant to this chapter is the inability of the main character, Gregor, to care in good faith. He was not a bad person; on the contrary, he may be aptly described as a do-gooder, or caring leader. However, he is guilty, Barnes observes, of being self-centered because in his unreflective acts of care he does not realize that in actuality he is stifling those around him along with himself.

Leadership studies often produce agent-centric theories, which is a problematic paradox for caring leadership as well. Barnes does not offer a step-by-step guide on how leaders may care in good faith; this approach would be contradictory to an existentialist one. Caring is an existential choice in the midst of encounters with others. As Barnes writes, 'These tasks do not rise up before us labeled in order or priority and with printed instructions. Taking care of the world is a strictly do-it-yourself project, and we are all amateurs together. . .' (1967, p. 46). From Kafka and Barnes, this chapter presents an examination of myth and Existential Philosophy that will reveal a paradox of care to avoid a banality of goodness, or unreflectively joining the bandwagon of caring leadership as the next attractive leadership theory.

KAFKA'S *THE METAMORPHOSIS*: CARING IN BAD FAITH

Kafka's *The Metamorphosis* intrigues readers because of its absurdity and ambiguity – common themes among Existentialists. In the beginning, we find Gregor, the main character, fretting not so much that he has transformed overnight into a monstrous man-sized vermin, but about his loathsome job as a salesperson. Gregor works tirelessly for a boss who not only ignores his devotion, accomplishments, and perfect attendance, but who also admonishes him without reason. Gregor dreams of the day, after he has paid his father's debts, when he can quit his job and set himself free from this misery. The first two pages of the story are devoted to this contemplation. Perhaps we could relate to his thoughts of 'take this job and shove it' if we weren't distracted by the strange situation in which these thoughts are pondered; that is, Gregor would be more relatable if his thoughts were instead: 'I'm freaking out because I've transformed into a giant insect!' In this absurdity, we can see how caught up in care a leader can become. That is, Gregor is not thinking of himself even in this state; his thoughts go to his responsibilities of his job and family, which intertwined, have engrossed him for many years. Now, literally, as a consequence of that preoccupation, he has become what he was figuratively as human 'the boss's creature, mindless and spineless' (Kafka, 1915, p. 8).

Gregor's self-centeredness is reflected in his lack of communication with others, even his family. In his state as an insect, he wants to express himself, but is always misunderstood. Barnes recognizes Kafka's symbolism, taken to the extreme, of the feeling that all people experience: communication is not perfect. Transforming into an insect is certainly a horrible thing, but perhaps most horrifying is the removal of his ability to communicate — the ability that makes us most human. Yet, as a human, Gregor did not communicate either. Thus, he did not embrace his existence when he had the opportunity to be present to himself and others because he 'had been smugly content with conventional human morality' or what he thought was the right way to care for others, which doesn't necessitate communication (Barnes, 1955, p. 125).

Arguably, Gregor's boss and workplace contribute to the unfortunate situation he finds himself in. As such, leadership scholars may focus on transforming the character of Gregor's boss, and organizational studies on the firm in which he worked, into better people and places. Kafka poses a question that these scholars could seize upon and to which they could apply ascribed theories: 'Why was Gregor condemned to serve at a firm where the smallest infraction was seized upon with the greatest suspicion; was each and every employee a scoundrel; was there no loyal dedicated man [*sic*] serving them?' (Kafka, 1915, pp. 11–12). Even though Gregor had never missed a day in his career, the firm was quick to send the Head Clerk to check on him this one day. To show her son's commitment to work and family, Gregor's mother says to the Clerk, 'It almost makes me mad at the way he never goes out in the evening; he's been in the city eight days now [for work], but he's been at home every night' (p. 12). The Clerk threatens Gregor's dismissal and recent highly unsatisfactory performance. This proclamation elicits fawning and groveling from Gregor, yet while the words are clear to him, they are unintelligible and sound like an animal to his family and the Clerk. Kafka has presented thus far in the story that the Firm does not care, even though Gregor has demonstrated great acts of care for the Firm. We also learn that his family did not care for Gregor when he was human, by his mother's use of 'almost' in the above quote, along with every family member's willingness to live a life of luxury while Gregor lives a life of misery for their benefit. Thus, while Gregor seems to fall into the conundrum of bad things happening to good people, Kafka may be offering us a paradox – Gregor's care is the bad thing, or in existential terms, bad faith.

In fact, Gregor is consumed by care. In his incoherent groveling to the Clerk, Gregor exclaims,

> A man [*sic*] can suddenly be incapable of working, but this is the precise moment to remember his past performance and to consider that later, after resolving his difficulties, he would work all the harder and more diligently. I am so deeply obligated to the Chief, as you well know. And besides, I am responsible for my parents and sister. (p. 17)

Gregor again ignores his current state of existence to imagine himself even more committed to care for his employer and family. Gregor was locked into this view of reality, and now even though his world has radically changed, he cannot envision the family members taking responsibility because he had always done this for them.

The new situation presents opportunities for the previously uncaring family to care for Gregor. For example, Gregor's sister, the only family member who could barely stand to look at his new disgusting form, attempts to give him a bowl of milk because she remembers it was his favorite drink. Unfortunately, as a cockroach, Gregor despises the taste of milk, and through trial and error of his sister serving foods, he realizes he has a new taste for only decomposing leftovers. Yet, even while eating garbage, his thoughts are still focused on caring:

> 'What a quiet life the family has led,' Gregor said to himself, and felt, as he stared pointedly into darkness, a great surge of pride that he had been able to provide his parents and his sister such a life and in such a beautiful apartment. But what if all the tranquility, all the comfort, all the contentment were now to come to a horrifying end? (p. 22).

In this moment, Gregor displays himself as a caring narcissist. He places himself at the center of what he deems to be good without recognizing the detrimental effects his caring has imparted on his family members as having no purpose of their own. Additionally, he is in denial that this situation he has created has come to an end. Even as he moves out of denial, his narcissism remains, because he sees himself as their greatest burden along with lamenting the loss of all he created for them.

The family also tries to hold on to these luxuries and does so through an amount of money that was set aside by the father and unbeknownst to Gregor. This news frustrates him because had he known, he would have been able to announce his intentions to send his sister to study the violin at the Conservatory much sooner; he had been saving and waiting for the announcement on Christmas Eve. Now this event that he was looking forward to would never materialize. Here Kafka teaches another lesson about caring. First, we cannot know everything about a situation, and second, we cannot predict the future. Again, by thinking alternatively, Gregor demonstrates his hubris in caring.

Eventually the maid, cook, and janitor are all let go while the family members take on these responsibilities to care for themselves. Additionally, each of the family members gets a job; however, Gregor does not believe they are capable. Having been out of work for five years, his father is seen by Gregor as old, sluggish, newly overweight, and incapable of doing much. Similarly inutile, he views his mother as incapable since she suffers from asthma and gasps for breath from even walking around the apartment, and he perceives his sister a child at 17 and accustomed to sleeping late, enjoying amusements, and playing the violin. Thinking about their new state fills Gregor with shame and grief. Yet Gregor, still focused on himself as care giver, misses seeing that his sister now has a greater purpose when his parents praise her efforts for being the only one to take care of him 'whereas earlier they had frequently been annoyed with her because she appeared to them to be a somewhat useless girl' (p. 29).

In this new role of caring, the sister finds herself in an argument with the mother over the care of Gregor's space, specifically whether to remove the furniture from his room. Would he like more room to crawl around or like to keep the items to remind him of his humanity? Although she begins the argument as Gregor's advocate, by considering what he may want, she changes her role to Gregor's expert, a newly found position of power in the family, where she makes decisions for him regardless of whether they are in his best interest or not. At first, Gregor likes the idea of having more room to crawl, but then he realizes his room will be no more than a pen. He cannot verbally communicate, so he climbs the wall to guard a picture in a frame that he made. This object is particularly important to him because in his human life he bought it for himself, and engaged in an activity, whittling the wooden frame, that wasn't work. As the argument intensifies, Gregor can no longer contain himself. He wants to express his agreement with his mother to keep his things in his room 'and plagued with worry and self-reproach he began to crawl, to crawl over, over everything, walls, furniture, ceiling, and finally fell in despair, when the whole room was spinning, onto the middle of the large table' in the living room (p. 34). The father, who had shown no care towards Gregor throughout this entire time, returns from work, arrives at the scene, and is furious. In his rage, he throws apples at Gregor and one becomes lodged in his back, seriously injuring him.

In the final section of the story, Gregor's injury contributes to his decline in health. We also learn that the family's recent caring was only 'in accordance with family duty, they were required to quell their aversion and tolerate him, but only tolerate' (p. 37). Yet, they leave the living room door opened so Gregor can view them sitting at the dining room table and feel part of the family. This simple act of care towards Gregor means more to him in this moment than all the luxuries he provided to them. He sees his father in his new work uniform, his mother sewing delicate lingerie for an apparel shop, and his sister, who had taken a job as a salesperson, studying French and shorthand to further her career. He also witnesses his mother and sister care for his father as they help him move from his chair where he has fallen asleep to bed to ensure he gets a good night's rest. Nevertheless, the family and Gregor continue to live in bad faith because they have not embraced, taken responsibility for, and fully chosen with freedom their existence.

Their bad faith is most exemplified in their persistent laments over their situation – the apartment is too large, and Gregor is too big to be moved, so he is keeping them trapped there. Gregor recognizes this bad faith because he knows that he could have easily 'been transported in a suitable crate with a few airholes; what truly hindered them was an utter hopelessness and belief that a plight had befallen them unlike any other . . . They carried out the world's demands on poor people to the extreme' (p. 39). However, Gregor is still unaware of his bad faith because even in his current state, 'he mulled over the idea that the next time the door opened he would take control of the family affairs as he had done in the past' (p. 39). He cannot de-center himself from the situation.

The relationship between Gregor and his family deteriorates to the point where their duty to care for him is broken; he is merely a task. The sister, who first gave him the bowl of milk, 'No longer concerning herself about what Gregor might particularly care for hastily shoved any old food through the door' (p. 39). Gregor's room is not cleaned as it had been before, and household items are shoved haphazardly in his room to make space for three tenants who could help cover the bills for such a large, costly apartment. Gregor is ill, not eating, and cut off from his family. The family and Gregor hit rock bottom in their disdain of each other. While this situation is one where all caring ceases to exist, good faith is budding in the family and in Gregor, and as Kafka writes, spring is coming.

Throughout the story Kafka illustrates how much more Gregor experiences what it is like to be human when he is an insect than when he was a human. As a human, he was nothing more than a worker bee continually gathering nectar for the hive or an ant building a hill. Conversely, as an insect, he was cared for by others, had emotions towards others, and contemplated his existence beyond work. Kafka illuminates humanity in the greatest degree in the scene where Gregor is mesmerized by his sister's playing of the violin. Without him even realizing, he is so caught up in the moment that he finds himself drawn out into the room where she's playing. In his human form, he was so focused on saving money to send her to the Conservatory, he missed the beauty of the music.

Finally, Gregor exposing himself to the tenants is his ultimate demise. His sister now refers to him as 'it' rather than by his name as her care for him ceases. If only Gregor could have realized his humanity and lived in good faith when he was human, perhaps he could have saved himself from this metamorphosis. Kafka's lesson by this point is clear: it was only his physicality that changed, he was an insect inside all along. As an insect, his existence aligned with his essence. When he finally has a real human experience in music, the metamorphosis truly occurs; he is free of his essence, but since he is still physically an insect, he must die.

Upon first reading of *The Metamorphosis*, one might see Gregor as the victim because he was the dutiful son – he *appeared* to care the most among all the characters in the story. He practically killed himself for the sake of his family and employer. Moreover, his family could also be looked upon as unappreciative since they live as sloths, and only care for him out of duty and tolerance when he becomes an insect. Yet, Gregor's caring is in bad faith hubris, righteousness, and as a glutton for punishment. Moreover, his caring stifles his family's existence. He assumed he knew what was best for them, but we learn at the end of the story that the family never wanted a big apartment. They also find that they actually like their new jobs. Thus, while the story does not seem to end positively, this is Kafka's paradox: Gregor dies in good faith, the family lives in good faith, and it is springtime. Barnes (1964a) describes this kind of paradox as tragedy and comedy working together. The paradox in these extremes comes together when the goal a person attains is never quite the same as the one projected. Barnes writes:

> By his acts he inscribes himself in a world which he can never fully control, which distorts and disappoints his projects, which he cannot comprehend any more than he can understand himself. Each person is a self-creation, but chance furnishes most of the material out of which he must make himself. In short, man is absurd, but he does not always find his situation laughable. (p. 125)

Gregor, in bad faith, thought he was in complete control by caring for every-one around him, and then life threw him the biggest existential curveball. He continued to live in bad faith by not accepting that 'suffering and anguish are essential facts of human existence' (Barnes, 1964b, p. ix).

A METAMORPHOSIS FOR LEADERS: CARING IN GOOD FAITH

Kafka's *The Metamorphosis* shows us what bad faith caring is. Sartre also dis-cusses at length the idea of living in bad faith with the concluding thought that others are Hell. Through her extensive work with Kafka's and Sartre's ideas, Barnes investigates how to live in good faith. This contribution is most salient for those in positions of leadership to ascertain because the existential calls us to embrace our human condition to choose — to go beyond living a bug's life and consciously realize or be awakened to our ability to be present to ourselves and others. Yet, we must be mindful and communicative with others to care in good faith. Following Kafka's caring in bad faith, Barnes's existential philos-ophy of good faith offers a valuable response to his paradox.

Altruism, or total commitment to care for the other or 'alter' is how Gregor cared for his family. His was in total sacrifice of self. Altruistic leaders have been praised for this servant leadership style.[1] Yet, altruism runs the risk of objectifying the self and other. If oneself becomes the sole object of care, as Barnes observes, we run the risk of becoming spoiled; if others become the sole objects of care, they may also become spoiled. The paradox of the self-sacrificing martyr is the stifling of those he thinks he is caring for. Gregor achieved what he thought was good for his family even though they never wanted a big apartment and were freer once he was dead. Why did Gregor behave in this manner? Kafka states in the story that when Gregor was younger, he was a good soldier. Gregor appears to cling to some lofty ideal of what it means to care – to be a good soldier, worker, son and brother, yet all the while his own life is miserable and no one else's life is flourishing despite his sacrifice. Gregor is ego-centric to believe he knows what this ideal is and the care needed to achieve it.

Caring is not assuming what others need. In the story, whether in human form or as an insect, no communication takes place between Gregor and his family; rather, Gregor believes he knows what is best for them. Good faith caring involves caring about another's projects, but becoming involved at the other's invitation. With Gregor's family, there is no invitation; Gregor completely colonizes his family with care. As such, communicating-with-others-in-the-world is fundamentally necessary for leaders to care in good faith. Ashman and Lawler (2008), through the lens of Existentialism, make an important observation that rather than viewing communication as a skill within leadership, the opposite may be true: 'leadership might be considered as an aspect of communication' or that leadership '*is* communication' (p. 253, emphasis in original).

As the story progresses and Gregor's family becomes more discouraged in the situation, lack of caring leads them toward authentic living. Without Gregor's caring, the family members are able to spread their wings and embark on a new path with the possibility of living in good faith. Leaders, like Gregor, may learn from this situation that they must leave room for others to care for them(selves). We all need to care and to be cared for, regardless of our business or family titles. As the good son and employee, Gregor ascribed himself false confidence that only he was in a position to care for others as the leader. To him, the company and his family would succeed because of his ability to care more than anyone else. Nothing could stop his one-way caring behavior, except the unimaginable, which Kafka shows will figuratively kill leaders of this sort as well.

If we imagine this traditional situation of caring, we might see two people facing each other. One is caring for the other who is receiving the caring act.[2] Barnes would have us reimagine this situation, where these individuals are standing side by side. Instead of seeing each other, they gaze out into the world. From an existentialist perspective, they see the same world of objects, but each of them sees the world from their unique subjectivity. Then, they communicate. Now their world is intersubjective. Because they are side by side, their own point of view changes because part of the other's has been woven into their own. Caring may now take place through dialogue and with the goal not to live and let live, but to mutually love and help live. We might imagine how Gregor's situation may have been different had he chosen to place himself beside his family and employer, rather than above and below them at the same time.

Barnes describes the life-world, a term derived from Husserl, as 'the world as it appears to each one of us within its "horizon of meanings," its values, its organization in relation to ourselves as vantage point and center of reference' (1967, p. 65). Leaders ought to realize that they and others enter into this kind of space, which Ladkin (2006), in Heideggerian terms, calls 'dwelling', where leaders may be better able to respond to issues in the midst. Communication grants a sharing of a leader's and others' lenses of the life-world.[3] As others open their worlds to us, the way we see our own world changes. Others allow leaders to get closer to their 'inner horizon' (Barnes, 1967, p. 73), which, iron-ically, is always at a distance from them. Others help leaders discover and care for their own projects as they are existentially called to care for them. As such, Barnes (1967) illustrates how projects are:

> intermeshed with the edges of the patterns of others — like the design of a paisley print. The satisfaction in a life may well result in large part from the sense that these intermeshings have positive significance for the individual pattern. There is another kind of satisfaction — that which comes from the knowledge that other persons have declared one's pattern good. Still a third derives from the realization that what one has done has helped make it easier for others to live patterns intrinsically satisfying to them. (p. 107)

Rather than a hierarchy, as relationships and organizations are typi-cally depicted, Barnes presents an alternative metaphor of a beautifully co-constructed tapestry, where each thread leaves behind a trace that has contributed to the cultural fabric by working collaboratively with others. The fabric is vibrantly alive and constructed through the meeting of existential moments. A sense of shared caring leadership emerges. Others validate us by making our well-being a part of their own projects, but they do not imprison us by being wholly self-for-other, as Gregor did. Barnes concludes, 'thus, in a curious way he [*sic*] makes me aware of my being-in-the-world without causing me to lose my sense of being-for-myself. And of course I do the same for him' (1967, p. 353). A commitment to care in good faith is, for Barnes, to love in good faith, which 'perilous though it be, demands the constantly renewed pledge that each will seek both his own and the Other's continued growth' (1967, p. 354). Envisioning the leader as de-centered in this manner is necessary for caring in good faith. Caring in good faith is a shared endeavor.

CONCLUSION

Kafka's example of caring in bad faith contradicts the agentic great man approach – even caring men. His is a cautionary tale for leaders who have good intentions but end up paving the path to Hell. Barnes opens up the possibility for a counterpart to this kind of familial and work relations where Heaven is Others in good faith relations (p. 341). Yet, caring in good faith is not prescriptive since the future and others' radical subjectivity cannot be known. Good faith caring accepts and celebrates this ambiguity and absurdity. Good faith involves caring deliberately — communicating and making the best choice at the moment without guarantee it will be the right choice. Thus, this chapter has not attempted to answer the question, 'what does it mean for a leader to care', but has attempted to open up understanding about caring in bad and good faith, which allows the question to remain.

NOTES

1. Eicher-Catt (2005) offers a feminist critique of servant-leadership and von Schlichten (2018) also has a different approach to servant leadership with his idea of 'a proto-feminist servant-leader'.
2. Noddings (1984) discusses 'caring about' as the universal attitude toward caring, and 'caring for' as the existential attitude toward caring (p. 112).
3. This relationship lends to the idea of empathy. For more on empathy and leadership see Jones (2018).

REFERENCES

Ashman, I. and Lawler, J. (2008), Existential communication and leadership, *Leadership*, **4** (3), 253–69.

Barnes, H.E. (1955), Myth and human experience, *The Classical Journal*, **51** (3), 121–7.

Barnes, H.E. (1964a), Tragicomedy, *The Classical Journal*, **60** (3), 125–31.

Barnes, H.E. (1964b), Schopenhauer, evangelist of pessimism, in A. Schopenhauer (ed.), *The Pessimist's Handbook: A Collection of Popular Essays* (pp. vii–xxxi). Lincoln, NB: University of Nebraska Press.

Barnes, H.E. (1967), An Existentialist Ethics, Chicago, IL: The University of Chicago Press.

Eicher-Catt, D. (2005), The myth of servant leadership: A feminist perspective, *Women and Language*, **28** (1), 17–25.

Gilligan, C. (1995). Symposium on care and justice: Hearing the difference: Theorizing connection, *Hypatia*, **10** (2), 120–27.

Jones, J. (2018), Edith Stein (1891–1942): Empathic leadership: Saint Edith Stein's phenomenological perspective, in B. Jones Denison (ed.), *Women, Religion, and Leadership: Female Saints as Unexpected Leaders* (pp. 155–77). New York: Routledge.

Kafka, F. (1915), *The Metamorphosis*, New York: Barnes & Noble Classics.

Ladkin, D. (2006), When deontology and utilitarianism aren't enough: How Heidegger's notion of 'dwelling' might help organisational leaders resolve ethical issues, *Journal of Business Ethics*, **65** (1), 87–98.

Noddings, N. (1984), *Caring: A Feminine Approach to Ethics and Moral Education*, Berkeley, CA: University of California Press.

Sartre, J-P. (1943), *Being and Nothingness: A Phenomenological Essay on Ontology*, New York: Washington Square Press.

von Schlichten, D. (2018), Saint Elizabeth Ann Seton (1774–1841): A proto-feminist servant-leader for the nineteenth century – and today, in B. Jones Denison (ed.) *Women, Religion, and Leadership: Female Saints as Unexpected Leaders* (pp. 100–118). New York: Routledge.

PART IV

The caring leader at work: security, sacrifice and self

10. Care and security in Vergil's *Aeneid*: an analysis of the politics of empire

Michèle Lowrie

Vergil's *Aeneid* tells a story about securing the state.[1] The poem first appears as a triumphalist declaration of empire, not so much a manual for governance as a document of Rome's foundation on moral principles, authorized by fate. Written during the first decade of the emperor Augustus' accession (c. 28 to 19 BCE), after he emerged victorious from the civil wars that tore apart the Roman Republic, Vergil's epic tells the backstory of the preeminent world power of the day and the principles on which it came to be. Trojan refugees flee their city, burned by the Greeks, under the leadership of Aeneas. Consistent portents direct him to found a new city in Italy. His lineage will spawn Romulus and Remus, who will in the plot's future found Rome. Their lineage will produce Augustus Caesar in turn, who will extend empire to the ends of the known earth through all time. The events of the poem guarantee Rome's foundation and set it on a course that comes to fruition during Vergil's lifetime. Aeneas offers a paradigm for leadership, taken up by Augustus, just as Rome offers a paradigm for power. The governing virtues are those inscribed on the honorific shield the Roman senate dedicated to Augustus in 27 BCE, around the time when Vergil began to compose his epic: besides virtue itself, clemency, justice, and reverent duty to gods and country.

The triumphalist narrative runs counter to the *Aeneid's* darker, mournful tone, one of pathos and longing, where cares and worries occupy the emotional foreground and much promise is unfulfilled – derailed, misdirected, or cut short before its time.[2] The poem stages one security crisis after another. Violence between the immigrant Trojans and the native Italians besets peoples who will join together in eternal peace and presages the civil wars in Rome's future. Aeneas undergoes a psychological breakdown as he devolves into fury in the poem's climactic scene, when he plunges his sword into the breast of his opponent Turnus. His heated act denies the Augustan virtues on whose very basis Turnus appeals to Aeneas: vengeance overwhelms clemency and only on the most nationalistic reading can justice and duty be said to be performed. From this perspective, the foundation told in the *Aeneid* sets up Rome's political turmoil to come and serves more as a warning than as anything deserving celebration. Empire comes at the cost of civil war and insecurity, emotional and political alike.

Vergil defines leadership in the *Aeneid* in part through the leitmotif of care (*cura*). It and related words have attracted little systematic attention, since scholarship on the *Aeneid* has favored flashier concepts such as fury (*furor*) or reverent duty (*pietas*). Defining how a leader should care, however, is central not only to Vergil's project, but also to the developing imperial ideology, according to which it was the emperor's responsibility to shoulder the cares of his people, to take care of their problems, and to provide them with security. Care has both a pragmatic and an emotional burden. In Latin, the verb etymologically related to care (*curare*) also means to get things done. The official duties of republican and imperial administrators included taking care of infrastructure: a (*pro)curator* oversaw a portfolio such as the grain supply or waters. The Romans conceived of the emperor's job not just as performing tasks, but also as providing emotional support. He became the state's and the people's primary caretaker. In Latin, however, the expectation that the emperor provide security through care produces a paradox.

Latin *cura* corresponds well to English "care." Like care, the sunny side of *cura* and its cognates pertains to acts of tending in personal, political, and cosmic contexts. Vergil's *Georgics*, a didactic poem on farming composed just before the *Aeneid* (late 30s to c. 28 BCE), opens with people caring for animals, gods for the landscape, and Caesar, soon to be named Augustus, caring for cities and lands. *Cura*, however, may also mean anxiety, care's dark side. This double valence leads to care undoing itself from within: we tend to things to alleviate our anxiety about them, with the result that *cura* in one sense relieves *cura* in another. Tending to self and others and lifting anxiety from self and others first appear both as desirable aims.[3]

The word for the relief of anxiety in Latin is *securitas* (security). Etymologically, *securitas* means being apart from care. The word falls into three parts. The prefix *se-* means "apart from," as in English "separate." *Cura* means care. In addition to anxiety and tending, *cura* may have erotic overtones: we tend to those we love, who may also cause us anxiety. The suffix *-tas* indicates an abstract noun. All together they produce an abstract state defined by its distance from an ambivalent term. When *securitas* is first attested in Cicero's philosophical works (40s BCE), it means peace of mind for an individual in a strictly psychological sense. A century later, it comes to pertain not just to persons, but to the state: the Roman historian Velleius Paterculus, writing during the late Augustan period and then under Tiberius (reign 14–37 BCE), refers to the security of the Roman Empire. Unlike the modern emphasis on national security, which stresses foreign threats, the perennial Roman worry was internal, specifically the outbreak of civil war. During this same period, *securitas* comes to have an additional meaning: besides the condition of being care*free*, it can mean being care*less*. The apartness indicated by the prefix may pertain not only to care's dark side, worry and anxiety, whose negation produces peace of mind, but also to its sunny side, tending and getting things done, whose negation produces reckless indifference. The erasure of care may mean the erasure of tending instead of the erasure of anxiety. The Latin etymology already hints that security measures may backfire.

Adding negation to an already ambivalent concept makes for a dizzying range of possibilities that must be adjudicated in context. Not all the meanings of security are operative in Vergil, but the *Aeneid* is a good text for examining Roman ideas about care and leadership. The poem sits at the historical transition from the Roman Republic to the Roman Empire, that is, from a more collaborative and contestatory form of distributed governance to de facto monarchy, and many of the actions and conceptualizations in this seminal text are formative for imperial ideas about leadership and national security. Some ideas it expresses overtly, some in inchoate form. In all cases, however, this poem helps establish concepts that receive greater development in the century to come. The poem asks who cares in multiple senses. Who feels anxiety? Who may legitimately express it? Who is authorized to act to alleviate it and for whom? Can a line be drawn between helpful tending and unhelpful anxiety? How leaders manage their own cares through self-discipline is as much at issue in Vergilian leadership as how leaders care for others in the interest of a larger whole. Leadership entails not just the reduction of external threats but also the alleviation of destructive internal passions.

Vergil sets up many paradigms of leadership in his epic, chief among them his protagonist Aeneas. Other characters who exercise leadership include men and women, gods and mortals: Dido, Jupiter, Juno, Latinus, Camilla, and Turnus, as well as less conspicuous figures. The poem's first simile sets in place a strong model of a statesman calming an angry mob against which to measure every other leader. A storm, roused by Juno, knocks Aeneas off course from Italy to North Africa. Juno has many reasons for stirring up trouble: she hates the Trojans and wants to capture Rome's fated greatness for her own city, Carthage. Neptune rises from the deep to calm the storm and save the Trojan fleet. The simile makes a parallel between the cosmic order of nature and the political sphere by comparing the turbulent waves to the outbreak of civil violence, the god to a political leader.[4]

> Just as when sedition arises in a great people, as it often does, and the vulgar mob rages in spirit, and now torches and rocks fly – fury supplies the weapons – if by chance they see some man, reverent, dutiful, and respected for his service, then they grow quiet and stand with ears ready to listen. He calms their spirits with his words and assuages their hearts. So the whole crash of the sea fell, after Father Neptune, looking out over the level seas and riding under the open air, turned his horses and gave them the reins, flying with the following winds behind his chariot. (1.148–57)

Vergil does not use the language of care or security here. He reserves the first mention of *cura* for Aeneas. But the model of quieting turbulence established in the simile corresponds well to security in both its psychological and political senses. Not a single character lives up to this ideal. Even Neptune cannot calm the winds and waves without almost losing his temper.[5] But the various characters fail to exercise care, manage cares, or achieve security in manifold ways that reveal much about how closely they approximate the ideal statesman.

Aeneas initially appears successful in repressing anxiety as he tends to his men. He is beset by various challenges, some of which he overcomes. As the poem's exemplary hero, his successes and failures stand as part for whole to those of the Roman Empire itself.[6] His management of his own cares bears a symbolic burden for national security. In the end, he succumbs before the highest test. The final scene inscribes all of security's ambivalences into Rome's foundation. Like Aeneas, so Rome. Far from a bright future of security understood as the successful management of anxiety, Rome will fail to contain worries of the worst sort and face the repeated outbreak of civil war.

STORM AT SEA, STORM AT HEART

In his first appearance in the poem, Aeneas pitches in the throes of a security crisis in all senses. Tossed in a storm at sea, thrown off course on his mission to found the city that will become Rome, he bewails his failure to die at Troy, where he could have perished with honor. His ship and all but one of his fleet survive. His management of his anxieties and the care he shows his men as he attends to their safety create a positive impression. Aeneas is a leader who surmounts internal and external obstacles. Although he by no means perfectly instantiates good judgment and self-control, he nevertheless appears trustworthy: he admits to and corrects mistakes and he creates solidarity within his band. Despite lacking charisma, Aeneas is a low-key but responsible leader Romans would willingly follow.

Vergil introduces his imperfect hero in light of a storm that stands as the image of psychic turbulence for Lucretius, a poet whose didactic epic on Epicureanism in the previous generation had a strong influence on Vergil. The second book of *On the Nature of Things* famously begins with a philosopher taking pleasure at not experiencing in person the storm at sea observed from the safety of land. The highest pleasure, and therefore aim, for the Epicurean turns out to be not tranquility in any absolute sense, but the negation of cares. The Latin *securitas* is the etymological correlate of the Greek *ataraxia* (lack of disturbance), valued by ancient philosophy of all stripes. *Securitas* does not scan in the meter, dactylic hexameter, used by Lucretius and Vergil. Both poets nevertheless convey the concept indirectly, but all the more powerfully by negating words for care. They demonstrate how security works without spelling it out. Lucretius emphasizes the enjoyment of "the pleasurable sensation when the mind is removed from care and fear" (2.18–19). Aeneas, who actually experiences the danger of the storm and the emotional turmoil it arouses, represses his anxiety once he reaches shore: "sick with huge cares, he puts on his face a hope he does not feel and pushes his pain deep down in his heart" (1.208–209).

Unlike the Epicurean poet, whose philosophy saw politics as a sphere of disturbance to be avoided for personal happiness, Vergil consistently turns psychological security toward a political end. Whereas Lucretius' philosopher himself takes pleasure in the physical distance between himself and turbulence, Vergil's leader reassures his rattled men: fate promises them a quiet place to settle and temporal distance will let them one day take pleasure in remembering these events. Aeneas thereby models not tranquility or fearlessness, but security and courage in the sense of care or fear overcome. Unlike the Epicurean philosopher, who overcomes anxiety for his own pleasure, Aeneas acts for the greater good of the group. He keeps their spirits up even at the price of his own feelings. The remark that he does not feel does not indict him of insincerity, a modern concern, but indicates that Aeneas performs the role of a better leader than he has yet managed to become. He is "good enough". The positive emotion to which he aspires remains beyond his reach, but he nevertheless succeeds in the political task: he forges cohesion by putting his team's feelings before his own.

Consistent parallels between men and gods, however, raise a disquieting thought: success in managing cares is an ideal beyond reach. Similar phrasing links Aeneas' actions here to the model of the statesman in the poem's first simile. Both assuage disturbed hearts and hold their political group together by doing so. For the statesman the group is a fully formed people, for Aeneas his companions. Vergil's political term for them, "allies," makes them a microcosm of the future Roman people. If Aeneas actually felt hope, that would be better, but he is at least on the right track. The god Neptune, however, the one explicitly compared to the statesman, threatens the winds with brute force before checking his temper when he calms the storm. His failure to live up to the ideal of the model statesman presages Aeneas' inability to keep his emotions in check later in the poem. It also suggests a larger problem. He is not the only god Vergil represents either struggling to manage cares – in Book 1 both Jupiter and Aeneas' mother Venus worry about Rome's future – or failing to contain passion. While knowledge that Aeneas is fated to reach Italy and found a new race reassures the divinities who back the Romans, yet another, Juno, rages against Aeneas with anger unabated until the poem's concluding scenes. The human leaders are held to a high standard of self-mastery, one the powers above fail to meet themselves. Even the favorable interventions of the gods seem inconsistent and arbitrary. Vergil's anguished question, "Do the heavenly spirits have such wrath?" (1.11), resonates throughout the poem, suggesting both the necessity and futility of human security before unmanageable forces of destruction.

The gods consistently unleash disturbing forces that overwhelm fragile humans who must live up to an impossible standard. Tending and security are necessary, but insufficient to guarantee either happiness or political order. In the face of crushing pressure from above and the needs of his wards below, the good leader nevertheless tries his flawed best. This turns out, unfortunately, to be not good enough.

LOVE AND GENDER

Patriarchy does not like women to exercise power, and the Romans were no exception. Vergil innovates on legend by having Aeneas and Dido, queen and founder of Carthage, fall in love. Their moving and tragic tale tells the mythic origins of the Punic Wars, from which Rome emerged victorious two centuries before Vergil's time. Defeating Carthage established Rome as an imperial power and the story of star-crossed lovers attests to central features of Roman identity with contrasting male and female models in managing cares. Erotic and political cares come into direct conflict. The woman's passions, concerns, life, and state all come to grief before the imperative of Rome's foundation. The episode allows masculinist self-control to win out – for the moment.

After the storm, Aeneas and his men wash up on the shores of Carthage and seek refuge with Dido. Divine intervention by the meddling goddesses Juno and Venus derails any possibility that Carthage and Rome could join in peace by stirring a new form of care into the plot. They beset Dido, initially intent on an egalitarian relationship between the Trojan refugees and her own new people, with a raging passion for Aeneas. The *Aeneid's* metaphorical register presents her love as a wound, a flame, and a care. Both Dido and Aeneas are afflicted with erotic cares. The difference is that the man successfully represses his when called, also by divine intervention, to a higher duty. Jupiter sends Mercury down to redirect Aeneas to his appointed task. By contrast, love destroys the woman. Dido asks repeatedly for relief from cares. Her inability to find release ends in self-destruction. She commits suicide with his sword when he leaves her, an act that presages Carthage's future ruin. Like Aeneas, she stands for her city. Like Aeneas, she offers a paradigm for leadership in her ability to manage cares. Where she fails by succumbing to turbulent emotions, he emerges as the better leader not because he does not care, but because he does not let his feelings divert him from his course. This is the second time Aeneas' leadership is defined by repressing cares.

The initial contrast between bad and good paradigms, however, founders before another security crisis. Aeneas may manage his own emotions, but he fails spectacularly in managing those of Dido, a woman he holds dear. He is a singularly bad listener. He succeeds at leadership only when his interests align with those of his interlocutor. He comforts his men who share his mission. He fails at comforting Dido, since his aims are at variance with hers. The personal becomes political. Violating the cares of the beloved in the name of establishing a secure foundation simultaneously engenders a deadly enemy. Dido curses Aeneas and his descendants and calls for an avenger to rise from her bones. Hannibal will answer her prayers and bring war to Rome during the Punic Wars. National security backfires when the repressed returns with a mission of vengeance. Dido's example warns the patriarchy: disregard women's cares at your peril.

AENEAS LOSES HIS COOL

In pursuing his mission, Aeneas' plunge ever deeper into psychological turmoil undermines the security of Rome's foundation. Far from overcoming Dido's failed model of leadership, he comes to resemble her more and more. War greets him once he finally reaches Italy. Turnus defends his promised bride, whose father Latinus instead gives her hand to the newly arrived stranger on the basis of omens. Aeneas seeks help from Evander, who rules at the site of future Rome and entrusts his adolescent son, Pallas, to Aeneas for training at the head of supporting troops. In symmetrical scenes that replay Homer's *Iliad*, Turnus kills Pallas as Hector kills Achilles' beloved friend Patroclus, and Aeneas takes vengeance on Turnus as Achilles does Hector. Aeneas rages at Pallas' death and succumbs to fury when Turnus pleads for clemency, appealing to respect for a father's care for his son. His psychological state, surpassing just anger in his loss of control, overrides the imperatives of patriarchal care and of self-governance, principles that justified abandoning Dido. Personal and national security come undone together in this climactic moment.

Political allegories in the poem track the state of Aeneas' soul. In Jupiter's prophecy in Book 1, personified Fury will be caged under Augustus in the temple of Janus, which was closed when Rome was at peace. Juno, ever a feminine figure sowing disorder, bursts open the gates of war and unleashes hellish forces once Aeneas arrives in Italy. In parallel, all the cares he masters in the epic's first half burst forth in its second. The times he does exercise leadership, he does so in terms of caring: he regrets killing Lausus, a young man who fell to Aeneas' sword while protecting his father, and respects his concern for burial. He himself is concerned to bury his own dead. But this gentler regard for others crumbles before his failure to protect his ward Pallas. Failing in this responsibility does not subdue him. Rather it magnifies his destructive feelings. He tries and fails to keep these under wraps.

Aeneas' feelings surge several times in the lead-up to the death of Turnus. Repetition at key points links him to Dido and sea imagery recalls the storm. "Her [Dido's] cares redouble and her love rages surging back again and fluctuates on a great tide of anger." (4.531–2). War's outbreak spurs the first parallel: "Seeing all this, Laomedon's heroic descendant [Aeneas] fluctuates on a great tide of cares." (8.19–20). Turnus' slipping his grasp, before they eventually face off, the second: "Alas, what should he do? He fluctuates in vain on a changing tide, and incompatible cares call his spirit in contrary directions." (12.486–7).

The poem's initial image of successful leadership based on self-governance already showed chinks in overriding Dido's cares with such destructive results. From a patriarchal perspective, women's concerns must simply yield to the demands of the political order. In the final scene, however, the sacred principle of a father's care also falls before uncontrollable emotions that Aeneas cannot keep in check. Rather than repressing destructive emotional forces, Aeneas' rage crushes tending care. Rome is founded on security, not in its positive sense of keeping anxiety in check, but rather in a heart-rending disregard of even masculine nurturing care.

The final scene enacts foundation on the wrong principles. The language of foundation (*condere*) returns from the poem's opening lines, which stress Aeneas' mission: "until he may found a city" (1.5); "it was such a great weight to found the Roman race" (1.33). Aeneas drives his sword into Turnus' breast, the seat of emotion, with the same verb *condere*, which means to bury as well as to found.[7] If his actions and feelings were simply his own, the *Aeneid* would tell a tragic story of a good man overwhelmed by destructive emotions. But his story belongs not just to him, but to Rome. The word Latin most often uses for civil war is "discord", which means a disturbance of the heart (*cor*). The Romans conceptualized the civil wars that ravaged Rome for a century, until Augustus' victory wiped out all opponents, as a matter of emotions run rampant. Dido's curse brings a foreign enemy against Rome, one overcome in the Punic Wars. But the replay of her abandonment in Aeneas' failure to regard not just a woman's concerns, but a father's, sets Rome on a course of civil war. Its security is threatened not from abroad, but by the domestic enemy that is the self.

CAREFREE AND POWERLESS

The *Aeneid* shows no way out. Self-mastery appears an impossible task, the trials of the world unsurmountable. There is no happy ending or even a didactic moral to this tale. For the ending, see Putnam (1999). Tending care appears attractive, but illusive. Self-mastery appeals – good luck with that. No one's cares are ever adequately addressed and some are even crushed before the notional good of the whole. The political order Aeneas' soul represents is riven by internal conflict. Vergil, looking back on a century of civil war, sees no way forward. In all Vergil's works, Augustus' job is never defined as caring for Rome or the Romans. Rather, he is to extend empire through warfare, to impose law and order on pacified foreign peoples. The Romans found two solutions to civil war: the centralization of power in one man and externalizing violence through conquest.

Later imperial ideology, however, highlights care as one of the emperor's attributes. He becomes the symbolic focal point for collective feeling. Inscriptions in the following century as well as literary sources attest to the idea that the emperor shoulders the cares of the empire, so imperial subjects may be carefree.[8] This sounds like bliss, but it comes with strings attached: he becomes the ultimate decision-maker. The younger Pliny, for instance, emphasizes the emperor's sole rule along with his taking over everyone's "labors and cares" (*Epistles* 3.20.12). Without responsibility, one may be as happy as a child, but that kind of security entails a loss of freedom. This paternalistic trade-off became a central obsession of Roman imperial literature. Emperors are judged good or bad on whether they could provide security without curtailing liberty (e.g., Tacitus, *Agricola* 1–3).

Through paradigmatic figures of both genders, Vergil's *Aeneid* shows the pitfalls attending leadership up and down the hierarchies. Leadership turns out to be about managing emotion, one's own and others', even more than achieving pragmatic goals. Aeneas succeeds in his mission of establishing a colony in Italy that will give rise to the Roman people, but at a price. He does better than Dido, whose passion destroys her city along with herself. Living up to the ideal of the calming leader is impossible, but failure to do so results in a discord that spreads from the leader's disturbed heart into the entire political order. The Latin word *cura* already shows ambivalence in meaning both worry and tending. Its negation in *securitas* reveals the complexity of alleviating cares through caring for both personal and group security. The strain on the singular leader is immense, but Roman history had recently demonstrated the perils of distributed leadership, so paternalism appears the only choice. As a literary text, the *Aeneid* is less interested in providing positive models than in exploring the ways in which, even in a success story, everything can go terribly wrong.

NOTES

1. This chapter condenses aspects of Lowrie (forthcoming) for a non-specialist audience. For a good introduction to the *Aeneid*, see Perkell (1999).
2. Johnson (1976).
3. Hamilton (2013).

4. Feeney (2014).
5. Quint (2018, 18–21).
6. Hardie (1993, 4–5).
7. James (1995).
8. Béranger (1973, 185–6): "The emperor 'takes on himself' the weight of cares; his life is laborious. Faithful to his post, he guards and watches over public safety. Work falls to him, to others leisure and rest."

REFERENCES

Béranger, J. (1973). *Principatus. Études de notions et d'histoire politique dans l'antiquité gréco-romaine*. Geneva: Droz.
Feeney, D.C. (2014). "First Similes in Epic," *Transactions of the American Philological Association* **144**(2): 189–28.
Hamilton, J.T. (2013). *Security: Politics, Humanity, and the Philology of Care*. Princeton, NJ: Princeton University Press.
Hardie, P. (1993). *The Epic Successors of Virgil: A Study in the Dynamics of a Tradition*. Cambridge: Cambridge University Press.
James, S. (1995). "Establishing Rome with the Sword: *Condere* in the *Aeneid*," *American Journal of Philology* **116**(4): 623–37.
Johnson, W.R. (1976). *Darkness Visible: A Study of Vergil's Aeneid*. Berkeley, CA: University of California Press.
Lowrie, M. (forthcoming). *Security and the Soul Political in Roman Political Thought*.
Perkell, C.G. (1999). *Reading Vergil's Aeneid: An Interpretive Guide*. Norman, OK: University of Oklahoma Press.
Putnam, M.C.J. (1999). "*Aeneid* 12: Unity in Closure," in C.G. Perkell (ed.), *Reading Vergil's Aeneid: An Interpretive Guide*, Norman, OK: University of Oklahoma Press, pp. 210–30.
Quint, D. (2018). *Virgil's Double Cross: Design and Meaning in the Aeneid*. Princeton, NJ: Princeton University Press.

11. Negative Capability and care of the self

Charlotte von Bülow and Peter Simpson

Bill Abbott worked for over thirty-seven years as a policy advisor and operational prison governor at two UK institutions: Pentonville and then Liverpool. When he retired, he gave a talk at the Tavistock Institute in London in which he shared his personal philosophy of leadership. He said,

> When I debriefed myself on retiring from the Service, I was surprised to understand how big a part death had played in the events of prison life. When the Chief Inspector offered me feedback in Liverpool from the staff it was to say that I was good at funeral speeches. I had spoken at three staff funerals. He did not offer feedback on whether they had said I was any good as governor. It is always interesting to know what matters in leadership and the professional training rarely prepares you for it. (Abbott, 2000)

Our purpose in quoting this rather strange reflection on death is to draw attention to the greater breadth of concerns than is typically considered a part of the leader's responsibility. We are also hinting at our central claim about caring leadership, which entails an engagement with the transformation of self in the world. This involves a renewed approach to the ways in which we typically understand leadership development and practice.

Through the particular lenses of Negative Capability (Saggurthi and Thakur, 2016) and Care of the Self (Foucault, 1990), we will argue that an aspiration to practise caring leadership involves a commitment to the development of self-knowledge. Following an exploration of our key themes, we will draw upon Abbott's reflections to illustrate how a phenomenological inquiry into one's experience of self may serve to heighten the quality of attention that leaders give in complex situations. In a sector increasingly dominated by systems and driven by targets and performance indicators, we suggest that Abbott's accounts reveal a dedication to re-humanising leadership by challenging his organisation to recognise that *being human matters*. This implies the need to develop a capacity for courage, trust and care in order to make decisions that are not driven by our personal agenda and fear of failure.

Caring and compassionate organisational leadership is often understood as necessary in situations where organisational members are experiencing difficulty, perhaps suffering stress or anxiety. The caring leader might be one who steps in to help out, providing comfort, resolving a problem. Such an understanding of 'care' is aligned with the etymological roots of the term in Old High German *chara* 'grief, lament' and Old Norse *kǫr* 'sickbed'.

We broaden the concept of care here and propose that it includes the development of an attitude of concern. 'Concern' derives etymologically from the Latin *concernere*: *con-* indicating heightened intensity and *cernere* meaning to sift or discern. This entails a heightened quality of attention. However, we challenge the notion that leaders merely need to learn to 'pay better attention' to what is happening within their organisation and its context. Leaders typically cast themselves as extremely busy and so it is important that we do not merely add to their 'to do' list by demanding that they 'be more caring'. By contrast, we suggest that the poet Keats' enigmatic notion of Negative Capability is a quality of being rather than a way of *thinking, feeling or doing*. As a consequence, it offers a radically different way of understanding care as a heightened quality of attention.

NEGATIVE CAPABILITY

Over the last two centuries, Negative Capability has influenced numerous fields of study – in literature, psychology, social work and leadership studies. Keats described it as when one is 'capable of being in uncertainties, Mysteries, doubts without any irritable reaching after fact & reason.' (Gittings, 1970: 43).

There are two important elements in Keats' description, both in a sense 'negative' but in different ways. The first is 'negative' in the sense that it is not a 'capability' at all, if by capability is meant that which we *think, feel or do*. In this first sense, Negative Capability is concerned with *being* in uncertainties, Mysteries, doubts. The second meaning of the phrase is 'negative' in that it is concerned with *not* feeling, doing or thinking: it is *being without* any irritable reaching after fact and reason. Negative Capability is thus *being* and *being without*. It is concerned with being rather than thinking, feeling and doing, and it is concerned with *being without* the forms of thinking, feeling and doing that we turn to in a search for the security of the familiar. We suggest that this is a *simple* interpretation of Keats' description of Negative Capability.

However, at another level there is something complex and inscrutable about this notion, demonstrated, for example, by the many interpretations of the phrase in the literature. Saggurthi and Thakur (2016) provide an interesting and informative review – and it is revealing that the various interpretations differ from one another and from what we argue here. To highlight the *complexity* of Keats' insight, we need say little more than that the nature of 'being' has absorbed the attention of some of the greatest minds since antiquity, from Aristotle to Heidegger, and that the related literature is notoriously difficult to understand. Rather than attempting to explain the nature of being, we seek an understanding of Negative Capability *in practice* through the lens of Keats' own philosophy 'on the pulses' (Gittings, 1970: 93), through which he gives attention to the phenomenology of his own experience.

To appreciate the contribution of Negative Capability to caring leadership requires an understanding that attention has more than one aspect (French and Simpson, 2014: 10ff.). We will consider two. The first is the ability to concentrate the resources of all (positive) capabilities (*thinking, feeling and doing*) on an object. This is closely associated with knowledge, both in guiding what to focus upon (the known object) and in determining the nature of the outcome from the practice of attention (learned knowledge). This is particularly relevant to a systemic understanding of organisation underpinning, for example, notions of evaluation, measurement and best practice. Caring leadership involving a heightened quality of *focused* attention will draw upon Negative Capability through a concern for the proper object of attention – *being without* those thoughts, feelings and actions that are a distraction. Negative Capability also contributes to caring leadership through the second – less commonly appreciated – aspect of 'evenly suspended attention', Freud's '*gleichschwebende Aufmerksamkeit*' (*ibid.*: 1). This implies an engagement with reality in a fuller sense: it does not focus on anything in particular but is open and receptive, scanning the inner and outer 'environments', mobilising an attitude of inquiry in the pursuit of 'truth'. This is an awareness of being, resting in 'uncertainty, Mystery, doubt', without requiring a sense of direction from existing sense, knowledge or action.

The value of making clear this distinction between focused and evenly suspended attention is that there is a tendency to favour the former, which requires knowledge and aligns with a desire for control. The latter is capable of being without control and involves the continuous letting go of the knowledge, feelings, practices and habits that have served us well in the past, tempting us to give them their attention through the illusory promise to remove the painful experience of anxiety and doubt.

Negative Capability, as a radical acceptance of *being* and *being without*, thus creates the conditions for giving a heightened quality of attention in all of its multi-dimensional complexity. We will now discuss how the Care of the Self can contribute to the development of Negative Capability, before exploring the implications for the practice of caring leadership.

CARE OF THE SELF

The Care of the Self (*heautou epimeleisthai*) is an ancient spiritual and philosophical practice of giving attention to one's own being. Foucault (1990: 49) cites the Stoic philosopher Seneca as asking 'people to transform their existence into a kind of permanent exercise'. In addition to general prescriptions for the care of the body (diet, health, exercise, etc.), the extensive literature across many traditions has many common themes. There are a number of related practices that have recently seen something of a renaissance in organisational thinking, including meditation, retreats, various kinds of study, conversation, friendships, and guides (e.g. coaches, consultants and advisers). The shift that is required beyond current practice is from a remedial focus *at the level of need* (e.g. stress management, career development, problem resolution) to the aspiration for a developmental transformation *at the level of being*.

Contrary to the solipsistic concerns of many modern approaches to personal and professional development, Hadot (1995: 82) asserts that by means of spiritual exercises, the individual is re-located 'within the perspective of the Whole'. This has important consequences for caring leadership in that a transformation occurs not only in being but also in the way in which things are seen. This emphasis of a shift in perspective indicates how caring leadership might arise from a change in quality of attention rather than a need to do more.

The development of a heightened quality of attention – referred to as 'vigilance' (*prosochē*) in the Stoic literature – is an exercise in its own right, which contributes to a range of other spiritual exercises. Hadot argues that attention 'is, in a sense, the key to spiritual exercises' (85). Hadot categorises the exercises that comprise the Care of the Self as meditations, 'remembrances of good things', intellectual exercises (e.g. reading, listening, research and investigation), and more active exercises (e.g. self-mastery, accomplishment of duties, and indifference to indifferent things). What we are suggesting is that the capacity for Negative Capability is an awareness arising from self-knowledge that can be developed through the Care of the Self: a range of spiritual exercises that 'have as their goal the transformation of our vision of the world, and the metamorphosis of our being.' (*ibid.*: 127).

It further helps our understanding of their developmental function to note that these spiritual exercises are often referred to as ascetic exercises. The notion of *spiritual* exercises encourages us to appreciate the development of that capacity of Negative Capability that is *being*. By contrast, we can associate the *ascetic* characteristics of the exercises as concerned with the development of a capacity for *being without*. However, it should be noted that the modern understanding of asceticism needs some refinement if we are to better understand the philosophical traditions of Care of the Self. Modern sensibilities recoil at the perception of asceticism as an austere, disciplined – perhaps even inhuman – process of self-denial. This is an understanding of *being without* as 'abstinence' or 'restriction' and, if left unbalanced, is entirely the wrong emphasis to apply. As the phrase 'Care of the Self' implies, these exercises are practised as a form of self-care, not self-abuse.

A more helpful focus for our purposes is found in the ancient roots of the term, which derives etymologically from the Greek adjective *askētikos*, meaning laborious, and the verb *askein*, meaning to exercise or work. *Askesis* was the term used in Ancient Greece when speaking of the athlete in training and has the connotation of a disciplined exercise regime. We can perhaps better translate 'ascetic exercises' merely as 'exercises' – albeit those with a serious, disciplined intent. It is, perhaps, also worthy of note, in passing, that the etymological roots of the term 'discipline' relate to learning (c.f. disciple as learner) rather than restriction. In ancient philosophy the term was used to refer to spiritual exercises that have not merely a moral, but also an existential value. These are not intended to be isolated practices but form part of an integrated regime: developmental activities not merely leading to improvements in moral conduct, but contributing to a philosophical life designed to achieve a radical transformation in self-knowledge, a fundamental reconstruction of one's being in the world.

An appreciation of the importance of discipline and training in organisational and leadership practice is not entirely absent, but there is a general neglect of the dedication required to become capable of dealing with particularly challenging situations. The ancient philosophical traditions suggest the need for a more disciplined engagement with one's own development in order to become capable of 'being in uncertainties, Mysteries, doubts without any irritable reaching after fact and reason'.

Foucault (1990) draws our attention to the range of 'exercise regimes' required for the transformation of existence into a 'permanent exercise', citing care in the political life (81ff.), of the body (97ff.), the soul (133ff.), and all manner of relations with others (145ff.). We are thus proposing an approach to caring leadership that emanates from the philosophical life, a developmental path to self-knowledge. Far from our typically modern association of asceticism with the experience of restriction and abstinence, the ancient emphasis was upon the (re-)generative potential of such work. It is possible, therefore, to understand the intention of ascetic practice as fostering a passionate care for whatever is considered to be of the greatest importance. This does not deny that such a practice will sometimes need to draw upon hard, sometimes painful, disciplinary practices in order to prepare for challenging situations – much like athletes must discipline their bodies to develop a capacity to compete against fierce and determined adversaries. However, as an act of self-care rather than self-denial, any price is deemed to be worth paying, any restriction worth suffering, for a new vision of the world and the capacity to remain true to oneself in the face of uncertainty, Mystery, doubt. Such training develops a capacity for care, arising from a metamorphosis of our being.

These ideas are alien to common understandings of leadership practice because of the pervasive influences of post-Enlightenment thinking (utilitarianism, rationality and empiricism). We do not engage with our being through the pursuit of usefulness, reason or evidence. The Care of the Self is not concerned with 'philosophizing' in the sense of constructing a system of productive ideas and efficacious knowledge, but is rooted in the ancient traditions of *theoria*, contemplation, which is a receptive form of knowing beyond theory. This is a knowing which is tested and proven by experience 'on the pulses'.

Giving serious consideration to ascetic work as Care of the Self through disciplined exercise opens up the possibility of an understanding of caring leadership as based on attention, awareness and the discernment of reality-oriented thought. From this perspective it is the work of philosophy to uncover this underlying motivation: an intention to establish or perpetuate goodness in the world, beginning with oneself. However, it is important not to let binary thinking dominate our understanding of the practice of Negative Capability and the Care of the Self. We are not suggesting that the leader who has given sufficient attention to self then has the capacity to give to others. The primary purpose of caring leadership is not to act in a caring way towards the other but neither is it to be undertaken as a solipsistic endeavour: these exercises are designed to give a perspective of the world and to develop a capacity for a heightened quality of attention that is always and inherently social: 'the work of oneself on oneself and communication with others are linked together.' (Foucault, 1990: 51).

Foucault is very clear that the tradition of the care of the self 'is not an exercise in solitude, but a true social practice' (1990: 51). In this regard, it is helpful to note the importance of social structures that both support and constitute the Care of the Self, for example, in drawing upon the services of 'the private consultant . . . a life counsellor, a political adviser, a potential intermediary in a negotiation . . . professor, guide, adviser, and personal confidant . . . kinship, friendship' (52).

It is in this sense that developing Negative Capability arises from the philosophical attitude. Through a commitment to living the philosophical life, the love of wisdom is awakened – not in an abstract sense but 'on the pulses' – and the phenomenological inquiry of the Care of the Self leads to the emerging realisation of a deep-seated care for goodness, beauty and truth discovered at the level of being. And this not with a narcissistic focus on the development of self-knowledge, but rather as a social process that fosters a rejuvenated vision of the world. It was such an awakening that led Keats to be radical in his acceptance of the uncertain, mysterious nature of reality.

CARE OF THE SELF AND NEGATIVE CAPABILITY IN PRACTICE

Keats had been schooled in philosophy from a young age and it can be observed that he had developed his own practice of Care of the Self. He is recognised as much for his letters as for his poetry and in these it is possible to discern the unsystematic development of a personal philosophy. These letters comprise meditations on his life and practice, personal reflections, the recollection of truths, revelations of the state of his soul, and requests for and gifts of advice. Whilst he lived only to the age of 25, there survive over 240 of his letters to family and friends. From these we know that he was in the habit of taking a regular retreat within himself and that his approach was to conduct an ongoing phenomenological inquiry into his own experience. This is one modern understanding of the ancient practice of Care of the Self.

We will now reflect on some aspects of the leadership practice of Bill Abbott, the prison governor who provided us with a tantalising reflection on death in our introduction. We will suggest that, like Keats, Abbott demonstrates a capacity for an ongoing phenomenological inquiry into his own experience. Importantly, in our view, both Keats and Abbott also demonstrate a capacity to develop their own approach to Care of the Self. It is our assumption that if ascetic/spiritual exercises are going to contribute to a developing practice of care then it is important that they are freely chosen and not experienced as an externally imposed regime of discipline and restriction. Moreover, the uniqueness of each person, role and circumstance means that every individual must take up the freedom to determine their own regime for the Care of the Self. This is obvious when one considers that the development of self-knowledge and the nature of the philosophical life will vary considerably between the 'philosopher' *qua* philosopher, poet, or organisational leader. However, this is not to say that everyone is left to work it out for themselves: we are illustrating in the philosophical traditions of Care of the Self that there are many resources upon which to draw – ancient and modern. We know that Abbott drew on the Tavistock tradition, rooted in psychoanalysis rather than philosophy, and was supported by a coach from the Tavistock Institute (see Armstrong, 2005).

Hadot argues that the Care of the Self is exemplified in Socrates who was an educational leader, who had no interest in best practice, 'Socrates had no system to teach. Throughout, his philosophy was a spiritual exercise, an invitation to a new way of life, active reflection, and living consciousness.' (Hadot, 1995: 157). We can see echoes of this in Abbott's practice, which consistently shuns a reliance upon 'best practice' and the demands of the system but demonstrates an attention to the present moment by means of a very human inquiry. In the following discussion, we select excerpts from Abbott's (2000) account that describe his own phenomenological inquiry, which is central to Care of the Self. We do not attempt a systematic analysis of his behaviour in relation to the practices of Negative Capability and Care of the Self. Rather, we present an illustrative narrative that might be considered a modern example of someone for whom these ideas have meaning. Further, we invite the reader to decide whether this presents a picture of something that might reasonably be thought of as caring leadership.

In the early days of his time at Liverpool Prison, Abbott argues that his approach to organisational leadership was less focused on the legitimacy of the managerial role and more an issue of being human . . .

> In my opening speech to staff I had concluded with a strong commitment to the individual . . . If there has been a significant but subtle shift in the Service, and perhaps elsewhere in society . . . it is a move away from the focus on the individual to a range of performance indicators . . . Within this shift there is a potential change of atmosphere – a less personalised world, a less warm world.
>
> . . . My view is that within the Prison Service the system – the organisation, its structures, and line management with a focus on delivery of a set of objectives – is most prominent. This is strengthening a managerial, descriptive version of the role of governor and strengthening the authority inherent in the office of governor. In the past and when I was governor . . . much of the authority was a personal one.

One of the attractions of managerialism of the kind that Abbott eschews is that it provides a safety net of certainty for the leader who is day by day facing uncertain occurrences. This safety is a defensive reliance on the collective knowledge of 'best practice', encouraging leaders to follow patterns of organisation that are prevalent in similar institutions. This fearful, anxiety-laden response to the challenge of leadership is precisely what Keats is alluding to in his phrase 'irritable reaching after fact & reason'. In taking up a 'personal authority', Abbott is accepting the responsibility and accountability of his role to himself. This is not to neglect existing knowledge, and the importance of learning from good practice, but it is to recognise that authentic behaviour will entail a recognition that it is particular and not general knowledge that will be most important in a specific situation. This approach to caring leadership demands a practice not merely of giving focused attention to the presenting issues, but also to practise evenly suspended attention, with a vision emanating from one's whole being, 'on the pulses' and not 'by the book'. This involves remaining in touch with being human, and it is this, which time and again in his talk, Abbott says, '. . . returns me to the central theme of individuality and the importance of understanding . . . person, role and system.'

Abbott's understanding of personal authority is not a narcissistic insistence on one's own ideas but is enacted through a commitment to taking responsibility for making discerning judgements, and not falling back on what the system dictates the leader should do. An overreliance on procedures and protocols in leadership constitutes a barrier to the development of a philosophical attitude. When leaders rely on externally determined factors, like performance indicators, attention is captured by predetermined outcomes in a way that can prevent the leader from paying attention and being receptive to what matters. Caring leadership requires the exercise of personal responsibility, courage and risk taking in the face of a systemic expectation to impose controls predicated upon standardisation, generalisation and an adherence to prescribed norms of practice.

In the following excerpt, Abbott describes attending to systems in a humanising way by taking up a personal authority, suggesting a resonance with a Care of the Self in the 'intellectual exercises' of listening and investigation (discernment):

> The important element of control in prison is the atmosphere. The atmosphere is what conditions the prison and it is difficult to put it into a performance indicator. I put greater emphasis on my emotional antennae than on performance indicators. The key elements in the individualist approach are compassion, listening, and the use of discretion, which prisoners set store by. It re-emphasises that the governor must take up the role using their own personality and focus on being creative for and with individuals. In the new managerial world, the governor cannot afford to be just a manager delivering a set of outputs.

By contrasting 'a strong commitment to the individual' with a shift in society towards 'performance indicators', Abbott is illustrating a tension created by *being without*. In this case this practice of attention leads him to want to imagine the possibility of counter-balancing the demands of performance indicators with a more humane sensibility, recognising that people want to be seen for who they are, and treated with appropriate compassion and understanding. In taking up his leadership role in this way he was signalling an intention to give a heightened quality of attention to what he refers to as the 'personal'. In this he is undertaking, with Negative Capability, the work of attending to the emotional 'data', sensitised to a wider array of factors than are typically contained within the systemic indicators of effective organisational performance.

We infer that Abbott has learned the importance of *being without* received certainties (e.g. guidelines for best practice) in order to give sufficient evenly suspended attention to a wider range of 'indicators' within his institution. In alluding to his 'emotional antennae' he is signalling a high level of confidence in his self-knowledge. This experiential dimension to the practice of Negative Capability – being in uncertainty and without imposing pre-existing, known solutions – is evident in Abbott's description of an approach involving 'compassion, listening, and the use of discretion'. This does not exclude the function of his role as 'a manager delivering a set of outputs' but demonstrates a commitment to avoiding the dangers of giving insufficient attention to the foundational reality of *being human* in an institution like a prison, for all the uncertainties of that reality and the systemic and societal encouragement to objectify and stereotype prisoners as something less than human.

Providing a specific example of the nature of caring leadership through heightened attention to the emotional atmosphere of the institution, Abbott talks about his practice of 'walking the landings' of the prison, illustrating the importance merely of 'being there':

> Above all else it provides the opportunity to feel the institution and having felt it to work with and on the feeling. The task is to absorb the emotion and thus allow people to take up their role free of negative emotion, which detracts from their performance. Often just being there will remove the emotion. Often just listening to the anger will move it.

We see this form of caring leadership described by Abbott when he makes reference to the 'personal attention' that he paid to staff, as well as the assertion that he 'cared passionately rather than managerially':

> Liverpool was proud of being the biggest prison. I used this and issued mugs, key-rings, pens with the logo 'Security and Care in the Biggest Prison'. It got the word care into the language of the prison. The personal attention I paid to staff deaths [in my funeral speeches] may also have contributed to developing staff concerns about death. This returns us to the complex relationship between staff and prisoners. Those who attempt suicide are looking to be cared for at one level. The prison was changing and prisoners themselves acknowledged this.
>
> The decision to allow them to wear their own trainers was a significant indication of change and care. The continual reiteration of the message that we cared may have reached them. A prison in a process of dramatic change sent a message of care. Making a lot of noise about suicide and about care was important. This is about organisational dynamics and about how the psyche of an organisation can affect individuals within them. It is also about the governor consciously holding the issues and working with them in the subconscious of the organisation. Perhaps the respect the staff and unions came to have for a governor that respected them was reflected in their greater respect for prisoners. Because I cared passionately rather than managerially the institution which represented me came also to care.

This is an example of how the Care of the Self can underpin a discerning and heightened quality of attention not solely towards individuals in need but also to the organisation as a whole. By using some very basic psychology – putting the word 'care' on the prison mugs – Abbott worked attentively with the organisational subconscious. Working intuitively in this way is one thing – working on these levels consciously requires a vigilant commitment to the development of self-knowledge.

And, again, Abbott returns to the theme of death. This is symptomatic of an experiential philosophy developed 'on the pulses' of an uncertain and precarious institution like a prison and it seems to us that nothing demonstrates the importance of Negative Capability more than when we dare to remember that organisational life includes many moments of death – literal and figurative. Hadot (1995: 95) makes clear that Care of the Self is a 'training to die to *one's individuality and passions*, in order to look at things from the perspective of universality and objectivity' (italics in the original). This is a social and not selfish practice. It is also concerned with a renewed vision of the world, for all its limitations, imperfections and difficulties. As Abbott illustrates with such eloquence, those who develop a high level of capability in *being* and *being without* are better able to provide a heightened quality of attention in their leadership in such testing conditions.

REFERENCES

Abbott, W.A. (2000). 'Prison management.' Unpublished paper presented at the Tavistock Institute Series, *Programme of Dialogues: Worlds of Leadership 2000*, London, 6 July.

Armstrong, D. (2005). *Organization in the Mind: Psychoanalysis, Group Relations, and Organizational Consultancy*. London: Karnac.

French, R. and Simpson, P. (2014). *Attention, Purpose, Cooperation. An Approach to Working in Groups Using Insights from Wilfred Bion*. London: Karnac.

Foucault, M. (1990). *The History of Sexuality, Vol. 3: The Care of the Self* (R. Hurley trans.). London: Penguin.

Gittings, R. (1970). *Letters of John Keats*. Oxford: Oxford University Press.

Hadot, P. (1995). *Philosophy as a Way of Life: Spiritual Exercises from Socrates to Foucault*, (A.I. Davidson, ed.) (M. Chase, trans.). Oxford: Blackwell.

Saggurthi, S. and Thakur, M.K. (2016). Usefulness of uselessness: A case for negative capability in management. *Academy of Management Learning and Education*, **15**(1): 180–93.

12. *Pater* figure: leaders, emperors and fathers in Seneca and Stoicism

Liz Gloyn

De Clementia, or *On Clemency*, was written by an influential teacher for a powerful pupil. In AD 56 the Roman philosopher Seneca addressed it to the emperor Nero, then eighteen years old and at the beginning of his reign. *De Clementia* is, in some ways, a forerunner of Machiavelli's *The Prince*, in that it tries to make its autocratic ruler more amenable to his subjects whilst making him think that it was his idea. Seneca uses images which combine Roman ideas about authority and power with the concepts of care and responsibility to highlight the advantages a leader can gain through exercising *clementia*. Practical tensions arise when trying to implement Seneca's advice in the modern world, not least in settings where everyone is understood to have equal agency. Yet by bringing out a leader's shared duties of care and guidance, Seneca argues that everyone benefits from a caring leader – not least the leader himself.

Seneca wrote from a position of trusted authority. Since AD 49, he had been Nero's personal tutor, summoned back from exile specially by the young man's mother. Following the death of the emperor Claudius, Nero's stepfather, in AD 54 and Nero's subsequent accession to the throne at sixteen, Seneca's role transitioned from tutor to close advisor. We know, for instance, that he acted as the adult Nero's speechwriter in this early phase of his rule. *De Clementia* shows every evidence of the close personal relationship between its writer and a young man at the start of what promised to be a glittering political career.

The ancient world saw virtues as desirable character traits that individuals possessed. *Clementia* was framed as a virtue specifically exercised by emperors after it was included on a celebratory golden shield placed in the Senate House at Rome, lauding Augustus' clemency alongside his courage, justice and piety. This dedication set out what Augustus wanted to present as the personal qualities essential for a successful ruler; later emperors put much effort into demonstrating they met the criteria that he established. *Clementia* also becomes, for Seneca, a response to the autocratic power which Augustus first began to consolidate control in the hands of himself and his family in 27 BC.[1] While the Roman senate functioned as a nominal set of checks and balances on the emperor's whims, in reality there was little opposition to his activities if they were clothed in judicial respectability. Both Nero and his subjects would benefit if the teenager could develop habits of restraint at this early stage of his rule.

One could see Nero and Seneca as offering two different models of the caring leader. Nero's leadership cares primarily about himself, focusing on self-interest and self-preservation, especially towards the end of his reign. Seneca's leadership focuses on persuading and enabling others, hoping to equip them with the tools which will enable them to function effectively – empowering rather than directing, as he does in arguing for the benefits of *clementia*. There is, however, a third model on which I want to concentrate, and that is the figure of the ideal leader that Seneca constructs in *De Clementia*, the person who is capable of exercising this virtue and thus acting as an example for his readers.

What, then, is *clementia*? Sometimes it feels as if Seneca is more comfortable with a negative definition, given how often he defines it by what it is not rather than by what it is. For instance, it is not giving in to a sense of personal outrage when you have suffered a personal injury; it is not doing harm simply because you can; it is not anger, which debases a king. It is the antithesis of cruelty and savagery (*crudelitas* and *saevitia*), which not only respond to situations irrationally and without impulse control, but which even seek out ways to be inventively vicious towards the victims of their excessive anger. Perhaps surprisingly, it is also not pity, or *misericordia*; when we fall into pity, we become sad ourselves because of the circumstances another individual is experiencing, and thus our own spirits cloud over even though we ourselves are not suffering anything. Someone demonstrating *clementia* can still be sympathetic to a person in bad circumstances, but will pay more attention to the underlying reasons and how that fits into the bigger picture.

The definition of *clementia* that Seneca eventually offers is as follows (2.3.1): 'Clemency is the self-control of the mind that has the opportunity to take revenge, or the gentleness of a more powerful person towards a weaker person in deciding punishment.'[2]

The ability to show *clementia* is intimately bound up with power over other people's lives, which makes it inherently paradoxical. You can only demonstrate *clementia* if you have the power to do harm, but the presence of *clementia* is the absence of that power being exercised. This follows the well-established distinction between power-over and power-to: rather than choosing to demonstrate how much you have power-over someone, *clementia* is choosing not to do that which you could do, making a deliberate choice to exercise your power-to-*not*. Perhaps this is why Seneca spends so much time talking about what *clementia* is not rather than what it is: it is a set of behaviours notable by their absence rather than their presence.

Clementia's relationship to care is complex. I define care here as caring about something, specifically about individuals over whom one has authority. Care thus functions as the opposite to the cruelty exercised when people with power give in to anger rather than deploying *clementia*. *Clementia* helps balance a weaker individual's interests with the needs of the more powerful person to, for instance, maintain order or enforce regulations. But there is not a unidirectional relationship between care and *clementia*. A reiterative relationship exists between the two: the more you exercise *clementia*, the more you enable care, and the more you care, the more you exercise *clementia*. This pattern echoes broader Stoic moral theory, which proposed that you could develop virtue by acting in the appropriate manner externally, so that you would encourage an appropriate internal disposition to help you act correctly in future.

Two possible objections arise concerning the usefulness of *De Clementia* to modern readers. First, one might argue that arguments for why a Roman emperor should exercise *clementia* have little resonance with the challenges facing modern leaders today. Seneca draws an explicit link between the ability to save rather than destroy life and the emperor's exalted status; even the most draconian terms and conditions of employment in the global north stop short of capital punishment. But Seneca is not writing just to Nero. While his focus may be on how the emperor can demonstrate *clementia*, he urges his reader to take lessons about how to wield great power from the way that lesser power is used; that is, you can put the lessons of *De Clementia* into practice if you hold any kind of authority over other people.

The second counterargument maintains that Seneca's roots in a patriarchal, sexist society limit the wider applicability of his advice. Why look for solutions to the challenges of the twenty-first century in a text written by an elite male to an elite male? Seneca has an answer here too. His thinking is rooted in the ancient philosophical system of Stoicism, a systematic way of explaining the world which believed that the only way to achieve virtue, and thus happiness, was to act in accordance with perfect rationality.[3] The distinctive characteristic of humans was the ability to contemplate and to reason. This intellectual potential needed proper training, but every human had the capacity to become virtuous. The Stoic Musonius Rufus commented that since men and women had the gift of reason, if we insisted on training women differently from men, we had only ourselves to blame for differing outcomes. Equally, while someone working for a living may not have the time to engage in the sustained study necessary to refine their reason, they have the same innate capacity for virtue as everyone else – a strong contrast to Aristotle's position that those engaged in manual labour are essentially slaves and thus cannot make full use of their reason. While Seneca and Nero may occupy the privileged pinnacle of their society, and *De Clementia* is embedded in a society dominated by patriarchy, the ideological underpinnings of the text see virtue, and this particular virtue, as accessible and relevant to everyone.

In order to make understanding *clementia* easier, Seneca uses a number of images to illustrate what it looks like in practice. Concrete examples of situations in which people exercise *clementia* thus help him past the difficult paradoxes of explaining the virtue in the abstract. Three of these images and how Seneca deploys them are of particular interest to us: the father, the doctor and the king bee.

Seneca illustrates the role of the good emperor by comparing it to the behaviour of a good father (1.14.1–2):

> So what is his duty? It is that of good parents, who should rebuke their children sometimes affectionately, sometimes threateningly, and sometimes even admonishing them with a beating. Surely a sensible man does not disinherit his son for a first offence? Unless a great many serious wrongs conquer his patience, unless he fears more than he condemns, he does not come to the definitive sentence. Before that, he tries many things to call back the wavering character, which is already in a worse place. As soon as the matter is given up for lost, he undertakes extreme measures. No one comes to requiring punishments unless he has used up all the possible remedies. What a parent must do, an emperor must do too.

Seneca finds this image useful because of parallels between how power is exercised in the father–son and emperor–citizen relationships. To get to the root of these, we need to understand the structure of the Roman family. A Roman *familia* was headed by the *paterfamilias*, the oldest male in the family; it included descendants through the male line, not the female; women who married men in that line through a particular kind of marriage ceremony;[4] and even enslaved people claimed as property by the household. The stereotype of the harsh *paterfamilias* became widespread because of the absolute authority he held over those under his control – *patria potestas*, a father's power, gave him the theoretical right to decide independent of any judicial process whether those in his *familia* lived or died.[5] The unlimited control that the father had over those in his *potestas*, in particular his son, makes him an excellent figure to think with when advising a man with complete authority over his powerless subjects.

Patria potestas was responsible for much of the conflict that Roman society saw embedded in the father–son bond. The Romans felt the father played a positive role in his son's moral development and could offer a behavioural model, but the danger posed by his unlimited authority always lurked in the background. The Roman conception of the dynamic between father and son was rigidly hierarchical, and had little flexibility. A son remained under his father's control either until he was legally released by his father or his father died; this meant that a grandson might in fact be under his grandfather's control rather than his father's. A son in his father's *potestas* could not legally own property, make a will, or have his own money, although there were technical work-arounds for these restrictions. That said, the possibility that a man might remain under his father's authority beyond young adulthood led to genuine concern that frustration and enforced incapacity might manifest in parricide. Despite idealised models of fatherhood, and even a comic stereotype of the over-indulgent and lenient father, there was no getting away from the fact that ultimately, when it came to making decisions, the father held all the cards.

The *paterfamilias*'s position at the top of the *familia* explains why Seneca uses the father as a way to help the emperor understand his duty and as one possible way of demonstrating *clementia*. The father, through his possession of *patria potestas*, can demonstrate self-restraint and moderation in determining the consequences of another person's actions. His authority may not extend across as many individuals as the emperor's, but in terms of scope, he legally has the capacity to impose punishments which are just as harsh. In the passage, Seneca leads us through the various stages of admonishment available to fathers – scolding, threatening and even corporal punishment.[6] The ultimate reprimand in his list is disinheritance, being cut out of your *familia* and losing your right to inherit property and wealth.

Yet Seneca is emphatic that the process of working through these various punishments is gradual and slow. Instead of hunting out sanctions, a father should try to help his son improve – again, power-to rather than power-over. Rather than seeing the current state of his son's morals and behaviour as evidence of an irreversible downward trend, the father should see the potential for recovery and improvement. In fact, as he thinks about when it might be appropriate to take the extreme measure of disinheriting someone, Seneca says that the father will only do that 'when he fears something worse than he has reprimanded' – that is, I think, a fairly clear allusion to wider social concerns about the constant risk of parricide that a father faced from a hostile son. It's telling that Seneca never mentions the right of life and death in this treatise as part of a father's powers, even though it is an important part of the cultural landscape he's evoking. This omission, too, is deliberate – by making disinheritance, the domestic equivalent of exile, the most extreme option in the father's disciplinary armoury, Seneca quietly omits the possibility of capital punishment. The implied lesson is that even though a father has the legal power to go this far, in reality he would never do so, and that the emperor would do well to do likewise.

In case this message was too subtle for Nero, Seneca provides a couple of examples to reinforce it. The first is of a Roman knight, Tricho, who flogged his son to death and was only just saved from an angry mob in the forum who tried to stab him to death with their writing pens (1.15.1). This father *has* taken his legal power to its limits, but his action generates public antagonism towards him for exercising those rights. He may have been *able* to flog his son to the point of death, but his decision to do so results in social condemnation so violent that his own life is endangered. Tricho's experience highlights the informal social restrictions which operate on the exercise of power; just because you can act in a certain way doesn't mean that your community will approve of it when you do. For Seneca, the underlying message to Nero is clear – as Tricho's failure to show *clementia* towards his son puts his life at risk, so Nero's decisions may lead to his life being endangered by the outrage of his discontented citizens. With the memory of the emperor Caligula's assassination in 41 AD still resonating, this was not an idle warning.

The second example focuses on the case of Tarius, whose son plotted parricide against him; after investigating the accusations, he sent his son into exile in Massilia (modern day Marseille) whilst continuing to provide him with a comfortable allowance (1.15.2). This example specifically evokes the fear of parricide, the worst domestic crime the Romans could conceive. However, Tarius does not seek revenge or exercise his right to an equally brutal reprisal in response. Instead, he opts for *clementia*, and both shows affection for the offender and acknowledges his guilt.

We can now understand why fathers provide powerful examples of how to show *clementia*. The emotional affection a father feels toward his son is supposed to moderate any urge towards retribution he may also experience; care felt towards a subordinate results in care being shown towards the subordinate, thus fuelling the repetitive expansion of both *clementia* and care. An emotional connection between two people is critical for creating the impulse towards *clementia*, not to mention a generally more beneficial environment for everybody concerned. Seneca elsewhere mentions that the ruler who is known to 'care about everything' will be 'loved, defended and respected by the whole state' (1.13.4); a leader who fosters and responds to emotional investment in others both demonstrates care and in turn becomes an object of care.

Seneca combines the image of the father with a second image to help illustrate the nature of care and *clementia*, namely that of the doctor (1.14.3, trans. Braund, 2009): 'Reluctantly would a father cut away his own flesh and blood; even after he had cut them away, he would long to restore them; and in the act of cutting them away, he would lament, after frequent and long hesitations.'

This image brings together that of the father 'cutting out' his son through disinheritance with that of a doctor amputating the limbs of a suffering patient. This image of care through cure appears frequently through *De Clementia*. Again, it is based on a hierarchical relationship: a good patient follows their doctor's instructions obediently. Indeed, a seriously ill patient in need of drastic medical intervention is unlikely to be in a condition to participate in a discussion about their own care, and is much more likely to be at the doctor's mercy. Thus a doctor has as much ability to cause harm to a patient's body as she does to help it; she stands in the same position of ultimate power over her patient's health and life as an emperor does over his subjects' well-being.

The combination of the father and doctor imagery in this passage emphasises the hesitation over incision, the regret for the action undertaken, the longing that the surgery could be undone. The combined image underscores the need for reluctance in taking extreme action, even when it is framed as curative; if a decision to operate is made to provide a cure, the act should be performed with reluctance and regret, by father and surgeon alike. The medical imagery adds another layer to our understanding of what *clementia* should be; it reinforces the idea that a person with authority should be thinking about curing rather than punishing, about improvement rather than condemnation.

Other images of the ruler as doctor reinforce this idea. At the beginning of the treatise, after reminding Nero that he is the mind of the state and the state is his body, Seneca first uses the surgery metaphor (1.5.1). He tells Nero to treat even blameworthy citizens like ailing limbs, and that if blood must be let, to take care not to cut more deeply than necessary. Once more this image forgoes the full power of the doctor, and indeed of the emperor himself; the comparison of wayward citizens with sick body parts suggests both are responsive to care and thus curable. Seneca's rhetoric of saving life takes on new force within the context of this medical image, particularly if we assume a doctor has taken the Hippocratic oath. In order to be considered a doctor in the ancient world, you had to convince your patients that you knew what you were doing; we do not know how many people actually swore the oath, or how common it was. That said, the oath has been hugely historically influential. The earliest extant versions require the doctor to swear they will always seek to heal the sick and never to carry out intentional injury or harm;[7] medical imagery implicitly evokes this expectation, and provides another way to conceptualise what committing to *clementia* in leadership means in practice.

What should the doctor do with diseases which seem incurable? Seneca's response dashes all hope of easy excuses (1.17.2):

> It is typical of a bad doctor to despair that he cannot cure. The person to whom everyone's safety has been handed over ought to do the same thing for those who are afflicted in their minds. He should not quickly abandon hope or pronounce signs heralding death. He should wrestle with vices and resist; he should reproach some with their particular illness, and deceive certain others with gentle care, so as to restore them to health quicker and better with false remedies.

There's no escape here for the leader who claims that the medical analogy collapses when faced with difficult people. The art of good doctoring, and thus the successful exercise of *clementia* and caring-for, is as much about psychological manipulation as it is about making a correct diagnosis. What's needed is patience, perseverance, a degree of cunning, and willingness to try different strategies to cure the sick person – being a caring leader requires hard work and ingenuity. Just as Tarius had to think of an appropriate yet clement response to his murderous son, so must the caring leader find a way to reach the wayward person over whom they have power. Some strategies will work for some people, but not for others; like the persistent doctor, the person with responsibility for others will not give up just because their first attempt hasn't worked.

The final image I want to explore occurs only once, but Seneca unpicks it at length (1.19.2–3, trans. Braund, 2009):

> Nature, after all, devised the idea of kingship, as can be understood from other creatures but especially from the bees. Their king has the most generous bedroom, situated in a central place of maximum safety. Besides, he is free from work himself but supervises the work of the others. When the king is gone, the community disintegrates completely.[8] They tolerate only one at a time, never more, and they discover the better in a fight. Besides, the appearance of the king is extraordinary and distinct from the rest both in size and in splendour. Yet the biggest difference is this: bees are highly irascible and, for the size of their bodies, very fierce fighters and they leave their stings in the wounds they inflict, but their king himself has no sting. Not wanting him to be cruel or to seek revenge that would cost a high price, Nature removed his weapon and left his anger unarmed. This provides an important model for great kings.

The Stoics often took models from nature because they believed that as this was the best of all possible worlds it showed us how things were ordered virtuously. Looking at the natural world as Seneca does here could provide us with cues for our own behaviour. That a hive was ruled by a king rather than a queen was a common claim in antiquity, found in authors as diverse as Aristotle, Xenophon, Pliny and Virgil. This popular belief allows Seneca to use the king bee as a parallel for the emperor, and offer Nero a valuable lesson about how he should behave.

The main point that Seneca highlights is that, despite not having a sting, the king bee remains central to the hive, and critical for its continued existence despite his apparent failure to make a substantive contribution to the community. His power is so great that he does not need a sting to maintain it. Seneca presents this example as nature's way of showing kings that they should behave as if their power, too, is so absolute they have no need of retaliation. Despite the resources upon which a king might draw, he should consider himself to be like a king bee – distinct from his subjects in splendour and magnificence, but without need of the tools to act upon his anger or seek revenge for personal insult. *Clementia* thus becomes an exercise in acting in accordance with nature (*secundum naturam*), which for the Stoics was a way of learning the lessons that a providential creator had placed within his creation for human instruction. Bees teach the ruler that it is possible to be at the centre of a kingdom without resorting to violence against one's subjects; as such, the exercise of *clementia* is in harmony with the natural order, which makes it desirable for a leader to demonstrate it.

These images – the father, the doctor and the king bee – each clarify a different aspect of the links between *clementia*, care and power. From the king bee, the leader can reflect on the possibility of authority and respect without the need for retribution; from the doctor, the responsibility to care and cure rather than wound and maim. Yet Seneca keeps returning to the image of the father as the most helpful way to conceptualise how to perform *clementia*. The delicate balance between genuine affection and hierarchies of power in interpersonal relationships, creating the reciprocal yet paradoxical flow needed to generate *clementia* and care, is best understood through the father–son relationship, given the legal rights of the Roman *paterfamilias* and their implications for family dynamics. The father, walking the fine line between authoritarian stringency and indulgent permissiveness, calls readers to create a genuine emotional engagement between themselves and those over whom they have power, and to build their relationships on care (in all senses of the word) rather than a pecking order.

Although Seneca would like to suggest that *clementia* is a vital tool for the emperor, the idea cannot be uncritically applied to modern leadership contexts. While there is some discussion of how to respond to those who have wronged others, the primary context for *clementia* is the emperor–citizen relationship. This setting means that *clementia* and the factors which affect it revolve around one specific relationship, where one individual is more powerful than the other. This focus is inevitable, and indeed helpful, in a text addressed to the emperor himself, written in an imperial political system. However, it also means that there is nothing said about how *clementia* plays out within a wider community, or where other people are affected by the behaviour of the person to whom *clementia* is granted. The leader may not be able to provide care for everyone for whom they have responsibility if they decide to grant *clementia* to someone who is causing sustained harm to others.

I suspect the Romans may not have seen a problem with this. As Seneca makes clear on several occasions, one of the primary benefits Nero would gain from employing *clementia* would be securing his own position, and eliminating threats of rebellion and assassination attempts. *Clementia* stops the emperor from getting killed by encouraging him to demonstrate his own magnanimity. The function of *clementia* is not to create justice or to ensure fairness, but to reinforce the emperor's pre-existing power. Seneca presents *clementia* primarily as a virtue worth cultivating because it is in Nero's best interests to do so, not because it has any inherent value in its own right; many of the passages where he praises the good king and condemns the bad tyrant rely on appeals to Nero's naked self-interest.

The challenges of incorporating *clementia* into the modern world, particularly when seeking alternatives to paternalistic models of management, does not mean that we must abandon what Seneca represents as one of the major qualities of good leadership. It does mean that modern leaders wishing to learn ancient lessons must now take their wider communities into account, and think beyond maintaining and advancing their own status. Deploying *clementia* requires commitment to the hard work of nurturing the interlocking cycle of caring in order to show *clementia* and deploying *clementia* in order to enable care. *Clementia* has the potential to be a transformative virtue which places care at the centre of a relationship otherwise destabilised by power – always provided that the caring leader balances it with justice, and can extend their vision beyond their own benefit to that of those about whom they care.

ACKNOWLEDGEMENTS

I thank Leah Tomkins for inviting me to contribute to this volume and for her help in developing this chapter's argument. Jane Broadbent and Bill Gloyn also offered valuable advice.

NOTES

1. Alston (2014) provides an accessible introduction to the history of the Roman empire in this period.
2. All translations are my own, unless otherwise stated.
3. Inwood (2018) offers a bitesize introduction to Stoicism.
4. A marriage *cum manu* transferred a wife into the *potestas* of her husband or his *paterfamilias*. A *manus* marriage occurred through the ceremony known as *confarreatio*; a fictive legal sale; or if a husband and wife lived together under the same roof for an uninterrupted year. Most marriages in Seneca's period were *sine manu*, where a wife remained under her father's *potestas*.
5. We have very few examples of this right being exercised. Shaw (2001) explores the construction of this myth, both in the sources and modern scholarship.
6. Saller (1991) argues that whipping was a humiliation for a free son, because of its frequent use as a punishment for enslaved people; it was a symbolic punishment that was inappropriate for fathers to use against sons. The fact that Seneca includes flogging before disinheritance is a sign of the extremity of making this particular disciplinary choice, which carried its own strongly negative connotations.
7. King (2002, 14–17) provides more on the Hippocratic Oath and the medical profession in antiquity.
8. This observation resonates particularly with the model of charismatic leadership.

REFERENCES

Alston, Richard (2014), *Aspects of Roman History 31 BC – AD 117*, London, UK and New York, USA: Routledge.

Braund, Susanna (2009), *Seneca. De Clementia*, Oxford: Oxford University Press.

Inwood, Brad (2018), *Stoicism: A Very Short Introduction*, Oxford: Oxford University Press.

King, Helen (2002), *Greek and Roman Medicine*, London: Bristol Classical Press.

Saller, Richard (1991), 'Corporal punishment, authority, and obedience in the Roman household', in Beryl Rawson (ed.), *Marriage, Divorce, and Children in Ancient Rome*, Canberra, Australia and Oxford, UK: Clarendon Press, pp. 144–65.

Shaw, Brent D. (2001), 'Raising and killing children: Two Roman myths', *Mnemosyne*, **54**, 31–77.

13. Through the prism of Sartre: taking care of our existential freedom

Peter Bloom

INTRODUCTION

The values and practices associated with caring for oneself or another are increasingly influencing how we conceive personal ethics and social relations. This highlights how the principles of support, attending to the needs of others, and reciprocity can add to the conception and implementation of economic development, human rights, and community well-being. Yet it is less clear how theories of care can enhance notions of individual freedom and social progress. More precisely, how can theories and principles of care help reimagine what it means to be free both individually and collectively?

To answer these questions, it is first necessary to get a better sense of what is meant by care. Traditionally, care refers to the relationship between a carer and someone being cared for. This can take the form of an official caretaker such as a health professional or an informal one such as friends or family members who care for one another during times of physical or mental illness. However, recently it has also been understood as a phenomenon that has wide-ranging social and even global implications (Held, 2006). It reflects differing perspectives for fostering greater empathy toward others. In doing so it offers the opportunity for rethinking current society for the construction of one that is more caring and just.

This expanded idea of care and caring also opens up new possibilities for thinking about selfhood. Holistic perspectives speak, in this respect, of a caretaker attending to the "entire needs" of the person they are caring for. For this purpose, this advocates that they use techniques such as storytelling in order to enhance the freedom and agency felt by patients over their own identity and existence. Yet these attempts can still be rather individual-centred – focused on helping promote personal rather than shared or social agency. By contrast, relational understandings of care are explicitly inter-personal in their emphasis, recognising well-being and, by association, freedom as a common and interdependent endeavour.

These insights point to the profound linkages between ethics and practices of care with notions of existential freedom – or the ability to choose how one exists in a socially constructed world. Caring for others and ourselves is turned into an "existential challenge" for individually and collectively enhancing this freedom to control our own destiny and not be stuck in a socially proscribed identity or social condition. This chapter will attempt to explore such possibilities of combining care with existentialism. In particular, it will show the importance of care and caring leadership for fostering existential freedom at both a personal and community level.

To do so it will draw principally on the existential philosophy of Jean-Paul Sartre. Using his famed concepts of bad faith and nothingness, it will explore existential freedom as linked to an ethos of caring for oneself and others. For this purpose, it associates notions of holistic care with Sartre's idea of a productive "nothingness" that continually obligates caretakers to care not only for our current selves but also our possible future selves. Furthermore, it shows relational care perspectives as a powerful leadership ethos, through helping people form the mutual support networks needed to overcome our "bad faith" in a status quo in favour of new and more empowering forms of existence. To this end, it reveals the importance of individually and collectively taking care of our existential freedom.

CARING ABOUT EXISTENTIAL FREEDOM

It is well understood popularly and by practitioners that freedom is a critical part of caring for others. The ability to apply care-based techniques and ethics for patients is crucial to their recovering their capacity for choice and augmenting their overall social agency. Recently, these rather standard medicalised approaches have been enlarged to include feminist perspectives that take into account issues of gender and sex-based discrimination. Specifically, it is not just about allowing people to have more control over their body but their sense of "who they are" and "who they would like to be".

These ideas challenge traditional notions of liberty, promoting ideas that are both more inclusive of marginalised voices and sensitive to existing power inequalities. Drawing on the work of the French critical thinker Michel Foucault, Roe Sybylla (2001) notes that it is always imperative to ask "Whose voice" is being heard and as such frames both freedom and care as a process of continual self-choice and creation:

> Empowerment, then, means the individual gaining a sense that she or he is not tied to an origin but has the capacity to choose new actions and behaviours, constructed in the present time of volition. Change becomes less a struggle against one's weakness, and more a taking of control over one's life, and, to achieve this, the collection

of knowledge, reflection, and a regime of practice, training, and drill carefully designed to cultivate the desired habits and strengths (2001: 77).

In the wider political context, this ethos of care and freedom has been used to expand understandings of human rights internationally. It asks governments and NGOs responsible for preserving these rights to pay more attention to the physical and mental well-being of citizens – especially those with impairments or disabilities – so that they can use these rights to enhance their overall feeling of being independent and autonomous. More critical are perspectives that explore how caring for others can be transformed into a broader ethos of resistance. These values make possible a distinct form of "compassionate resistance" which derives its inspiration and call to action not from earthly authorities but from a higher power and universal ethos of love. Such an ethos can challenge established notions of "pastoral care" that often reinforce under-lying values of sovereignty and power imbalances while gesturing toward the potential to create new and more caring social structures and values.

Significantly, this assumption of care as resistance sits alongside emerging efforts to critique established liberal conceptions of freedom prioritising personal rights at the expense of material security and collective agency. Previously celebrated ideas of "self-determination" are now placed under scrutiny as reinforcing market-based inequalities and tyranny. These speak to fundamental attempts to foster greater existential freedom both at the personal and societal levels. These attempts focus on the ability of people to choose how they exist, encompassing but going beyond rights- or market-based choices of where to work and what to buy. While based on expanding one's positive agency to "take a leap of faith" and live authentically, this also highlights the cultural and economic barriers people face in actually doing so. Looking beyond the realm of the personal, this gestures towards questions of how much freedom societies have in choosing their economic, social and political systems that largely define their shared existence.

Missing from these perspectives, though, is an understanding of the impor-tance of care in supporting such existential freedom. Notably, how can values and practices associated with caring for others be a force for enhancing each other's autonomy over deciding fundamentally how we live and find meaning in an otherwise meaningless existence?

As discussed above, the values associated with care have become increas-ingly important for understanding and potentially transforming our inner selves and external world. While traditionally relegated to the field of either health or ethics, over the past several decades care is helping to shape broader ideas of personal spirituality and social relations. However, it is also gesturing toward the possibility of redefining human existence. If this sounds ambitious, it is because for many the ethos and practice of care has the potential to radically redefine how we live or, to use common existential terminology, our "way of being". Caring for others opens up new possibilities for helping others exist differently, allowing them to subvert and transcend social barriers and prejudices.

These perspectives allow, in turn, for new ideas of freedom that are imbued with and indeed strongly informed by care ethics. This shifts the focus of freedom to how we care for each other's perceived and real social agency. Here the notion of care and caring is understood to be essential to the creation and preservation of a "free society". Reflected, in turn, is how care becomes an entire way of living within and changing the world. At stake is a fresh approach for theorising and practically realising existential freedom. Highlighted is the ability to draw on care perspectives to enhance autonomy in all spheres of our existence and throughout our life (Pritchard-Jones, 2017). Care, in this respect, serves as a vehicle for radically rethinking the possibilities of existential freedom, both individually and collectively.

CARING FOR OUR EXISTENTIAL SELVES

Thus far this chapter has shown the important but relatively underexplored relationship between care ethics and existential freedom. It is crucial, in this respect, to understand how care can positively contribute to authentically choosing how we exist and find meaning in an otherwise absurd and meaningless world. This to an extent echoes the ideas of the previously referenced French critical theorist Michel Foucault in his belief in "the ethic of care for the self as a practice of freedom" (quoted in Fornet-Betancourt et al., 1987). Yet while Foucault focuses on care for the body and self as a site for contesting power, others have viewed it as opening oneself up to an "existential identity crisis" (Senkevich, 2016). This chapter will now turn to the theories of French existential philosopher Jean-Paul Sartre to investigate the ways in which care ethics and perspectives can enhance and expand existential freedom.

It is tempting, perhaps, when thinking of existentialism to take a rather narrow view of the self. It seems to be fixated on an individual who makes a decision about who they want to be and then seeks to live as authentically as possible according to this choice. Yet for thinkers such as Sartre, existentialism takes a more holistic view of selfhood similar, though not necessarily identical, to that of care theorists. Understanding the existential self requires a comprehensive understanding of the various social contexts in which one is born and by which one's identity is influenced. Existential freedom, in turn, is the ability to recognise – to paraphrase the German philosopher Martin Heidegger who inspired Sartre – the world we have been "thrown within" so that we can either freely choose it or seek to break free from it.

Existentialism, then, is to a certain extent a practice of discovering and caring for one's whole self. It involves an exploration of different spaces and aspects of oneself to determine who one currently "is" and who one would most like to "be". As such, caring ethics which foster such exploration – like those found in otherwise taboo places such as women's bath houses – can open people up to their previously unseen existential potentials. This entails creating "existential spaces" for giving people the tools to discover and care for their "holistic selves". Equally important is creating spaces where we can support others in their own exploration of their "holistic self", often in the face of rather daunting power dynamics and entrenched institutional processes.

Drawing on care ethics and perspectives to overcome issues of individual and collective bad faith is at the heart of these efforts. Sartre defines bad faith as the continual commitment to and embrace of a life and self that you have not freely chosen. In recent times this can be expanded to societies as well (see Bloom, 2018). Collectively we continue to invest and have faith in systems like the free market that we know are problematic. This is not as a result of any true belief or evidence, but rather because we cannot conceive of any other option, or lack imagination, which leads us to even more passionately act out and accept these seemingly religious forms of existence.

By contrast, a true commitment to existential freedom would be to take responsibility for our individual and collective existences rather than surrendering to such bad faith. There is a profound societal component to this existential commitment. It is the willingness to put lived experiences above mechanistic processes, thus empowering people to feel as if their lives and choices matter, as opposed to feeling helpless in the face of depersonalised structures and organisational prerogatives. Care is a central component of such efforts, as it entails fostering a culture where people's unique experiences and journey are prioritised and cared for. At the broader level, this form of existential care would allow us simultaneously to accept each other's own choices and differences while being willing to jointly and frequently overcome those shared identities and norms which are preventing us from truly confronting our shared existential dilemmas as a society.

It is imperative for such radical forms of personal and collective self care to grapple ironically with who we are not – at least yet. Sartre titled his philosophical magnus opus "Being and Nothingness", as he was as much interested in what "is not" as he was in what presently "is" and previously "was". The reason for this embrace of negation and ultimately nothingness is that a key part of existential freedom is to continually be willing to let go of your current self, your existing experience of being, for something new and different. To overcome the inherent meaninglessness of our existence it is necessary to transform this nothingness into an exciting possibility of continual becoming. It is a willingness to reflect on who you "are" and to consider who you may instead "become". There is also a profound responsibility of care for this "non-self". The holistic self, hence, transcends our current existence and includes future existences as well. Taking care of our existential self means granting us the freedom to choose who we are today as well as who we could be tomorrow.

TAKING CARE OF OUR EXISTENTIAL FREEDOM

Existentialism is often portrayed, at least within the popular imagination, as individually focused. It is the courage of a single person to take their own personal "leap of faith" and live authentically. Freedom, similarly, is discussed most commonly as ultimately individual in nature, in terms of personal liberty and rights. This focus on individual autonomy is increasingly being complemented by a more social vision of freedom, in particular, through critically asking which types of agency, capabilities and licence certain organisational and societal configurations permit, as well as which they minimise, outright prevent, or make impossible even to conceive. This socialised understanding of freedom creates, in turn, the potential to envision a collective experience of existential freedom – one that is rooted in theories and practices of caring leadership.

Helpful, in this regard, are perspectives that explicitly combine existential and humanist philosophies. These centre on exploring how a current way of being impacts our well-being and that of others. Here individuals are tasked with forms of "self-leadership", managing their own existential development. Hence, everyday experiences of travel and tourism can be transformed into "personal journeys" exploring new ways of living and being free. More broadly, this makes it possible to question commonly accepted, shared identities, like those associated with nationalism, in order to investigate different forms of collective existence. This can also serve as the basis for protests against governments and other authorities who are seen as caring for the existential freedom of one group while ignoring or actively reducing the existential freedom of other groups – such as witnessed in the recent Black Lives Matter protests.

Less immediately apparent, however, are the concrete social conditions conducive to such existential freedom; in particular, what type of social, organisational and cultural values are conducive to promoting individual and shared existential freedom. Care perspectives and practices are crucial to fostering the comprehensive and concrete conditions for individual and shared existential freedom. Indeed, existential freedom always had, even if sometimes only implicitly, a sense of sharedness and relationality. Central to existential philosophy and politics of the brilliant existential philosopher Simone de Beauvoir, for instance, was solidarity between oppressed people and groups. More recently, scholars have highlighted the existence of global care chains, those which, if properly utilised, could promote a transnational ethos of "freedom, responsibility and solidarity".

In practice, this means creating new forms of care-based governance both at work and politically. These would not only lead to more ethical and "caring" types of authority and sovereignty but also expand the agency individuals and groups have for questioning and changing their present existence. Indeed quite literally it can provide the opportunity to craft a radically different relationship with our physical world, promoting the transition from ecological "care to citizenship" that eschews desires for control and exploitation in favour of co-existence and conservation (MacGregor, 2004). Personally, existential psychotherapy can help individuals realise the therapeutic value of activism and effective civic engagement in their own lives (Greenslade, 2018). In the not-so-distant future, the caring ethic can guide the governance of technolog- ical enhancements to our body and mind for both our moral benefit and as a means for augmenting our existential freedom.

At stake, though, is the transformation of essentialised notions of "us" into existential conceptions of "we". More precisely, this involves forging a sense of solidarity based not on any inherent characteristic such as race or gender or even historically entrenched ones associated with national belonging, but instead on a shared and universal potential all of us have to shape our existence and discover new ones that have not yet been born into existence. Doing so means forging a culture and politics premised on care for each other – built on a commitment we have in our mutual realisation of this existential freedom. This existential care for our freedom can take many forms. It can be, for instance, in guiding an individual's "spiritual journey of meaning making" or "working through existential anxiety toward authenticity". It can similarly inform "action research" perspectives which engage in deep and shared critical reflections of our common "way of being" in different social roles and how this reflects our individual and common understandings of "what was and what is" as well as "what could be" (Feldman, 2002: 233).

The notion of caring leadership is important for realising these lofty aims. Here leadership is not necessarily captured in an all great and powerful leader. Instead, it is personified by the figure of the caretaker. Yet unlike notions of "pastoral power" associated with religious leaders, this caretaker ethos does not proscribe pre-determined values and moralities for people. Instead radical changes to the status quo act to open up the possibilities for others to explore and discover their own evolving experience of "the good life". It is additionally mutually supportive. In this existential vision of caring leadership, individuals and communities take turns supporting each other's existential freedom, some- times being the existential caretaker for others and sometimes allowing others to help care for their existential freedom.

This combining of existential freedom and caring leadership extends beyond conventional politics. It also encompasses a wide range of social and organisational relationships. Already within many societies, there has been an implicit shift in the purpose of parenting, moving from discipline and training to empowerment and freedom. In this respect, parents are meant to nurture their children's creative spirit while also protecting them from harm in order that they may fully explore who they are and what they would like to be. This model can certainly be applied to other contexts as well, such as in the workplace. Managers, for instance, can focus on helping employees not just to achieve organisational objectives or their own personal goals but actually to attain the existential freedom to reconceive their working conditions and thus their economic existence. Political leaders can also directly challenge those structures and ideologies that endorse austerity or the free market, which decrease and bar people's existential freedom socially.

Significantly, leadership ethics is, from this perspective, refocused on the mutual promotion of existential freedom. Critically, it emphasises the positive possibilities of "nothingness". It means leading people to accept that what currently exists is not all that can exist. Thus it concentrates on constructing discourses and institutions that are oriented to helping to make "what is" better and "what is currently not" possible. Additionally, it means leading in order to help others individually and collectively resist "bad faith" identities and ideologies. This does not mean that any dominant social belief or system should be a priori rejected. Rather, it means that leaders have a special responsibility to ensure that they are being freely chosen based on their merits rather than simply accepted as an inevitable and permanent social reality.

The emphasis on caring and leadership also gestures toward a more positive and less traumatic experience of our existential freedom. Traditionally, Sartre would assert that while we always have the freedom "to choose", it is most likely we would take advantage of this freedom during times of extreme personal crisis or social hardship. He unironically proclaimed that it was during the Nazi occupation, for instance, that the French people were the most free, in that:

> Since the Nazi venom snuck even into our thoughts, every correct thought was a conquest; since an all-powerful police tried to keep us silent, every word became precious like a declaration of principle; since we were watched, every gesture had the weight of a commitment. . . The very cruelty of the enemy pushed us to the extremity of the human condition by forcing us to ask the questions which we can ignore in peacetime" (Sartre in Gerassi, 1989, also quoted in Hoagland, 1999).

While certainly shocking, his point is that it is during times of duress, when our other liberal and social freedoms are most at risk, that we are willing to have the courage to truly question who we are and who we could possibly be. However, through the introduction of caring cultures and leadership, it is possible to begin imagining a world where solidarity and support are there to continuously foster our personal and shared embrace of existential freedom.

REFERENCES

Bloom, P. (2018). *The Bad Faith in the Free Market: The Radical Promise of Existential Freedom*. Cham: Springer.

Feldman, A. (2002). Existential approaches to action research. *Educational Action Research*, **10**(2), 233–52.

Fornet-Betancourt, R., Becker, H., Gomez-Müller, A. and Gauthier, J.D. (1987). The ethic of care for the self as a practice of freedom: An interview with Michel Foucault on January 20, 1984. *Philosophy & Social Criticism*, **12**(2–3), 112–31.

Gerassi, J. (1989). Jean-Paul Sartre: Hated conscience of his century, Chicago, IL: University of Chicago Press.

Greenslade, R. (2018). Existential psychotherapy and the therapeutics of activism. *European Journal of Psychotherapy & Counselling*, **20**(2), 184–98.

Held, V. (2006). *The Ethics of Care: Personal, Political, and Global*. New York: Oxford University Press.

Hoagland, S.L. (1999). Existential freedom and political change. In J.S. Murphy (ed.), *Feminist Interpretations of Jean-Paul Sartre*, University Park, PA: Penn State Press, pp. 149–74.

MacGregor, S. (2004). From care to citizenship: Calling ecofeminism back to politics. *Ethics & the Environment*, 9(1), 56–84.

Pritchard-Jones, L. (2017). Ageism and autonomy in health care: Explorations through a relational lens. *Health Care Analysis*, **25**(1), 72–89.

Senkevich, L.V. (2016). Phenomenological and process dynamic characteristics of existential identity crisis. *Global Media Journal*, 19.

Sybylla, R. (2001). Hearing whose voice? The ethics of care and the practices of liberty: A critique. *Economy and Society*, **30**(1), 66–84.

PART V

Reshaping the contours of leadership:
relationship, community and democracy

14. Educating caring leaders: a paradox of collective uniqueness

Ann L. Cunliffe and Matthew Eriksen

It is the last class of my Leadership Development course. We had just completed the 5-minute meditation we do at the beginning of each course to transition into our time together.

'I would like to start with my favorite question: Which two classmates are you most appreciative of because of the impact they've had on you over the semester? Who are they and what was his/her impact on you? Who wants to go first?'

As I am completing my question, Jeff's hand shoots up. I'm surprised at his enthusiasm and thank him for going first.

Jeff begins 'You. . .'

I quickly interrupt him, saying 'I appreciate that you chose me but please choose a classmate. I know we are not in the practice of publicly appreciating the impact of our peers on us, but think of it as a practice in which effective leaders engage.'

My curiosity is piqued. Over the first three-quarters of the semester Jeff had continuously challenged my comments during class and offered cursory responses to questions. Only in the last few weeks has he become more engaged in the course – a change that seemed to emerge after completing an assignment in which students had to take responsibility for improving one of their relationships that they cared about. He chose his relationship with his sister and had witnessed a positive impact from his efforts.

I add, 'I'll make an exception because I am very intrigued as to why you chose me.'

'It's because you stuck with me. You never gave up on me.'

I'm pleased as I realize my newfound commitment 'to meet students where they are' – which resulted in me being more patient and caring – has had a positive impact on a student that I might have 'lost' in the past.

The next student to respond says 'Jeff and you. Jeff because he spoke out about things I was thinking and feeling but didn't have the courage to express. And you because you were always respectful and patient with him. You never shut him down or gave up on him.'

For the first time in my 15-year academic career, I am beginning to understand the importance of my caring on students' learning and development. Not just the student with whom I interact, but also those students watching the interaction unfold.

As the students continued sharing, Jeff is the student most chosen by his classmates. Interestingly, the most 'challenging' student was the most impactful on his fellow students' learning and development.

We begin with this reflection from Matthew because it exemplifies a number of issues we raise in this chapter, that: (1) care and relational leadership are interwoven; (2) care is about connecting uniqueness and embeddedness within a community; and (3) we can educate students to become more caring leaders. Matthew's reflection is from an undergraduate Leadership Development course designed to develop students' practical wisdom and ability to become relational leaders (Cunliffe and Eriksen, 2011). It aims to facilitate learning from and through experience by encouraging students to engage in a reflexive questioning of course readings, experiential learning exercises, and of the unique moments of their emerging relationships with each other and with people in their lives (Eriksen and Cooper, 2018) – all within the context of leadership. Throughout the chapter, we weave theoretical observations from philosophers of moral education with comments from students about care and leadership. These comments are from a questionnaire containing open-ended questions about leadership and caring that Matthew asked the MBA students from his Fall 2018 Self-Leadership Course to complete. The questionnaire was designed with this chapter in mind.

INTRODUCTION

> In saying 'our interests first, who cares about the rest!' you wipe out what's most valuable about a nation, what gives it life, what brings it alive, what leads it to greatness and what is most important: its moral values. (Macron, 2018)[1]

In practice, we expect our leaders to be knowledgeable, competent and to provide moral leadership. The latter is being brought increasingly to the fore in today's political and business world climate, where polarizing rhetoric, self-interest, ethical scandals, and environmental disasters give an increasing sense that the moral compass of leadership is being eroded. It is a climate well noted in President Macron's comment on Armistice Day, 2018 (above), in which he observes that caring is essential to moral values. We celebrate instances of caring leadership, such as the compelling action of England's football team manager, Gareth Southgate, putting his arm around Colombian player Uribe, consoling him after his missed penalty which led to England's win. Caring and leadership are not terms that are often equated in the leadership literature or in leadership education, and when they are, caring is often seen to be instrumental in the sense of improving commitment through creating meaningful work. Perhaps the nearest equivalent to caring is work around leadership and ethics, particularly in relation to transformational, servant, spiritual, and authentic leadership where an ethics of care or compassion are seen as integral.

Much of this work focuses on the virtues, behaviors or attributes of leaders, or normative principles of ethical leadership (see Eisenbeiss, 2012 for an overview) and one result is the development of instruments that measure one's degree of authenticity, caring, and so on – a 'dumbing down' of complex ways of being in the world (Tomkins and Simpson, 2015). Such measures often form a key component of business school education and leadership training. In this chapter, we are not concerned with defining or categorizing 'care' as a system of morality, a virtue, personality construct, neural mechanism, or a practice, for as Shotter (2016, p. 4), a social philosopher, notes, these are after-the-fact and beside-the-point generalizations. In line with Shotter, we argue instead for thinking about care as before-the-fact hermeneutically-structured possibilities, which we create and in which we express caring every day in our relationships, conversations and interactions with others. For many years Shotter has challenged our understanding of the nature of our social world, our place within it, and how we generate knowledge about our experience. In his last book (2016), he examines what it means to be a participant in a holistic, chiasmic world in which we can make a difference that matters. This, we suggest, is a key concern of leaders who care, and care is central to relational leadership. As such, we position leadership and caring as a way of being in the world rather than a set of practices or techniques. As one of Matthew's MBA students noted:

> Being a leader is not all about skills. A lot of it is about the relationships we are able to form with others. If we can be leaders for each other in this class – where we came from different industries and backgrounds – surely we can be leaders in our own lives if we approach it with the same attention and dedication.

We begin by elucidating the interwoven nature of care and relational leadership and go on to discuss three related paradoxes. We then discuss how we may educate caring leaders using illustrations from Matthew's course.

CARE AND RELATIONAL LEADERSHIP

> Shedding light on the value of the common and shared features of human life . . . [and] . . . clarifying the value of what is irreducible and unique about human beings. (Hansen, 2011, p. 2)

This quote from Hansen, a Professor of Philosophy and Education, relates to his definition of a cosmopolitan orientation to education – the need for teachers to be open to the world around them. We suggest it applies equally well to thinking about caring because it draws attention to our uniqueness and agency as individual human beings whilst being embedded within a community. His comments have particular implications for leadership education and practice, where the continuing trend is towards normalization and rationalization.

Students are taught how to implement 'efficient' techniques to categorize, measure and manage employee performance in order to achieve organizational goals, often without any moral debate around their impact or consideration that such techniques objectify people and their performance. The underlying paradox is that while 'rational' is assumed to be objective, unemotional, neutral and something that 'good' leaders and managers display, from a critical and reflexive perspective rationality is ideologically-infused, based on a set of values and beliefs about what is true, right and justifiable and determined by those in power (Cunliffe, 2014). Rationality and care are often deemed to be antithetical. So how can we think about leadership in more caring ways, recognizing, as Hansen notes, both our uniqueness and embeddedness? How can we educate our students to be caring leaders? We address these questions through the lens of relational leadership and by drawing illustrations from Matthew's MBA Self-Leadership course, which are based on the values of relationality and care. We begin by briefly defining care and connecting care with relational leadership.

BEING CARING

We situate our position in relation to the concept of an ethics of care. While there is a body of work around Foucault's notion of care of the self, which emphasizes the need to understand ourselves through self-reflection and care of the body, we focus on Gilligan's ethics of care, which is fundamentally underpinned by the idea of relationality (see Hawk, 2011 for an overview of various approaches to the ethics of care). Situated within a feminist epistemology, Gilligan differentiates between a feminine care ethic and a feminist care ethic. The former is about selfless interpersonal relationships that bow to patriarchy; the latter is based on an intersubjective view of the social world (Cunliffe, 2011) in which we live always in relation with others in 'a myriad of subtle and not so subtle ways' (Gilligan, 1995, p. 122). From a feminist ethics of care perspective this is a voice of resistance to the 'ego', and therefore to heroic leadership. Gilligan argued that, 'hearing the difference between a patriarchal voice and a relational voice defines a paradigm shift' (p. 120) in terms of listening to marginalized voices – a paradigm shift that we have not yet grasped within mainstream organization studies, particularly in the leadership literature where, despite critiques of heroic rational models of leadership, individualized conceptions still prevail. Noddings' (1984 [2013]) work in the philosophy of moral education is particularly relevant to our position because she situates caring as a way of being in relation to others, occurring between particular individuals within moments of time and place. As such, the nature and form of caring is not about rules or behaviors, but depends upon the specific context. She argues that genuine caring involves attentiveness to others as a means of understanding who they are. The importance of this relational aspect of caring was expressed by an MBA student as:

> You truly want what is best for everyone in the room. A deep feeling of connectedness, wanting everyone to grow, come to find meaning and develop a greater self-understanding leading to them being their best-self.

What is notable about this comment is that the student expresses that it's not just wanting the best for others, but also having a 'deep feeling of connectedness' ourselves. In other words, being caring involves self-care as well as care for others. Further, as we will argue later, cultivating genuine caring in the classroom is a means by which we can facilitate caring leadership.

We talk about caring for each other as individuals, caring professions, caring communities, caring for our environment, for freedom and justice. When asked what it means to be a caring leader, students in Matthew's MBA class commented that it means having a genuine interest in someone or something, appreciating every moment, making someone feel like they matter, listening to understand not just to respond, empathy, and respect. They also observed that caring meant becoming more vulnerable, speaking up, taking more risks, and being allowed to make mistakes and to learn from failure. Care is therefore not just about caring for others, but also ensuring that others are able to respond to that care, that is, the ethics of reciprocity – about *'aiming at the "good life" with and for others, in just institutions'* (Ricoeur, 1992, p. 172, italics in original). Discussing what this means for leading organizations can be a starting point for thinking about caring leadership.

We are therefore proposing that there are connections between an ethics of care, relationality and leadership. However, there are also paradoxes in terms of how relational and caring leadership is theorized, practiced and taught. We go on to highlight three paradoxes which, we argue, emerge from crucial differences in the leadership literature around how relationality is construed. We begin with the paradox of caring about objects or people because it sets the scene for our core paradox of collective uniqueness by highlighting the assumptions underpinning care-less and care-ful approaches to leadership education.

PARADOXES OF CARE IN RELATIONAL LEADERSHIP

Paradox 1, Care-less or care-ful leadership: The growing body of work around relational leadership can be broadly split into two streams that carry very different assumptions about the nature of social 'reality' and what it means to be human in that reality, that is, ontology. One, which we argue is care-less leadership, is situated in an objectivist ontology (Cunliffe, 2011) where social and organizational realities are assumed to exist independently from people and experienced in similar ways. In relational leadership research, the focus lies on the relationships within or between networks, practices, systems, or the social processes through which leaders get things done, that is, people play a minimal role and are treated as objects. The second, less common care-ful approach, arises from more subjectivist and intersubjective ontologies – that social realities are created and maintained between us in our everyday interactions and conversations – and focuses on the interactions and relationships between leaders and others (Cunliffe and Eriksen, 2011). This second approach, particularly an intersubjective one, emphasizes the need to pay attention to and respect our relationships with people around us, not in terms of using them as resources, but rather (as Hansen notes above) treating them as unique human beings. This is counter to much of what we teach in business schools, particularly in Human Resource Management, which is about objectifying, categorizing and measuring people.

Noddings' focus on relationality reinforces the need to address this paradox of treating people as objects. She argues that when we move into an objectivist realm, problems and issues become impersonal and we lose not only the 'one cared-for' but also ourselves as the 'one-caring' (1984 [2013], p. 36). One MBA student implicitly addressed this interrelationship in his/her observation that: 'You also not only have to care about others and a cause, but also yourself and your own well-being.'

Of course we live in a material world, but this doesn't mean that we need to turn people into objects to be studied or materialities to be manipulated. This paradox therefore raises the question of how we can encourage students to be leaders who care about their relationships with people and the world around us, not just about the bottom line and their career. This brings us to what we see as the central paradox in educating caring leaders – that of relating our uniqueness as individuals to our inseparability from those around us.

Paradox 2, Collective uniqueness: Much of the work around collective and relational leadership focuses on collective action in interconnected networks where agreement is reached. From this objectivist perspective, the collective is paramount, becoming a single agent – discursively represented in language such as 'the HR Department' and 'the Senior Management team' – in which individual differences and diverse attitudes are combined into one. In these conceptualizations, 'the idea of us as persons, as beings living in relation to all the others and othernesses around us, capable of creating in our "works" so many different ways of actualizing and expressing amongst ourselves our humanness [. . .] does not seem to be needed' (Shotter, 2016, p. 60). Not needed because our representational, referential and objectivized ways of theorizing and managing organizations ignore the uniqueness of each person and their lived, embedded experience. The paradox of collective uniqueness is experienced within organizations when individuals are expected to be a homogeneous collective, good at everything, and evaluated against collective norms. We experience this within academia where we have to be simultaneously good teachers, administrators, researchers, and solicitors of funding.

We argue that relational leadership addresses the paradox of acknowledging uniqueness within a community (team, group, organization), because from an intersubjective perspective, the notions of uniqueness (difference) and embeddedness in a community are inseparable and require a concern for 'unfolding movements of feeling, rather than with patterns and repetitions' (Shotter, 2016, p. 160). This requires us to be attentive to the hermeneutic possibilities of particular situations, understanding them as *'uniquely themselves'* (p. 161). Three students implicitly recognize this relationship – that they are unique individuals embedded in a community – in the following quotes:

> I think everyone's caring nature impacted my learning and development because I could trust them. It allowed me to be more open with my thoughts and feelings because I didn't fear there would be any judgment.
>
> It made me more invested in my co-students – I wanted them to learn and grow and be happy.
>
> [The course] helped me develop and learn far more about myself than I could've alone. I was challenged to push myself and answer questions to reveal more about myself than I initially knew.

They also acknowledge that in a caring and non-judgmental community we can be 'more open' in terms of our individual thoughts and uniqueness as well as being 'more invested' in others. Addressing the paradox of collective uniqueness means recognizing that we are social beings living in a community that influences us as we influence others, that is, what is often theorized as a social constructionist way of thinking and acting.

Paradox 3, Being/becoming human: We can learn to act more prudently and deliberately in our relationships if we think about ourselves and what we do as '*coming into being* as human beings in the world' (Shotter, 2016, p. 69, italics in original) rather than as ready-formed with fixed identities. Shotter talks about this as 'relational becoming'. While it might be argued that becoming human is an individualized activity, we suggest it inherently engages our collective uniqueness in that we do not become human alone because we are embedded in a context and community. Much of leadership education and training is based on becoming a better, more effective leader, but this is often judged against the after-the-fact representations that Shotter cautions us against. In other words, I can develop a better leadership style, transformational characteristics, be more authentic, and so on, if I do a, b, or c. This form of education is still self-oriented, concerned with an individual managing the impressions of others by performing 'charisma', 'emotion', or 'care'. Instead, as one student observed, being caring is about bringing humanness to actions and interactions:

> There is a human aspect that goes unnoticed and disregarded in many corporate cultures. Good leaders are human too (and show this) and don't forget that others are humans too with thoughts, feelings and wants.

In our relational leadership article we highlight the importance of what we called *relational integrity*, which we define as the moral task of treating people as human beings and understanding their differences. Relational integrity embraces all three paradoxes in that it calls upon leaders to be 'both responsive to differences and responsible for acting on them' (Cunliffe and Eriksen, 2011, p. 1439) and emphasizes the ethicomoral nature of our relations with others and with the world around us (Ricoeur, 1992). Relationality fills the spaces between us at many levels and is therefore implicated in the notion of caring as collective uniqueness. Given that there is little work around caring leadership, especially from an intersubjective relational perspective, how can we educate students to be care-ful leaders? We now go on to address this question.

EDUCATING STUDENTS TO BE CARING LEADERS

We contend that the issue of 'caring' in business education is important, for as Gabriel (2009) observes, without caring, education is little more than incarceration and consumerism – going through 1–4 years of attending classes and meeting requirements in order to satisfy student-customer career aspirations. Literature around care in the classroom is more prevalent in the field of Education than in Organization and Management Studies (OMS). For example, Louis et al. (2016) talk about a caring teacher–student relationship involving attentiveness, acting in a selfless way, situationality, mutuality and authenticity – all occurring in a safe learning environment. Within OMS, critiques of current practice are often situated within Critical Management Studies where education is framed as a political activity that is ideologically saturated, whether we are aware of it or not. For example, in business and management schools, teaching is mainly underpinned by an instrumentalist managerialist ideology rooted in rationality, efficiency, and the pursuit of profit and productivity (Cunliffe, 2014) in which there is a danger of losing 'the logic of care' (Gherardi and Rhodeschini, 2016, p. 267). Education is also a moral activity (Hansen, 2011) in that the theories, models and principles that we teach carry implicit norms and values relating to what are right, wrong, and/or acceptable methods, actions and ways of treating people. We, along with other critical and reflexive management educators, question the assumptions underpinning such models, arguing for a pedagogy that engages with difference, power and the relational and ethical nature of leading and managing organizations.

We now turn to the implications of the three paradoxes we identified for educating caring leaders. Noddings (1984 [2013]) identifies four aspects of moral education based on an ethics of care: modeling moral/caring behavior; creating genuine open dialogue; providing opportunities for caring practice; and confirmation. The latter involves helping a student understand how s/he can move from an unethical act towards being her/his best ethical self. Matthew was sensitive to these aspects when designing the MBA Self-Leadership course and to embracing the paradox of collective uniqueness. In their ethnography of care in a nursing home, Gherardi and Rhodeschini (2016) argue that caring is a collective knowledgeable doing and that we learn how to do, be and talk about caring as we work together. Matthew built this principle into his course by emphasizing everyone's inherent moral responsibility for how they interact with one another, the importance of supporting one another's learning and development, and the need to share personal experiences with each other in non-judgmental ways, trusting that, as one student commented 'each person wanted to offer guidance to help me succeed', that is, a collective caring. For the first class of the course, students write and share an identity-based story that explains why they are taking the course. In their feedback, students have expressed that listening to their classmates' stories precipitates caring, for example:

> Sharing stories on the first day of class made it impossible to NOT care. I was in awe as I listened to others share such personal and profound stories. This created the ideal environment for this class. In turn, I got to know my classmates in this class more so than any other class I have taken. I cared about their growth and genuinely wanted the best for them in this class and in life. I also developed a desire to stay connected with people.

One study of MBA students in a business school found that 44 percent of the students felt that a faculty member had 'given up' on them at some point in the programme (Hawk and Lyons, 2008). 'Giving up' was perceived by students as a lack of respect, communication, caring, recognition, trust, and ignoring questions by the faculty member. The importance of this issue was highlighted in our introductory illustration where Matthew's student commented, 'You never gave up on me', and where another student observed that Matthew was respectful and patient.

This raises an important issue – that educating leaders to be caring involves being a caring educator, which means caring for students, facilitating open dialogue, and creating a caring community in the classroom (Noddings, 1984 [2013]). Matthew's awareness of this increased as he continued to teach the course. While he had designed the course around our work on relational and reflexive leadership and an ethics of care, he realized that this alone was not enough and that he had to be reflexive about his own relational becoming. This meant working to change his defensive responses to students who questioned the course or disagreed with his comments – to be the caring leader/educator they were talking about in class. It required the same degree of vulnerability that he expected from his students and that they expressed:

> It made me feel free to be vulnerable and to explore my journey without fear of judgment. It allowed me to explore the texts more deeply because I knew that my classmates were counting on me in the same way I was counting on them.

He now commits to 'meeting students where they are', not where he wants them to be, that is, appreciating unique and different points of view within the caring classroom community he was encouraging students to engage with. For both students and educators this 'requires an awareness of one's habitual ways of responding and their associated consequences, while identifying alternative responses that may be more effective and experimenting with these new ways of responding to develop practical wisdom' (Eriksen and Cooper, 2018, p. 473).

FINAL THOUGHTS

As we have elaborated above, and also as Matthew's story at the beginning of our chapter illustrates, some key considerations emerge in relation to what caring and care-ful leadership means: listening, inquiring, humanness, imagination, responsiveness, responsibility, and understanding our world in relational, reflexive and intersubjective ways. Caring relates to the nature and quality of our relationships with others. Care-ful leaders acknowledge that we are embedded within a community and therefore understand the importance of paying attention to the nature of our relationships with others. Explicitly expressing one's care in words and actions were also noted by students as important:

> Yes, I cared about the others in this class. I thought about them often outside of class time – about something they wrote or said or how they were doing achieving their goals. It made me feel more comfortable sharing my own experiences, because I hoped it would help them. It made me listen more closely to their tone and inflections and understand more.

Educating leaders to be caring means finding ways of 'touching' others by exploring our and their uniqueness and embeddedness by somehow connecting our experience to theirs, by thinking and speaking 'from within a flowing circumstance in which we open ourselves up to being "moved" by that flow'

(Shotter, 2016, p. 72). As one student commented: 'By relating with similar struggles/obstacles/hardships and successes, I felt connected to and cared for by classmates.'

This, we argue, connects caring with relational leadership because it involves acknowledging that we are always selves in relation with others, that is, an intersubjective understanding of social and organizational realities that foregrounds the paradox of collective uniqueness. Finally, educating students to be more caring in the classroom as a collective knowledgeable doing emphasizes the need to be genuine in our relationships with others and extends beyond the classroom. To give a student the last word:

> It made me think of leadership with more flow and less rigidness. To be successful in leadership and have others follow you, you need to show a genuine interest in what others have to say. You have to be engaged and present. Not everything is a competition, collaboration is critical.

NOTE

1. French President speaking on Armistice Day, accessed 24 January 2019 at https:// onu.delegfrance.org/Emmanuel-Macron-s-speech-at-Commemoration-of-the -centenary-of-the-Armistice.

REFERENCES

Cunliffe, A.L. (2011), 'Crafting qualitative research: Morgan and Smircich 30 years on'. *Organizational Research Methods*, **14**(4), 647–73.

Cunliffe, A.L. (2014), *A Very Short, Fairly Interesting and Reasonably Cheap Book About Management*. (2nd edn) London: Sage Publications.

Cunliffe, A.L. and Eriksen, M. (2011), 'Relational leadership'. *Human Relations*, **64**(11), 1425–49.

Eisenbeiss, S.A. (2012), 'Re-thinking ethical leadership: An interdisciplinary integrative approach'. *The Leadership Quarterly*, **23**(5), 791–808.

Eriksen, M. and Cooper, K. (2018), 'On developing responsible leaders'. *Journal of Management Development*, **37**(6), 470–79.

Gabriel, Y. (2009), 'Reconciling an ethic of care with critical management pedagogy'. *Management Learning*, **40**(4), 379–85.

Gherardi, S. and Rodeschini, G. (2016), 'Caring as a collective knowledgeable doing: About concern and being concerned'. *Management Learning*, **47**(3), 266–84.

Gilligan, C. (1995), 'Hearing the difference: Theorizing connection'. *Hypatia*, **10**(2), 120–27.

Hansen, D.T. (2011), *The Teacher and the World: A Study of Cosmopolitanism as Education*. London: Routledge.

Hawk, T.F. (2011), 'An ethic of care: A relational ethic for the relational characteristics of organizations'. In Hamington, M. and Sander-Staudt, M. (eds) *Applying Care Ethics to Business*, New York: Springer (pp. 3–24).

Hawk, T.F. and Lyons, P.R. (2008), 'Please don't give up on me: When faculty fail to care'. *Journal of Management Education*, **32**(3), 316–38.

Louis, K.S., Murphy, J. and Smylie, M. (2016), 'Caring leadership in schools: Findings from exploratory analyses'. *Educational Administration Quarterly*, **52**(2), 310–48.

Noddings, N. (1984 [2013]), *Caring: A Relational Approach to Ethics and Moral Education* (3rd edn). Berkeley, CA: University of California Press.

Ricoeur, P. (1992), *Oneself as Another*. Blamey, K. (trans.). Chicago, IL: University of Chicago Press.

Shotter, J. (2016), *Speaking Actually: Towards a New 'Fluid' Common-Sense Understanding of Relational Becomings*. London: Everything is Connected Press.

Tomkins, L. and Simpson, P. (2015), 'Caring leadership: A Heideggerian perspective'. *Organization Studies*, **36**(8), 1013–31.

15. Caring leadership as collective responsibility: a dialogue with Arendt and Heidegger

Rita A. Gardiner

INTRODUCTION

One day when I was walking to campus last summer, I noticed a new sign outside one of the university colleges. The sign read "Leaders with heart since 1863." I wondered what this message was trying to convey to passers-by. Was it some sort of postmodern riff on zombie leadership? Unlikely, I thought, given that this particular College has a reputation for conservatism. What, then, was the purpose of this sign that informed passers-by that this institution had a proud tradition of electing caring leaders? Perhaps it was a signal to the rest of the community that care was integral to how this particular College perceived its leaders? Of course, a cynic might remark that this particular College has had four different leaders in ten years. Although its leaders may have hearts, they certainly do not appear to have institutional sticking power. And sticking power would seem to be a vital component of institutional leadership, along with a tenacity of purpose and a willingness to care for others. These musings led me to ask: what constitutes caring leadership within a university environment?

To address this question, I explore Hannah Arendt's ideas about care, or lack thereof, as it emerges in university life. She (1958) was adamant that leadership founded on care and mutual respect was rarely to be found in most bureaucratic environments, which encouraged a kind of "no man's leadership," whereby employees hide behind policies and procedures rather than connecting with each person on an individual level. Moreover, Arendt (1994) contended there was a kind of professional deformation that pervaded academic life, encouraging and rewarding self-interest over collective well-being. This professional deformation, she argued, leads some professors to live in a fantasy world, whereby they fail to recognize how their actions exemplify self-regard over and above regard for others. In short, caring for one's academic career can result in a carelessness toward others. This was particularly noticeable, Arendt argued, when some intellectuals became institutional leaders. The issues that she raises are, I will argue, still relevant today.

This chapter unfolds as follows. First, I will explore the meaning of care, demonstrating how this common phrase has multiple and, seemingly, contradictory meanings. Second, I will explore current research on care and leadership. Here we find that, unlike other institutions such as health care or the corporate sector, there is little scholarship that examines care and leadership within higher education institutions. I want to delve into what it means to care within the higher education context, and why caring matters to leadership in these spaces. In much of the literature on care and leadership, there is an assumption that caring matters to leaders. But, is that care borne out in practice? In answering this question, I explore examples of caring leadership, or lack thereof, focusing on university life. Martin Heidegger plays something of a "fall guy" in this exploration. In his writing, he shows how important care is to the human condition; yet, when it came to his own leadership praxis, it appears caring for others was overshadowed by his visionary desire to effect institutional change. In the final section, I explore Arendt's understanding of care and leadership to sketch out how an Arendtian approach can offer insights into what it might mean to lead caringly.

CARE

Care is a funny old word when you think about it, with lots of different meanings. For example, I often end my emails "take care." I am not sure when or why I began to use this particular salutation; I think I was bored with putting "best wishes," or "regards" at the end of my emails. In any event, to take care suggests that you want the recipient to look after themselves. When we use care in this way, it can also refer to alerting others to mind how they go. For example, we might tell someone to "take care," so as to alert them to a possible danger ahead, or when we sense that a friend or colleague is under undue stress. In taking care, then, we show concern for the other person's well-being.

An alternative way of speaking of care is to say "She doesn't have a care in the world." Here, to be free of care is something that we might wish for others, or be envious of, since to be carefree is usually deemed to be fortunate. Somewhat confusingly, however, a popular saying among North American students is "I could care less," which leaves the hearer somewhat befuddled as to whether care, or its converse, is implied. This befuddlement is also apparent "across the pond" in the UK context, whereby the North American phrase "I could care less" is translated into "I couldn't care less." No wonder that second language learners have problems with English idioms, for it seems that we are unsure whether we care a lot, a little, or not at all.

Care's meaning alters radically when we say that someone is careless. To be perceived as careless is not the same as being free of care. Rather careless, and its mate carelessness, suggest a lack of concern with what one is doing, and a lack of consideration for others. To be careless, then, seems to infer a certain selfishness in one's attitude. Alternatively, we sometimes say that someone is careful, which does not mean that they are overwhelmed by care but rather risk averse, an attribute usually seen as a negative quality for a leader. Besides, for some readers, being careful might conjure up memories of characters from literature such as Casaubon in *Middlemarch*, whose carefulness was a kind of pedantry. In any case, one has to be careful about the ways in which we enact, or fail to enact care.

By exploring different linguistic usages of care we see that, as Heidegger tells us, words are wellsprings whose meanings change constantly. In short, care shows up differently in different contexts. This contextual aspect of care is something that I now want to explore by looking at how leadership scholars have conceptualized care. Through this exploration, we may gain insight into what current scholarship can teach us about what constitutes caring leadership, or lack thereof, in an organizational context.

CARE AND LEADERSHIP

In a recent library keyword search, I discovered 14 800 articles that mentioned caring and leadership. The bulk of these articles focused on leadership and health care. In that same search, only ten articles specified higher education, care and leadership. Given that education is one of the caring professions, it seems surprising that few scholars have reflected, in print, about care in these spaces. Much of the scholarship that does exist is underpinned by popular psychology (Tomkins and Simpson, 2015). A good example is a study conducted by Uusiautti (2013) that connects caring leadership with positive organizational scholarship. In her comparative study of higher education administrators in Finland and the USA, Uusiautti asked her research participants to describe caring leadership. Most participants described caring leadership as involved in turning a personal vision into reality. Caring leadership was also described as action oriented, and leaders described the importance of celebrating success through campus events, and the importance of dealing with difficult situations promptly. These leaders viewed care through giving and receiving timely feedback. This type of caring leadership, it is argued, enhances productivity among followers, resulting in a positive work environment.

Uusiautti further asserts that caring leadership is about "leaders' ability to use their position in a manner that exemplifies love-based action" (2013, p. 4). She sees leaders' loving action as connected with a Platonic idea of the good. However, Arendt (1958) contends that emotions like love are private concerns.

As such, a focus on love is inappropriate for the public space because loving relations privilege particular persons over others. Thus, the ideal of a campus enriched by loving relationships is not one that Arendt would share, since such relationships may not only privilege some persons over others, but also restrict dialogue and debate, key aspects of a flourishing environment.

For Akbari et al. (2016), sharing is at the heart of caring leadership. Their research, based on surveys and interviews with 70 university teams, indicates that, when leadership is shared amongst different people, there is greater potential for an enriched working environment. As such, sharing leadership creates an environment that promotes functional, as opposed to dysfunctional behaviors. Thus, these scholars conclude that sharing begets a caring approach.

Yet ideas of caring and sharing in leadership are complicated when gender identity is foregrounded. In her reflections on chairing a department, Acker (2012) notes how gendered assumptions affect leadership. Women leaders, for example, are expected to act in caring ways, expectations that male leaders do not have to the same extent. From her perspective, being perceived as a caring leader is shaped by attitudes toward gender norms. These attitudes, in turn, influence societal discourses about caring and leadership.

Care is a vital aspect in how followers judge leaders (Gabriel, 2015). Followers, it seems, expect leaders to use their moral courage to promote collective, rather than selfish, ends. What this suggests is that many followers desire careful rather than careless leaders. Considering how caring enriches leadership is important, because it places an emphasis on how followers prefer leaders who are willing to develop nurturing relationships with others. From this perspective, choosing to lead in a caring way demonstrates concern for others' well-being. Such concern requires an attentiveness to one's environment, and the diverse needs of those within it. This way of leading requires leaders not only to be effective in their duties, but also to respond to others in a sensitive manner (Ciulla, 2009).

Such sensitivity to the needs of others is not always apparent in university life. Some scholars contend that higher education institutions demonstrate a lack of care, primarily as a result of the neoliberal turn in universities (Dowling, 2017). The neoliberal model places the emphasis on economic metrics whereby students are regarded as consumers, and faculty as mobilizers of particular forms of commodifiable knowledge. For their part, institutional leaders face increasing pressure from government funders and Board members to enhance specific metrics, such as growth in student numbers, international reputation and fund-raising revenue. At times, the pursuit of institutional success can cover over a deeper understanding of the purpose of education. Too much focus on individual success can lead to calls for learning that is socially relevant and market driven. But this desire for learning to connect with the marketplace encourages a reduced understanding of education (Paolantonio,

2016). It also encourages the single-minded pursuit of a particular kind of institutional success, one that can be measured through international rankings or specific research output. But these numerical aspects of university life sit uneasily with another prevailing discourse, that of institutional well-being and student flourishing. In short, there is intense competition affecting what university personnel should care about.

Increasingly, ideas of caring leadership are connected with efforts to promote student well-being. Improving student well-being is deemed critical, especially given the rise in student anxiety and mental health concerns. At my university, I recently attended an event where a Vice President announced a new approach to combat student mental health issues. Instead of long waiting lists, common in many North American universities, students would now be seen quickly as a result of the introduction of a new step care program. No longer will it be necessary for each student to meet with a counsellor, which not only takes too long but is, apparently, a costly endeavor. Instead, students will be provided with a menu of options from which to learn to manage their self-care. The fact that long waiting lists are being dealt with effectively is an important step forward in dealing with the mounting crisis of student mental health. However, when I inquired whether the links between student debt and increased anxiety were being explored as one possible cause of student distress, I was met with silence. But if we care for our students' well-being, wanting to see them thrive rather than strive, we need to address how financial insecurity is a major cause of student anxiety.

In pointing to links between student indebtedness and mental health issues, Lazzarato (2015) argues that the cost of university education, especially in the United States, is leading to a life of indebtedness. Student indebtedness is partly a result of a lack of government funding and the concomitant need for ever-growing funds to fuel university growth. This increased focus on revenue has led to administrators seeking new ways to keep students in school. But this may not be the most responsible or caring course of action for university leaders to pursue. Caring for each student's personal well-being may require having frank conversations as to whether higher education is the right path for them. In short, universities, and those who work within them, do some students a disservice in failing to encourage them to consider alternative career paths, ones that do not lead to a life of indebtedness.

Showing care requires us to focus on the individual student, rather than seeing students as a category. In Arendtian terms, this would mean that we focus on the "who" rather than the "what," thereby considering each individual in a holistic manner. Yet this change of emphasis would take time and effort, something that many organizational leaders have little enthusiasm for because they are judged by different metrics, such as their talents as fundraisers and as organizational cheerleaders.

Furthermore, to act in a caring manner requires leaders to take care that their personal desire for success does not lead to hubris. Perhaps it would be useful at this juncture to compare Arendt's ideas about care and leadership with those of Heidegger. Specifically, I focus on how his desire to overhaul the university system in Germany led Heidegger to act in a manner that lacked care for others.

HEIDEGGER, CARE AND LEADERSHIP

In *Being and Time*, Heidegger (1962) maintains that "Dasein's *Being* reveals itself as care" (p. 227). It is through an acknowledgment of care that we can engage in the world without trying to dominate others. Tomkins and Simpson (2015) argue that Heideggerian notions of care can deepen our understanding of how caring manifests itself. They contend that Heideggerian care is grounded in everyday practice. Within organizational life, for example, they perceive two distinct types of care intervention. The first type is when a carer leaps in to take responsibility to resolve an issue. The second type is when a carer leaps ahead to explore future possibilities. Tomkins and Simpson further contend that a Heideggerian approach to care critiques notions of best practices in organizations, such as following rules, rather than thinking for ourselves. Indeed, they argue that caring leadership, rather than flourishing as other scholars maintain, is a fragile affair in organizational life. Finally, they suggest caring leadership is primarily "an organization of self rather than an organization of others" (2015, p. 13). Too much focus on self can demonstrate a mode of being-in-the-world that ignores care. This is the mode of indifference. In displaying indifference we demonstrate a carelessness toward others. Such careless indifference was demonstrated by Heidegger when he took on an administrative leadership role, to which I now turn.

In April 1933, Heidegger was elected Rector of Freiburg University. In his Inaugural Address, he argued that the purpose of the Rectorate was to provide "spiritual leadership," and an unwavering commitment to the university's mission. To achieve this goal, Heidegger (1985) maintained that what were needed were "leaders and guardians [who] possess the strictest clarity of the highest, widest, and richest knowledge" (p. 476). Such leaders needed to hold fast to their specific vocation, and keep a resolute stance. He called for a complete transformation of the university from a "technical organization-institutional pseudo-unity" into a genuine place of learning. However, Heidegger had little opportunity to realize this vision, because his leadership proved unpopular with faculty, students and his Nazi overlords. After just over a year, in April 1934, he resigned.

Reflecting upon this leadership experience, Heidegger (1985) states that his unpopularity as a leader was because of his indifference to the minutiae of institutional life. Instead of focusing on administrative issues, it was his spiritual vision of a renewed form of educational life that propelled him forward. Thus, Heidegger's purpose in becoming Rector was to effect wholescale institutional change in higher education. In modern parlance, we might say that he wanted to become a change agent, instilling his particular vision in all aspects of university life. Forging caring relationships was less important to him than establishing a modern university based on Platonic ideals. What Heidegger's reflection reveals, however, is how leaders with strong personal visions can become myopic in their visionary zeal. Such myopia can result in a lack of care for others, as well as poor judgment. This lack of judgment can be seen in Heidegger's own admission of his indifference to others (Gardiner, 2015).

Heidegger's stated indifference to others highlights something that Gabriel (2015) argues is critical to followers, namely, a leader needs to demonstrate care for those around them. Those leaders who are propelled by a particular vision may not fully recognize the importance of ensuring they not only stay in touch with, but demonstrate care for others. I suggest this demonstration of caring leadership is relevant to how Arendt perceives the activity of leading.

CARE AND LEADERSHIP THROUGH AN ARENDTIAN LENS

Care was an important aspect not only of how Arendt (1958) perceived leadership, but also how she perceived relationships more broadly. In her view, our commonplace ideas about leadership stem from an obsession with leaders. Instead of being focused on the leader, for Arendt, leadership functions best when it arises out of individuals working together. When individuals find common cause, they discover the strength that emerges from their collective action (Gardiner, 2015). Yet thinking about leadership as collective action is, Arendt argues, overshadowed by the modern emphasis on leaders. Arendt (1958) traces this way of thinking about leadership all the way back to Plato. She maintains he wanted to create a society founded upon laws to assuage the problems caused by the unpredictability inherent in action. But along with Plato's emphasis on law-making, the notion of the sovereign leader emerged. When the focus is on the sovereign leader, Arendt argues, we become enamored by the notion of a strong man who can help us deal with whatever predicament we face. But too much focus on any one person is dangerous to our collective well-being since it separates that individual from others. This separation introduced a kind of hierarchy, which Arendt argues is not leadership, but a form of rulership (Gardiner, 2015). When we privilege the individual in this manner, it leads to a hierarchy in human relationships that Arendt regarded as anathema to human flourishing.

Today, this hierarchical approach is apparent in much of the leadership literature whereby one person is denoted as unique (the leader) while others are seen as interchangeable (the followers). Yet this way of thinking contradicts something basic to an Arendtian view of the human condition, namely, that we are all unique individuals living in a plural world. When we view people as followers, we view people as an amorphous category, rather than as unique individuals. Conversely, too much focus on the leader can encourage a lack of responsibility on the part of others. That is, followers may be more inclined to leave decision-making to those in charge. A leader's separation from others can create an atmosphere of fear and suspicion. Such an atmosphere can lead to people obeying the leader's demands, without thinking through their full implication. Such unquestioning obedience can result in devastating consequences, as Arendt showed in her study on totalitarianism.

To sum up, for Arendt a focus on the individual leader covers over the original meaning of leadership as collective action. Such a view of leadership is founded on the importance of gathering a plurality of viewpoints. When this plurality of perspectives is not apparent, then the focus on care may be eroded. But what then might constitute caring leadership in an Arendtian sense? Perhaps Arendt's own actions may offer insight into this matter.

ARENDT AS CARING LEADER?

Arendt (1994) did not view herself as a leader, caring or otherwise, arguing that leadership was unbecoming to women. Yet, despite her prejudice against women leaders, Arendt often demonstrated care and leadership, as can be seen from the following examples. First, concerned for their well-being, during the Second World War she sent food parcels to Max Weber's wife, Marianne, and to Karl and Gertrude Jaspers. Second, Arendt worked tirelessly to get Heidegger's work published in English, and his reputation was redeemed, in part, because of her efforts on his behalf. That said, Arendt was not without criticism for her former teacher and lover, especially in regard to some of his leadership actions, which she argued demonstrated not only a lack of care, but also a lack of judgment.

Such a lack of judgment is exacerbated by a willingness to go along with a particular regime without considering the consequences for others. In reflecting upon the events in Nazi Germany, Arendt (1994) describes how what most disheartened her was how intellectuals cooperated with the Nazis, voluntarily stepping in line. As she states, "I still think that it belongs to the essence of being an intellectual that one fabricates ideas" (p. 11). Some intellectuals actually believed in Nazism, Arendt argued, because they were trapped by their ideas. Here it is difficult not to see her comments as a rebuke for Heidegger's leadership actions. Commenting on his actions as Rector,

Arendt stated that what shocked her most was Heidegger's betrayal of Edmund Husserl, his former mentor. As Rector, Heidegger signed a letter dismissing all Jewish professors. Arendt contended that Husserl would have been indifferent if the letter had been signed by someone else. But, in signing the resignation letter, Heidegger demonstrated a profound lack of care toward his former mentor. In his desire to instill a leadership vision onto the university, Heidegger failed to enact his own philosophy, namely, that care is fundamental to being-in-the-world. And such care, as Arendt (1958) teaches us, is always founded on our relationships with others.

Many leaders arrive at organizations with grand ideas and a single-minded desire to fulfill their leadership vision. In Heidegger's case, his leadership action in trying to revision the German university serves to demonstrate a resoluteness of purpose over and above a care for others. Yet both resoluteness and care are essential if leaders are not only going to stay true to their principles, but also to demonstrate a caring attitude toward others. Furthermore, a leader's desire to be resolute in their decision-making can belie a more caring approach to leadership. For a leader's action to have organizational depth and breadth, it must take into account both resoluteness of purpose and care for others. And that means enacting leadership that not only cares for self, but also cares for others.

We need leaders to have the sticking power that enables them to deal with positive and negative situations. That stickiness is enhanced by the attachments leaders develop through their relationships with others. Building an environment where all can flourish is not an easy task, but it is one that has the potential to enrich the lives of others. And that, ultimately, seems to me an essential component of leading in a caring fashion.

CONCLUSION

I began this inquiry by asking what constitutes caring leadership within a university environment. The argument I have put forward suggests it is not how we conceptualize care that matters; rather, it is how we enact care in, and through, our relationships that counts. This relational approach to caring represents a key distinction between Arendt and Heidegger's response to the topic of care. In particular, Arendt implores us to remember our collective responsibility to care for the world before ourselves. Yet her reminder seems odd at a time when too many leaders, in universities and elsewhere, chose to place self-care over and above caring for others.

Part of the problem is an over-reliance on leaders, caring or otherwise. Before his death Heidegger gave an interview to *Der Spiegel*, where he stated "only a God can save us." In simple terms, this statement highlights an overreliance on the leader-as-savior – a dangerous idea that encourages demagoguery. Alternatively, Arendt (1958) teaches us that we do not need a god to save us. Instead, we need to take up our collective responsibility to care for one another and the world. Collective responsibility necessitates a desire to care, not founded on specific rules or regulations, but enacted through everyday interactions. This way of being requires us to refrain from placing self-care before caring for the world.

At the heart of an Arendtian leadership ethics of care is a responsiveness not to self, but to others (Gardiner, 2014). This form of leadership requires educators and leaders to be willing to combine an ethic of critique with an ethic of care (Gabriel, 2009). To foster a caring environment, we must not only be willing to critique those in power, but we must also care for those most vulnerable. Critique and care are fundamental aspects of caring leadership, and complement Arendtian ideas of collective leadership. Although the ethic of care has been maligned, some educational leaders would benefit from a reminder to place caring for others above caring for self. In practical terms, this would mean rethinking notions of what constitutes leadership success in educational spaces. Instead of caring about external accolades, the institutional focus needs to be on the community's well-being. Whether most leaders are willing to do the necessary work this type of caring demands remains unclear.

REFERENCES

Acker, S. (2012), Chairing and caring: Gendered dimensions of leadership in academe. *Gender and Education*, **24** (4), 411–28.

Akbari, M., Kashani, S.H. and Chaijani, M.H. (2016), Sharing, caring, and responsibility in higher education teams, *Small Group Research*, **47** (5), 542–68.

Arendt, H. (1958), *The Human Condition*, Chicago, IL: The University of Chicago Press.

Arendt, H. (1994), The language remains: A conversation with Gunter Gaus. In Jerome Kohn (ed.), *Arendt: Essays in Understanding 1930–1954*, New York: Harcourt, Brace and Company, pp. 1–24.

Ciulla, J.B. (2009), Leadership and the ethics of care, *Journal of Business Ethics*, **88** (1), 3–4.

Dowling, D.B. (2017), U.S. higher education and the crisis of care, *Humanities*, **6** (32), 1–14.

Gabriel, Y. (2009), Reconciling an ethic of care with critical management pedagogy, *Management Learning*, **40** (4), 379–85.

Gabriel, Y. (2015), The caring leader – What followers expect of their leaders and why? Leadership, **11** (3), 316–34.

Gardiner, R. (2014), Telling tales out of school: Gender, authentic leadership and care. *Values and Ethics in Educational Administration*, **8** (4), 1–8.

Gardiner, R. (2015), *Gender, Authenticity, and Leadership: Thinking with Arendt*, London, UK and New York, USA: Palgrave Macmillan.

Heidegger, M. (1962), *Being and Time*, trans. John Macquarie and Edward Robinson, Oxford: Blackwell Press.

Heidegger, M. (1985), The self-assertion of the German university and the rectorate 1933–34: Facts and thoughts, *Review of Metaphysics*, **38** (3), 467–502.

Lazzarato, M. (2015), The American university: A model of the debt society. In *Governing by Debt*, trans. Joshua David Jordan, South Pasadena, CA: Semiotexte, pp. 61–90.

Paolantonio, di M. (2016), The cruel optimism of education and education's implication with 'passing-on,' *Journal of Philosophy of Education*, **50** (2), 147–59.

Tomkins, L. and Simpson, P. (2015), Caring leadership: A Heideggerian perspective. *Organization Studies*, **36** (8), 1013–31.

Uusiautti, S. (2013), An action-oriented perspective on caring leadership: A qualitative study of higher education administrators' positive leadership experiences, *International Journal of Leadership in Education*, **16** (4), 482–96.

16. Caring leadership as radical ontology: Eastern philosophies of non-separation

Vinca Bigo

Heroic, top down, and often charisma-based understandings of leadership have over the last few decades been amply questioned and criticised for being incomplete (naive at best and disempowering at worst). Meanwhile other conceptions of leadership that have seen the day suggest that we cannot understand leaders if we do not also take into consideration their followers. The latter are seen to play an active role in both choosing and co-determining the nature of their leaders. Followers are no longer theorised as passive and subservient, but as actively co-creating.

Theories that suggest more relational forms of leadership have emerged in response to certain observed changes in leadership taking place, including in more mainstream profit-driven organisations. The change is at least in part a response to a world that is becoming faster, more complex, more ambivalent and less certain, than it previously was. It has been shown that leaders are in the long run more effective in addressing organisational challenges when they are able to listen, delegate, encourage participation and even serve their employees (Carney and Getz, 2009; Laloux, 2014). Such relational approaches to leadership have been variously branded as participative leadership, collaborative leadership, delegating leadership, democratic leadership, servant leadership, value-based leadership, ethical leadership, opal leadership, socio-cratic leadership, humanist leadership, liberating leadership, caring leadership, listening leadership and silent leadership, amongst other denominations.

These more relational conceptualisations of leadership have certainly contributed to developing a fuller insight into what leadership entails. My contention is that there is scope for a still deeper and more complete understanding of the subject. I suggest, in particular, that drawing on the Eastern based concept of non-separation (or non-duality) as found in the Advaita Vedanta may help us gain further subtlety in conceptualisations of leadership as a process in which particularly care as a way of being, care of self and care for others matter deeply. My motivation for engaging with Vedantic thought is twofold. First, it offers potentially fresh non-Western perspectives on managerial practices, thus furthering current research. And second, the Advaita Vedanta provides a powerful ontology for transcending binary thought and practices in general, and in leadership in particular. By ontology I mean the study of the fundamental features, or most basic structures, of reality.

The chapter is structured as follows. First, I examine how the current managerial literature engages with non-dual philosophical thought. This is followed by a section to describe my process of inquiry. I then introduce a number of key tenets of Advaita Vedantic philosophy, followed by an exploration of the non-dual philosophy through three binaries: body–mind, self–other and action versus non-action. The last section offers concluding comments. Let me at present examine theoretical advances in the domains of leadership, care and non-dual thought.

THE LITERATURE SO FAR

Relational understandings of leadership espouse, whether explicitly or not, a relational ontology, in which human beings, in virtue of their being to various extents (a matter that will vary from one concept to another) related to one another, depend on each other for their survival, their identity and ultimately for their flourishing. It follows that, if some form of flourishing is envisaged, people should in some way care for one another. So too, or perhaps especially, leaders need to set an example in caring for others, but also for themselves. The need to cultivate self-care to lead a life of virtue is advocated in (non-dualist) yogic teachings, in ancient Greek philosophy (Socrates), amongst other philosophical traditions. The idea that before leaders can lead others, they need to be able to lead, master and care for themselves is thus not new.

Now, whilst the weight of oriental scholars and/or studies using Asian data in leadership studies is definitely on the rise, contributions tend to draw on existing Western frameworks of analysis rather than introducing Eastern perspectives. This is true even when other disciplines, including sociology, ecology and theoretical physics are actively engaged with oriental frameworks (including the Advaita Vedanta) (Kakkar, 2018). And the deficit in Eastern perspectives on leadership in organisations is not due to the absence of Eastern practices in Asian organisations (or even elsewhere).

Eastern cultural and philosophical backgrounds are in fact important to make sense of certain Asian leadership practices, such as the fact that ambidexterity is both easily and commonly embraced in Asian organisations (Barkema et al., 2015). Ambidexterity has been described as an organisation's ability to balance current demands and maintain future adaptability by pursuing contradictory goals of exploration and exploitation simultaneously (Tushman and O'Reilly, 1996). Thus, leaders are challenged to combine *paradoxical* injunctions, such as the need to maintain *both* a holistic perspective *and* proximity with employees; treating employees without discrimination *and* allowing for individuality; embracing changes that maintain *both* stability *and* flexibility; and giving direction *and* autonomy to employees. Ambidextrous leadership is most compatible with, when not located in, oriental culture espousing Daoism, and yin–yang cosmology.

Non-dual thinking is thus clearly relevant to leadership. It is well grounded in Eastern philosophy, but perhaps especially so in the Advaita Vedanta. This is my motive to dig deeper and explore how the latter may help us to understand and practise care in leadership. I conjecture that the Advaita Vedanta may turn out to be particularly pertinent to approach these concepts. Let me first say a little more about my process of inquiry.

INQUIRING

Mine is a philosophical approach, which places an emphasis on modes of being, thinking and acting. For those familiar with Heideggerian philosophy, it is interesting, whilst not all that surprising, to see how the latter resonates with the Advaita Vedanta, in particular the notion of *Dasein*, with its profound and quasi mystical take on Care (*Sorge*), as concern for being. In fact, Heidegger, whilst not directly drawing on Eastern non-dualism in his work, in the end appears to recognise the limits of Western thought. According to Steffney (1956), Heidegger comes close to embracing Zen Buddhist thinking:

> For what is Heidegger's final message but that Western philosophy is a great error, the result of the dichotomizing intellect that has cut man off from unity with Being itself and from his own being... Heidegger repeatedly tells me that this tradition of the West has come to the end of its cycle; and as he says this, one can only gather that he himself has already stepped beyond that tradition. Into the tradition of the Orient? I should say he has come pretty close to Zen. (Steffney, 1956, p. xii)

Heidegger's implicit critique of Western philosophical dualistic and dualising tendencies constitutes an invitation to explicitly adopt a non-dualist framework in my exploration of care and leadership. My choice to engage with oriental non-dual philosophy at its source through the Advaita Vedanta is at any rate motivated both by the radicality and simplicity of its non-dualist ontology. Its ontological foundations appear to offer solid and powerful, though remarkably little explored, ground for advancing leadership theory grounded in care.

The Advaita Vedanta constitutes a working framework through which to examine three dualities in particular, chosen for the ways in which they bear most fundamentally on care and leadership. The first binary is the one posited between mind and body. If its relevance is obvious to the study of care, it may in the first instance seem less so to conceptualistations of leadership. Second, my interest lies in a non-dual reading of the usual opposition posited between self and others. It seems that relational understandings of leadership (and, it goes without saying, of care) need to encompass the relation between self and others. The third binary I wish to examine is between action and non-action. In contrast with the body–mind binary, the topic of action and non-action is possibly more obvious to questions of leadership than care.

I am aware that my project is beyond paradoxical. For in using language to write this chapter, I engage in a world of conceptual distinctions, be they temporary and illusionary, to convey an ontology of complete oneness. I shall nonetheless embrace the paradox. The following section is about exploring the sometimes surprising ways in which Advaita Vedantic philosophy traverses and transcends binaries, before considering how it sheds new light on leadership in relation to care.

ADVAITA VEDANTA

Whilst the Advaita Vedanta is attracting a certain attention from organizational scholars, it is still under-researched and ill-understood. This is particularly so in elusive domains, such as our present subject of non-duality, where language acts as a limitation to an embodied feeling and grasping of matters in hand. Let me now take a closer look at Vedantic philosophy.

One of the key elements of Advaita Vedantic philosophy is the way it sustains a radical form of relationality. For indeed, on its conception, there is in the end only *one* entity, termed Brahman (meaning "the vast"). The following passage spells this out clearly: "According to the Advaita interpretation of the Bhagavad Gita, the ultimate reality Brahman, is non-dual. This means that it is the only existing reality, there being no second entity apart from it." (Sarvapriyananda, 2019, p. 1).

Advaita Vedantic ontology is *radically* relational in so far as it truly eschews all dualism. It specifically suggests that (ultimate) reality simply has *no* attributes, qualities or properties distinct from itself. Put differently, "It is not that Brahman exists, but that it is existence itself. Not that Brahman is a conscious entity, rather it is consciousness itself. And not that Brahman is happy, it is bliss itself." (Sarvapriyananda, 2019, p. 3).

Not only is the profound nature of reality not divorced from its manifestations, it is free of any possible kind of further differentiation, whether from its under constituents, or from any (dis)similar entities. Advaita literally signifies *without second*, a term that conveys its fundamentally non-dual nature (or ontology). As noted, verbal and written language with the formidable exception of poetry, as opposed to, say, artistic language such as music, dance or sculpture, is in many ways limited and inadequate to describe the absoluteness of such a world. The former operates "within the dualistic world of appearance [and] is incapable of expressing the non-dual Brahman" (Sarvapriyananda, 2019, p. 1). The rational mind, which both produces and mirrors language, unsurprisingly struggles to grasp this, as it typically falsely apprehends the world as dual. The mind interprets and imagines reality as binary, as made up of mutually exclusive polarities.

To accommodate this state of affairs, Vedantic philosophy accepts, if only as a heuristic device, that there is a reality that can (temporarily) be distinguished from the mind (only) in so far as the mind appears to be too limited to grasp such a reality. This contrasts with (pure) idealism. The latter denies the existence of a reality over and above or beyond the mind, one that we may be mistaken about, one that we might misperceive (Kakkar, 2018).

The apparent contradiction in the Vedantic ontology between unity and its use of dual and/or plural language merits brief clarification. Kakkar (2018) offers a convincing explanation when arguing that the Advaita Vedanta proffers differentiation to be *temporarily real representations* of a single underlying consciousness. He adds, "A representation is real because it is an impression of the underlying denominator. Yet, it is not completely real because without the denominator itself, the representation has no existence of its own (Kaplan, 1983)." (Kakkar, 2018). This is ultimately coherent with Advaita's position on consciousness, namely that a single consciousness underlies all phenomena, and all perceived dualities are representations of such consciousness (Indich, 1995).

In a further and final move towards introducing Vedantic philosophy, let me contrast it with that other, perhaps more familiar, non-dual thinking we find in Dao philosophy that works with the yin–yang polarities. The latter also embraces a deeply relational ontology of things and beings in the world, and considers the world as a balanced harmony *between* polarities. Daoism, as mentioned above, actively embraces paradoxes. Yet Vedantic thought makes a more radical move, and takes us one stage further, since it argues that difference and distinction are illusionary altogether. The Advaita Vedanta thus describes transcendence as liberation from the ignorance of perceived duality (Chinmayananda, 2018). Advaita Vedanta, like Daoism, espouses apparent contradictions and embraces paradoxes, but polarities, whilst conceptually (through illusion) separate, are in fact versions of a single underlying consciousness, and so ultimately *neither* opposite, *nor* different.

How then, in the light of our discussion, can the Advaita Vedanta help us conjugate leadership and care? I propose exploring the three noted aspects of the philosophy. The Advaita refutes any form of separation, and a first application invites careful engagement with the *body* to clarify mental and emotional processes in an endeavour to connect with the world as it is. I am interested here in how such thinking plays out for (necessarily) embodied and potentially caring leaders. Second, the Advaita Vedanta invites us to reflect on the non-separation between self and others. This proposition sustains a notion of leadership in which leaders care deeply for their followers, as well as for themselves. Third, non-dual philosophy blurs the boundaries between action and non-action, and embraces the idea that a leader's caring actions and benevolent non-action may be joined in one. I address the first binary below.

THE BODY VERSUS MIND BINARY

Running with the body–mind binary for a moment, the mind is mostly associated with intellect and rational thought, which in turn is associated with the brain, and stands in opposition to the body. This in itself is problematic, since the neurons, we now know, are not just situated in the head, but also in the gut and further in the heart. It appears more generally that cells around the body carry consciousness of some kind, so that abstract activity is not restricted to the cerebral zone. In other words, the body supports *every* human experience, ranging from obvious physical activity, such as running, to more subtle activity involving thoughts and various other states of consciousness.

Thus, to be *disconnected from one's body*, or to lack a relation with one's body, raises the question as to precisely which part(s) of the human being is (are) disconnected from the body, and whether we are ever not going through embodied processes. The disconnect would appear to be then more about the *awareness* of the various bodily processes, or lack thereof as the case may be, involving the familiar expressions of being cut off from one's feelings, numb in the body, living in the head, and so on.

Vedantic discipline encourages active use yoga (as a form of sense perceiving oneness). The connection between Vedantic philosophy and yoga becomes clearer on realising that yoga means union. Practising yoga thus means practising union in its various forms, working with the body, working from visible "postures" to ever more subtle ones, such as breathing, and simple silence and mere focus, so called meditative practices, to experience *ever more subtle levels of oneness*. Note that meditation is in the end not destined as a punctual, sit-down protocol-based experience, but as a permanent way of being.

In yoga, the disciple thus adopts bodily (asanas), including finger (mudras), postures and movements, and breathing exercises (pranayamas) as well as sound (using mantras and other sounds), to reconnect profoundly with *sense perception*, before and beyond mental interpretations. To experience sensations consciously involves careful listening to signals sent by the five senses. Note that the invitation to meditate with eyes closed is due to the fact that sight is the sense that is most associated with the feeling of control, which in turn is associated with the intellect, or so-called ego mind.

An obstacle to experiencing oneness, for which we must at the very least connect with the present (the here and now), is *the constant ping pong game between thoughts and emotions*. Thoughts are connected with a vast reservoir of already lived-through labelled stuff that is, in turn, connected with certain emotional patterns. The mind feels safe in believing it recognises what is coming its way, so it can respond in familiar ways, thus maintaining its sense of control. As thoughts get triggered, past emotions are activated. Emotions themselves generate thoughts, and so it continues. The result is a thought–emotion feedback loop that takes protagonists away from opening up to the novelty of actual experiences.

In sum, Vedantic teachings suggest that the illusion of separation may be overcome by dis-identifying from transient mental and emotional states (some rooted in fears and neuroses), whilst accessing more enduring features of reality. Inspired and coherent leaders learn to relax into their sense perception, rather than pursue the illusion that the mind can know and control all. The state of presence that emerges gives leaders true power to notice and act on that which matters. The point is crucial, for moving into conscious sense perceiving determines a leader's ability to be *responsible*. Responsibility here means the ability to respond (response able) to things as they are, and not as they are willed or imagined.

THE SELF VERSUS OTHER(S) BINARY

The Vedantic disciple learns to bridge the perceived separation between her different bodies: her mental, physical, emotional and other bodies. And in the process, she may begin to sense that there is no self entirely distinct from others, either that there is only oneness. Grasping the deeply relational nature of the world is a very real condition for looking after it. Now, the notion of non-separation sustained by Advaita Vedantic philosophy is, as noted, quasi absolute. The Vedanta states that "Brahman, being non-dual, has no second entity to which It can bear some relation" (Sarvapriyananda, 2019, p. 8). And when considering the individual (here in the sense of not being divisible from the rest), it too is not separate from other things and beings. It is inseparable from the whole. The profound implication entails that so long as even one living being (or soul) experiences suffering, there can be no true and complete happiness for any one. The deeply relational ontology behind such thinking anchors mutual care as a central feature of flourishing.

On my path as a yoga practitioner, I am gradually developing an awareness of my being as a unique expression of universal being. However abstract and lofty that may sound, my practice is bringing this home to me. I am learning that, no matter how much I meditate, so long as others suffer, that suffering is bound to manifest in ways that will sooner or later affect my personal balance through the human chain that make up the planet earth. And probably most of us have experienced that feeling of getting absorbed in the caring for another, that quasi sense of freedom that comes with serving another selflessly. In fact, heartfelt care and service is in most spiritual traditions a place of transcendence, the possibility to become *one with*, to experience deep connection and unity. The spiritual journey is one that certainly appears relevant to making sense of, and looking after, the world and its people.

Vedantic philosophy hence takes the notion of leadership to another level, where leaders are inseparable from their followers. To reach out to others, leaders need in the first instance to chip off the illusion of a separate self. There is a sense in which we need to take sufficient care of ourselves to even be able to consider caring for others. At the same time, when we care for others, a part of us is being healed and completed. The movement is fluid. If leaders are to care, they should truly cultivate care for others and themselves without differentiation.

THE ACTION VERSUS NON-ACTION BINARY

The last of my three binaries is action versus non-action. Action tends to be a taken-for-granted feature of leadership, at least in more standard Western control and results-oriented versions of leadership. The topic of action is an important tenet of Vedantic philosophy, and offers further subtle guidance for understanding leadership in relation to care.

The notion of action as control espouses a mechanistic understanding of the world as a reaction to obscurantist medieval thinking that emerged with the *Siècle des Lumières* (Age of Enlightenment). The aspiration was for a social order that would achieve human flourishing through rational thought, careful planning, controlling of resources and populations.

The notion of leadership as *controlled and controlling action* over others and resources is not, at least at first hand, necessarily opposed to a relational conception of leadership. Yet, when considering the radical relationality and oneness supported by the Advaita Vedanta, it would appear that action as the endeavour to achieve control is but a further illusion. If a non-dualist take on the world espouses the idea that all things (including persons) are connected to each other, it follows that, in a dynamic world, all things also constantly act on one another.

Action is, as it happens, central to the Advaita Vedanta, a surprising story of intense battling in the world, as transpires in the following passage: "The Bhagavad Gita can be read as the Vedantic philosophy of action. Arjuna's questions arise in the field of action (the battlefield) and are concerned with his moral dilemma about the nature of the actions which he is about to undertake, viz., fighting a war." (Sarvapriyananda, 2019, p. 2).

Espousing Advaita Vedantic ontology, however, yields a very different take on action, one in which action and non-action come together in the most intimate ways, and where the boundaries between the two become blurred: "He who perceives inaction in action, and action in inaction, is wise among men" (The Bhagavad Gita, 4.18, cited by Burke, 2019).

To arrive in such a place is demanding. It is a masterful act of self-leadership from which just (or fair) action is possible. The leader is now like an orchestra conductor. She is deeply receptive and guides so as to best serve the players and the music. It is her quality of presence that matters above all. Some conductors barely move, or even drop their baton. There is a sense in which she is being acted through and upon. Vedantic action is of a most subtle kind. The conception of action here closes in on non-action. It prepares for a kind of leadership capable of care through subtle and gentle (non) action, seeming passive yet subtly active.

Vedantic philosophy suggests that action includes being still, listening to and hearing the as-yet unheard, encountered in the eye of the cyclone, in a place of innermost silence (Bigo, 2017). Innermost silence lies beyond the silent mouth, and beyond the silent mind. In it one discovers, one intuits, what is present, things likely less familiar and unknown, or perhaps those we have always known. Here things profoundly other can emerge, not as a projection, but as yet another version of the past. That quality of silence is creative of possibilities based on a deep sense of what is. The powerful relation between silence, action, non-action and just (fair) action is clearly described below. Here action means minimal interference, in which sometimes mere presence suffices. Action is:

> no more action prompted by dissatisfaction, but there could very well be altruistic action. There could be the most intense action for the welfare of the world . . . The karma yogi, in the midst of the greatest silence and solitude, finds the most intense activity, and in the midst of the most intense activity finds the silence and solitude of the desert. (Sarvapriyananda, 2019, p. 9)

In experiencing the intimacy of silence, solitude and (non) action, leaders can manifest in a profoundly subtle, and yet powerfully efficacious, manner.

In fact, the more I pull in one direction, the more the opposite tends to manifest. The invitation is to observe and dwell rather than react, and to act from a place of non-reaction. Action now involves a holding of space or field to allow the (best) course of events to flow (Chia and Holt, 2006). Planning and control are modes of functioning that tend to involve shutting out and removing that which "gets in the way", the weak signals that, with hindsight, often prove crucial in order to avoid accidents and/or seize opportunities. To listen deeply to and intuitively hold the host of elements that constantly emerge in the present takes proactive relaxing into the moment.

The degree of subtlety inherent in the Vedantic understanding of (non) action is *full* of care. It certainly requires *careful* consideration of life in general and humans in particular. It invites a capacity to relax, listen and tune in, so as to, in a sense, act by being acted upon. The silent presence of a wise person, a monk or other dignitary, can make all the difference to what people say and do in any given circumstances. Such *engaged non-duality* finds its place in a world that is increasingly challenging to navigate as well as in trust-based, collaborative leadership that requires care of self and others.

CONCLUDING COMMENTS

Motivated by the evolution of understandings of leadership in relation to care, I have selected an Eastern lens. My motive for engaging with Advaita Vedantic philosophy, in particular, is the radical relationality it sustains, recognising and then working through and beyond dualities. The Advaita Vedanta sustains that, prior to being enlightened, human beings hold dual conceptions of reality, as the ego mind holds onto the illusion of being distinct. Misrepresentations and distortions of the world thus stand in the way of responsible leadership. Spiritual practices are in effect forms of self-care designed to *calm the mind*, and the *emotional reactions* to the constant flow of thoughts at the expense of experiencing the present as is. Re-involving the five senses means placing flesh at the heart of the world once more (Merleau-Ponty, 1968), reinstating the sensing body as truth-teller. Gradually, the disciple reaches towards intuitively understanding that previously held distinctions are illusionary, and begins to embrace oneness.

The Advaita puts a certain form of care, involving a subtle, careful presence, centre-stage in leadership, as it sees body and mind, self and others, action and non-action as temporary, illusionary mind-based phenomena that emanate from a single underlying consciousness. Consistent with Vedantic ontology, leaders may develop their sense perception as they work to dissolve mental illusions of distinctness and separation. The emotional and mental bodies come to rest, much like sand settling on the bottom of the seabed.

The truth-telling body comes alive through sense perception. Corpo-reality takes on meaning. Leaders care for self and others, because self *is* other. Leaders further exert care to engage in the most just and subtle actions, listening to what is, knowing through intuition, cutting through complexity, and relaxing into being acted upon. I find Vedantic philosophy thus challenges some of the most engaged relational thinking around leadership.

Further inquiry is warranted in an endeavour to build bridges with other philosophies, such as with more recent Western philosophers. I also believe research engaging with other spiritual traditions, with which to compare and contrast the Advaita Vedanta, may provide further insight. Initial avenues of exploration may involve Daoism, as well as looking closer to home at

Christianity, as the passage below resonates with the Oneness I found in the Advaita Vedanta.

> When you make the two into one, and when you make the inner like the outer and the outer like the inner, and the upper like the lower, and when you make male and female into a single one, so the male will not be male and the female will not be female . . . then you will enter the Kingdom. – Yeshua. (Thomas, 22:4, The New Testament)

Not surprisingly, value-based, humanist dimensions of leadership, including the caring dimensions, are proving better suited for organisations to survive and prosper in a highly complex, fast-changing world than command and control-type leadership cultures (Carney and Getz, 2009; Laloux, 2014). Transcending binaries is particularly challenging in a world in which the mind is constantly solicited. Some say the mind is a thousand times faster than God, and many times faster, too, than the soul. The mind analyses the world, remembers, develops "knowledge", to try and predict and control that which, in truth, escapes it. It meanwhile hangs onto the illusion that mind is distinct from the body, and from other bodies, and further imagines that individuals are separate, and that action involves control rather than relaxation. There are lessons to be gleaned from the Advaita Vedantic journey that offer interesting responses upon which leaders, many of whom live on the brink of burn-out, may wish to take time to reflect.

REFERENCES

Barkema, H.G., Chen, X-P., George, G., Luo, Y. and Tsui, A.S. (2015). West meets East: New concepts and theories. *Academy of Management Journal*, **58**(2), 460–79.

Bigo, V. (2017). On silence, creativity and ethics in organization studies. *Organization Studies*, **39**(1), 121–33.

Burke, G. (2019). The mystery of action and inaction. Accessed 10 January 2019 at https://ocoy.org/dharma-for-christians/bhagavad-gita-for-awakening/the-mystery -of-action-and-inaction/.

Carney, B. and Getz, I. (2009). *Freedom, Inc.: Free your Employees and let them lead your Business to Higher Productivity, Profits, and Growth*. New York: Crown Business.

Chia, R. and Holt, R. (2006). Strategy as practical coping: A Heideggerian perspective. *Organization Studies*, **27**(5), 635–55.

Chinmayananda, S. (2018). *Kindle Life*. Cochin, IN: Central Chinmaya Mission Trust.

Indich, W.M. (1995). *Consciousness in Advaita Vedanta*. New Delhi: Motilal Banarsidass Publishers.

Kakkar, S. (2018). The goblet and two faces: Understanding transcendence and paradox from the perspective of Advaita Vedanta. *The Learning Organization*. Accessed 23 January 2019 at https://doi.org/10.1108/ TLO-04-2018-0052.

Laloux, F. (2014). *Reinventing Organizations*. Brussels: Nelson Parker.

Merleau-Ponty, M. (1968). *The Visible and the Invisible*. Trans. by A. Lingis. Evanston, IL: Northwestern University Press.

Sarvapriyananda, S. (2019). Non-duality and the language of paradox in the Bhagavad Gita. Accessed 22 January 2019 at https://www.academia.edu/35135632/Non--duality_and_the_Language_of_Paradox_in_the_Bhagavad_Gita.

Steffney, J. (1956). Zen Buddhism: Selected writings of D.T. Suzuki, ed. William Barrett. New York: Anchor.

Tushman, Michael L. and O'Reilly, Charles A. (1996). The ambidextrous organization: managing evolutionary and revolutionary change. *California Management Review*, **38**, 1–23.

17. Care without leaders: the collective powers of affective leadership

Iain Munro and Torkild Thanem

> Today's leadership problem is really a symptom of a profound historical transformation, one that is currently in midstream – modern organizational forms have been destroyed and adequate replacements have not yet been invented.
> (Hardt and Negri, 2017, p. 8)

In this chapter we articulate a concept of 'affective leadership' based on the capacity to increase our collective powers of action. Doing so, we show how leaderless movements and organizations can foster their participants' powers of action by cultivating active affects which are independent of individual leaders. Although the effectiveness of leaderless organizations and movements has already been subject to some discussion (Crevani et al., 2010; Graeber, 2013; Sutherland et al., 2014), the present chapter explains their power in terms of their ethical and affective constitution.

Indeed, it is possible to start unfolding the power of collective leadership through ongoing discussions about the ostensible virtues of individual leaders. Here, good leaders are often portrayed as possessing special social competencies such as good organizational skills, excellent skills of persuasion as well as a host of other desirable traits such as being 'caring', 'authentic' and even 'transformational'. It is typically these social skills and virtues that legitimize the position of leaders at the top of the social or corporate hierarchy and justify that they are rewarded with status and high pay. Meanwhile, the leadership literature often celebrates the charismatic leaders of social and religious movements who are driven by ideological and altruistic aims rather than personal gain. Christ, Mohammed, Gandhi, Martin Luther King, Malcolm X and Harvey Milk have all been acknowledged as archetypal great leaders with virtually superhuman abilities to change the world for the better (see Bass et al., 1987).

However, in practice, in any large organization or social movement very few of its members will have any prolonged contact with their purported leader; for the most part the leader will have a largely symbolic role within the movement, as the embodiment of a particular set of ideas and affects. So, it must be that in good leadership something else besides the personal traits and abilities of the so-called leader is doing the work. Although a leader may be the perceived embodiment of certain ideas and certain affects such as intelligence, love and martial prowess, the work of leadership is not performed until these ideas and affects start circulating beyond the body of the leader. Indeed, leadership is always a collective effort in which the spread of ideas and affects plays an important role in the movement itself and in followers' perception of their leader.

Building on these elementary observations, this chapter outlines a concept of 'affective leadership' which does not rest on an individual endowed with special virtues and competencies. Once we realize the affective nature of leadership, leadership is necessarily a leaderless endeavour which involves enhancing our collective powers and capacities for action.

In order to map out the concept of affective leadership, we will revisit our previous work in this area and draw further on the writings of the 17th-century philosopher Benedict de Spinoza (Munro and Thanem, 2018). While Spinoza's 'joyful affects' bear some resemblance to some of the virtues endorsed by contemporary arguments for 'caring leadership', he teaches us that our capacity to enhance such virtuous affects is always a collective effort which exceeds the ostensible virtues of individual leaders. Through illustrative examples, we will then contrast how affective leadership is actualized within social movements by examining what kinds of virtues and affects they thrive on. Whereas affective leadership within social movements has increased their members' capacity for action, supposedly virtuous and caring business leaders have done little beyond enhancing their own wealth and social status. Finally, we argue that social movements and organizations striving for genuine change will need to 'immunize' themselves against individual leaders to stand a chance of enhancing their collective powers of action.

AFFECTIVE LEADERSHIP

Elsewhere we have defined affective leadership as a radically democratic practice devoted to enhancing our collective powers of action (Munro and Thanem, 2018). Drawing on the ethical and political writings of Spinoza, we have formulated a number of basic principles of this form of leadership, which may be summarized as follows:

1. Affective leadership diverges from the idea of the leader–follower relationship, which ultimately rests on the virtue of obedience.
2. Affective leadership is based on collective action without interference from purported 'ethical leaders'.

3. Affective leadership entails the cultivation of joyful affects such as love and courage, which increase our collective powers of action, and the avoidance of sad passions such as hatred and pity, which decrease them.
4. Our collective capacity for action develops from good encounters that accord with our reason and enhance our capacity to affect and be affected. In turn, our capacity to affect and be affected is enhanced as we experience and understand the limits of our freedom and the causes of joyful affects.
5. Thus, affective leadership involves the organization of good encounters through the cultivation of friendships that enable people to pursue their common advantage and welfare and the development of democratic relations that enable people to think what they wish and say what they think. Not to be confused with the nepotism flourishing in homosocial executive networks, we are more likely to enhance our affective capacities by crafting amicable relations with people who are different from us yet share our desire for the common good.

There are some important affinities between our notion of affective leadership and current arguments for caring leadership which more or less explicitly draw inspiration from the virtue ethics of the Ancient Greeks and Ancient Romans (see Knights and O'Leary, 2005). Care is often associated with the ability to be kind and compassionate towards others. Spinoza defined compassion and kindness as joyful and virtuous affects that enhance our power to affect and be affected by others. He viewed compassion as a form of love where one is gladdened at someone else's fortune but saddened by their misfortune (DefAff24). However, one key difference between the two concepts is that caring leadership is historically grounded in a notion of pastoral care, which, emphasizing the patriarch's power to care for himself and his household, pacifies those who are subject to his care.

While care as such may be associated with 'interdependency, mutual assistance. . . [and] solidarity. . .' (Kittay et al., 2005, p. 465), talk of 'caring leadership' comes with managerialist and hierarchical connotations that risk entrenching the practice of care in conditions of exploitation and a gendered division of labour. As Kittay and colleagues have argued (Kittay et al., 2005; Kittay, 2006), the system of care-work on which our society is grounded does not require 'caring leadership' but relations of solidarity and 'mutual care'.

Not only are such relations at the core of Spinoza's ethical sociality; Spinoza explains how they may be crafted and cultivated. Assuming that virtue is itself a form of power, he maintained that our collective powers of action are strengthened through social interactions which enable us to use and develop our reason, learn from each other, and foster convivial relations with others across and in spite of our differences. Whereas contemporary calls for caring leadership continue to frame care primarily as a virtue characteristic of individual leaders, Spinoza insists that the cultivation of any virtuous affect – and the good life as such – is necessarily a collective accomplishment that rests on our joint capacity to cultivate and use our collective powers. Through what he calls the 'principle of common life and common advantage' (EIVP73Dem), '. . . everyone who is led by reason desires for others also the good he wants for himself' (EIVP73S). Let us therefore not be tricked by Spinoza's seemingly brutal equation between power and virtue.[1] Recognizing that our capacity to live a good social life depends on our agreement with others (EIVP38, 40), he argues that we strive to join others 'in friendship' in order 'to lead. . . [ourselves] and others by the free judgment of reason. . .' (EIVP70Dem).

It is worth dwelling a bit with Spinoza's notion of reason, because this too is profoundly embedded in his affective system. As Deleuze (1992) pointed out in his thesis on Spinoza, reason is our strongest affect (EIVP40-73). What Spinoza teaches us, then, is that we cannot enhance our reason and know the causes of good encounters with others without appreciating how such encounters affect us 'through our bodies' as well as our minds (Munro and Thanem, 2018, p. 60). The more we seek to cut ourselves off from our affects and embodied experiences, the less we care about the consequences of making unreasonable and resentful claims that turn others into enemies rather than friends. Indeed, 'it is only through our embodied experience and knowledge of our appetites that we might try and modify them so as to seek joyful encounters and avoid sad encounters' (Munro and Thanem, 2018, p. 60).

Hence, affective and caring leadership share the assumption that we must cultivate our collective powers of reason in order to understand how we may live well and work well with others. Under such conditions, the very notion that leadership is exercised by individual leaders disappears. As people engage in 'mutual caring' (Graeber, 2013) to be of 'mutual assistance' (Kittay et al., 2005) to one another, we flourish despite, rather than because of, individual leaders. Concern with the traits and virtues of individual leaders becomes little more than a distraction from the task of democratic self-governance.[2]

Affective leadership therefore does not preclude all acts of compassion or care for others. However, they only constitute joyful affects insofar as they involve a sense of 'collective responsibility' (Kittay, 2006, p. 338) that enhances everyone's capacity to act and care for each other. The challenge is to strengthen our capacity to organize good encounters between people. Developing our judgment and reason as a collective is central to this endeavour. By means of illustration, let us now discuss some of the virtues and affects that are actualized in radical social movements.

AFFECTS IN LEADERLESS SOCIAL MOVEMENTS

One case which illustrates the affective power of social movements is the anti-Vietnam war movement during the 1960s and 1970s in the United States. A pinnacle event in the development of this social movement was the march on the Pentagon, where up to 200 000 protestors attempted to surround and occupy the heart of the US military industrial complex. Norman Mailer's (1994) account of this march is instructive on the role of affects in the organization of the march and the attempts to disrupt and break the protest by US authorities. Mailer describes how feelings of solidarity, bravery and mutual respect drove the protestors as well as their indignation at the conduct of the war.[3] This indignation is expressed both in protest at the actions of the state and in language itself: 'the use of obscenity was indeed to be condemned, because the free use of it would wash away the nation – was America the first great power to be built on bullshit?' (*ibid.*, p. 201).

In response to these protests against the war, the bureaucracy of the police and military apparatus unleashed aggression and open violence on the protestors, as well as using techniques of humiliation to undermine the movement. Mailer describes the joy at the forward momentum of the march, the urgency in not stopping until their goal was achieved – the numerous acts of individual and collective bravery in the face of police violence, arrest and imprisonment. He describes the fear at witnessing the violent beating of a young woman at the hands of the police – the despair and impotence of her companions. He talks of his open admiration of his cell mate, the academic Noam Chomsky – 'a slim sharp-featured man with an ascetic expression, and an air of gentle but absolute moral integrity' (*ibid.*, p. 178). What is largely absent from this exceptional account is the direction of any leaders, where instead the role of a variety of affects takes priority – solidarity, joy, obscenity, indignation, bravery, fear, humiliation.

Mailer observes how the affective life of the organization was not only a part of the anti-war movement, but also the police state against which it fought:

> For years he had been writing about the nature of totalitarianism, its need to render populations apathetic – its instrument the destruction of mood. Mood was forever being sliced, cut, stamped, ground, excised or obliterated. Mood was a scent which rose from the acts and calms of nature, and totalitarianism was a deodorant to nature. (*ibid.*, p. 117)

The bureaucratic machine of state – the coldest of all monsters – is designed to destroy mood and in particular the dangerous affects of those individuals and groups that it considers to be a social enemy both at home and abroad:

> The American corporation executive who was after all the foremost representative of man in the world today, was perfectly capable of burning unseen women and children in the Vietnamese jungles, yet felt a large displeasure and fairly final disapproval at the generous use of obscenity in literature and in public. (*ibid.*, p. 49)

Burned bodies were unseen and deodorized in the publications of the RAND Corporation, and the unending reports of military campaign victories in the US media. Along with these counterfeit measures in a system awash with bullshit, the destruction of mood was essential to prevent the mobilization and self-organization of the people against these crimes. But the movement grew as the authorities lost their ability to deodorize their own stench, their mood intensified, and effects of outrage, indignation and solidarity moved the protestors against the machinery of the state. Perhaps one of the most surprising things about Mailer's account today is just how effective the corporate executive and state has itself become in mobilizing mood – and how similar crimes continue to be committed by the same state today in country after country – from Afghanistan to Iraq, from Libya to Syria.

A more recent account of the role of affect in the leaderless leadership of a social movement has been given by a number of participants of the Occupy movement. Harcourt (2013) reports that some participants of Occupy described it as being a 'leaderless' movement, whereas others called it a 'leaderful' movement, where everyone could be understood as exercising leadership. The role of leadership was questioned by the Occupy movement in terms of both its ethical limitations, to the extent that hierarchical structures could undermine democratic participation, and its strategic limitations, to the extent that leaders offered a focal point and weakness that could be attacked by state authorities. David Graeber's (2013) insider account of the Occupy Wall Street movement of 2011 describes in detail the variety of organizational practices that were developed by participants to ensure horizontal networks of democratic decision-making in the movement, but also the absolute importance of practices to organize basic everyday living, such as the provision of food, sanitation and living space. This was crucial in the creation of 'a community without money' based on principles not just of democracy but on affects of mutual caring, solidarity and support.

The Occupy Movement created new practices for enhancing its collective affects, such as the 'human mic' where the protesters would repeat each line of any speech made to amplify the message to all those present and enhance collective participation and solidarity. Harcourt (2013, p. 59) also observed how

the human mic had 'the effect of undermining leadership. It interrupts charisma. It's like live translation: the speaker can only utter five to eight words
before having to shut up while the assembled masses repeat them.' Techniques
of massage and meditation were also used by the protestors to help relax, ease
anxieties and foster feelings of solidarity (Schneider, 2011). At the same time,
Graeber's account observes the difficulties in maintaining solidarity when
confronted with the militarized tactics of the police who attempted to break up
the movement and destroy the new social space that they had created. Thus,
he bears witness to a range of intimidation tactics, including beatings, the use
of pepper spray against non-violent protesters as well as micro-aggressions of
degradation and humiliation.

In response to such tactics, the movement itself had required a great deal
of attention to its affective dimensions. With an immense creativity which
directly informed their tactics of protest, the Occupiers fostered a collective
atmosphere of carnival where 'love and caring was our primary weapon'
(Graeber, 2013, p. 258). This was not just a revolutionary challenge 'to the
power of money but to the power of money to determine what life was supposed to be about. . . for that brief moment love had become a revolutionary
act' (*ibid.*, p. 127).

What these two examples show is that it is not individual leaders imbued
with special powers or competencies that are acting as leaders, but the collective affects that are part of the social milieu of these movements. We will
now turn to a closer examination of the ambivalent role of leadership within
leaderless movements and organizations.

IMMUNIZING AGAINST LEADERS – ENHANCING
COLLECTIVE POWERS OF ACTION

The principle of a leaderless movement or organization is absolutely fundamental to the source of its power and its increase (Sutherland et al., 2014).
Hardt and Negri (2017) argue that the social movements of the recent past
that have fought for the increased freedoms and democratic powers of their
participants are increasingly immunizing themselves against the 'leadership
virus' and the hierarchical social relations that this virus brings with it. This
does not mean that such movements do not have coordinators who help to
facilitate public assemblies and consensus decision-making, or mutual carers
who help to defuse tension and bolster solidarity, or temporary spokespersons.
But, to understand these roles in terms of being a leader is to misconceive their
fundamentally collective and affective nature.

For example, in the Occupy movement of 2011, the lack of leaders gave the
movement strength both in removing them as strategic points of weakness that
could be focused upon by the police to undermine the movement, and in the

stimulation of collective assemblies as decision-making bodies, which helped to increase the affective commitment of the participants in the movement. The principle of leaderlessness also embodied the ethical idea of radical democracy that the movement stood for, in contrast to the corrupt representative democracy against which it was directed. However, other examples can be found which equally demonstrate the ethical and tactical importance of leaderlessness in fostering the power of any movement.

One of the most famous military 'leaders' of World War I, T.E. Lawrence, confessed that he was not really a leader and had little control over the events and the victories which others ascribed to him. Instead, he explained his role in the events as a 'mock primacy', emerging largely from the fact that many of the reports and interviews about the events were either written by him or based upon interviews with him. While it is no doubt true that he was a phenomenal organizer and a superb tactician, he left the leadership role to others (i.e., to General Allenby and Prince Faisal). Lawrence's account of the tactics of guerrilla war explained that it had far more in common with the practice of a general strike than with a traditional military campaign. His strategy of guerrilla warfare implicitly rejected the need for a leader; as the irregular forces that made up their rebellion could not be counted on to follow a leader for any length of time, his strategy focused on making it impossible for the adversary's leaders to mobilize *their* forces effectively. The leading was done not by him as an individual but through an assemblage of affects – through an idea of freedom, a Bedouin way of life, and the desert. Hence, one might understand Lawrence's 'mock primacy' in the revolt in terms of what Skeaff (2018) calls an 'intermediary', where the role of the 'leader' is little more than a symbolic and affective idea, rather than issuing from the capability or character of a particular individual.

Skeaff (2018) elaborates the role of the intermediary through the example of another historical figure who is routinely celebrated as a charismatic leader: Moses. The figure of Moses played a peculiar role in the creation of the Jewish nation, in that he is cast as both a charismatic leader and someone with no power of his own. Moses simply follows the order of his God and helps to organize a division of powers within a federation of autonomous tribes, which constitutes 'a republic in which no single individual or group in society exercised command over the people as a whole' (Skeaff, 2018, p. 102). Notwithstanding the commanding and un-reasonable nature of the Decalogue that Moses received from God on Mount Sinai, Skeaff argues that the chief commandment which came to organize this new society was the principle whereby its members agreed to live according to the dictate that they should love their neighbour. As such, Moses was not the leader of the Israelites but the mediator of God's laws; 'strictly speaking, no-one ruled' (p. 106). Again, the idea of God plays a purely symbolic and affective role – it is an empty signifier but one which is attributed immense powers.

More specifically, this principle led the Israelites to establish a system of checks and balances between the tribes, including rules which militated against the accumulation of economic power, such as the right of a jubilee whereby debts were forgiven and properties redistributed after a period of seven years. Rather than simply expressing a moral duty, this system, and its underlying principle of neighbourly love, involved an ancient form of radical democracy which rested on the power of the community. In Skeaff's words, 'loving one's neighbour as oneself is . . . a necessity to take one's power to the limit through an alteration or exchange with the powers of others' (2018, p. 117).

Instead of focusing on the magical powers of the individual charismatic leader, Skeaff observes that the institutionalization of new ways of living is always a result of judgments and actions made by the collective itself. According to Skeaff, the power of judgment plays a fundamental role in the creation and circulation of affects, which are formed and refined in common by means of mutual interaction. Skeaff explains that the power of judgment is fundamental to the constituent power of any social group and is essential to the formation of true democracy. Even when an individual acts in obedience to another they can never give up their power of judgment because this is our inalienable, constitutive power. According to Skeaff, 'these judgments carry a vital normativity, a constituent power transgressing established norms and creating new norms more conducive to the common endeavor of becoming maximally free, rational, powerful' (*ibid.*, p. 87).

Indeed, the creation of new forms of living in common is the explicit aim of social movements, such as the Civil Rights movements, LGBT movement, the Occupy movement, and Black Lives Matter. Erica Edwards explains that the glorification of individual leaders is detrimental to such movements, and is both 'politically dangerous . . . and historically inaccurate' (quoted in Hardt and Negri, 2017, p. 30). Writing about the Black civil rights movement in the US, Edwards argues that the mythology of the charismatic leader is grounded in a stereotype of heteronormative masculinity which presents a sanitized and inaccurate historical account of the development of social movements. Frederick Harris (2015) has also argued that dependence on individual charismatic leaders such as Malcolm X or Martin Luther King was a strategic weakness of previous social movements. Having said that, it is inaccurate to claim that there are no leaders in Black Lives Matters (Chatelain and Asoka, 2015). However, these organizers do not act as charismatic leaders but as community organizers who help to organize protests and express the collective will of their communities from below. To avoid being dragged down by a cult of individual leaders, social movements whose aims are radically democratic have therefore sought to develop immune systems that attack signs of hierarchical authority. For instance, the recent Black Lives Matter movement which has emerged in response to police violence against blacks in the United States is self-consciously organized from the bottom-up, with great skepticism of the power of individual leaders (Hardt and Negri, 2017).

CONCLUSIONS

This chapter has drawn on a number of examples of leadership in order to refine a conception of 'affective leadership', which enhances our collective capacity for action. Doing so, we have been strongly critical of the concept of leadership in general, particularly how it continues to be grounded in a mythology symptomatic of hierarchical social forms, masculine stereotypes and individual saviours. This mythology gives a largely inaccurate portrayal of the affective dimension that leads people to act in ways that enable genuine progressive change.

If anything, the individual leader plays a largely symbolic role in the organization, as the living embodiment of a particular set of ideas and affects. In good leadership something else besides the personal abilities of the purported leader is doing the work – it is always a collective effort through the spread of ideas and affects such as intelligence, love, solidarity and courage. It is these ideas and affects that are performing the work of leadership beyond the body of the leader. In order to enhance our collective powers of action, the mythology of the individual leader and leadership *per se* must therefore be abandoned. Instead, we must examine the social relations and collective affects which are circulating within organizations. In a world where horizontal networks of organization have found new forms of expression, it is time to reveal that the capacity of leaderless movements and organizations to increase the power of action of their participants relies on active affects that are independent of individual leaders.

Three such affects are care, reason and judgment. Although social movements are often formed as a response to painful experiences of violence and injustice, what makes them powerful is their ability to transform these experiences into joyful affects which enhance their capacity to achieve change. It is not sufficient to be dismayed and enraged by witnessing and experiencing injustice. We must learn to act together, in ways which produce the change we care about, so much so that we end up being gladdened by our joint collective fortune. Creating this new vital normativity may require courage and cheerfulness. But it also requires that we cultivate our affective powers of judgment and reason – to be able to judge and understand what is good, not just for ourselves, but for all. This task cannot be off-loaded onto individuals in leadership positions but is something we all must learn through social interaction, with our bodies, by living and working in common. As our freedoms are under attack by unreasonable forces, we must learn to cultivate our power to affect progressive change by using our judgment, enhancing our reason, and transforming sad affects into joyful affects of care, courage and love at a collective scale.

NOTES

1. The equation between power and virtue is most explicitly articulated when he claims that 'the more one strives, and is able, to seek his [*sic*] own advantage, that is, to preserve his [*sic*] being, the more he [*sic*] is endowed with virtue' (EIVP20; see also EIVP22C).
2. Kittay's feminist conception of care frames this not in terms of leadership but in terms of mutual relations, in which the autonomy and decision-making capacity of the other is fully respected (Kittay et al., 2005; Kittay, 2006).
3. Norman Mailer's account of the march on the Pentagon does mention some of the virtues of its leaders, but he takes pains to emphasize the role of its collective and affective dimensions rather than the qualities of specific individuals. Mailer himself was one of the key spokespersons for this event and a prominent voice in the antiwar movement itself.

REFERENCES

Bass, B., Avolio, B. and Goodheim, L. (1987). Biography and the assessment of transformational leadership at the world-class level, *Journal of Management*, **13**(1), 7–19.

Chatelain, M. and Asoka, K. (2015). Women in Black Lives Matter: An interview with Marcia Chatelain, *Dissent*, Summer, 54–61.

Crevani, L., Lindgren, M. and Packendorff, J. (2010). Leadership, not leaders: On the study of leadership as practices and interactions, *Scandinavian Journal of Management*, **26**(1), 77–86.

Deleuze, G. (1992 [1968]). *Expressionism in Philosophy: Spinoza* (trans. M. Joughin), New York: Zone.

Graeber, D. (2013). *The Democracy Project: A History, A Crisis, A Movement*, London: Penguin.

Harcourt, B. (2013). 'Political disobedience' in W. Mitchell (ed.), *Occupy: Three Inquiries in Disobedience*, Chicago, IL: University of Chicago Press, pp. 45–92.

Hardt, M. and Negri, A. (2017). *Assembly*, Oxford: Oxford University Press.

Harris, F. (2015). The Next Civil Rights Movement, *Dissent*, Summer, 34–40.

Kittay, E. (2006). The concept of care ethics in biomedicine: The case of disability, in Rehmann-Sutter, C., Düwell, M. and Mieth, D. (eds), *Bioethics in Cultural Contexts*, Dordrecht: Springer, pp. 319–39.

Kittay, E., Jennings, B. and Wasuna, A. (2005). Dependency, difference and the global ethic of longterm care, *Journal of Political Philosophy*, **13**(4), 443–69.

Knights, D. and O'Leary, M. (2005). Reflecting on corporate scandals: The failure of ethical leadership, *Business Ethics: A European Review*, **14**(4), 359–66.

Mailer, N. (1994). *Armies of the Night: History as a Novel/The Novel as History*, New York: New American Library.

Munro, I. and Thanem, T. (2018). The ethics of affective leadership: Organizing good encounters without leaders, *Business Ethics Quarterly*, **28**(1), 51–69.

Schneider, N. (2011). From Occupy Wall Street to Occupy Everywhere. The Nation, 12 October.

Skeaff, C. (2018). *Becoming Political: Spinoza's Vital Republicanism and the Democratic Power of Judgment*, Chicago, IL: Chicago University Press.

Spinoza, B. de (1994 [1677]). *The Ethics and Other Works*, edited and translated by E. Curley, Princeton, NJ: Princeton University Press.

Sutherland, N., Land, C. and Böhm, S. (2014). Anti-leaders(hip) in social movement organizations: The case of autonomous grassroots groups, *Organization*, **21**, 759–78.

18. Caring beyond kinship: applying Jane Addams' social ethic to the organizational domain

Donna Ladkin

As an approach to ethical engagement, 'care ethics' has largely been seen as appropriate to the realm of the personal: within family relations, health and well-being contexts, and education, particularly that of young children. Principle or justice-based ethical approaches, with their emphasis on fairness and universal applicability, have been seen as more apt orientations to use within organizational contexts. The kind of particularized attention central to an ethic of care is potentially problematic within contexts in which treating everyone 'equally' is a guiding principle.

Basing ethical action in care rather than justice can even be seen as a soft option. It is often associated with the way women relate to one another: putting feelings and friendships before the hard realities of truth. The grandfather of moral development theory, Lawrence Kohlberg, rated such attention to relationships (as often practiced by young girls) inferior to the way 'morally developed' boys adhered to truth and risked hurting their friends' feelings in the process (Kohlberg, 1971). The association between the ethics of care and a female approach is further strengthened by its appropriation by feminist ethicists. This alignment can further marginalize it as 'women's business', something that has limited applicability to the 'real world' of industry, organizing and leading. After all, what happens to organizational standards of fairness when care gets involved?

This chapter argues that contrary to the view that care has limited value within organizational settings, it has an essential role to play in all ethical human relations, wherever they are situated. Whenever human beings come together, caring for one another provides the social glue that holds endeavors together; it is 'an important nonstructural component in maintaining social cohesion' (Hamington, 2007: 150). Drawing on the social theorist Jane Addams' work, it further contests that care in ethical relations is not a soft option, but demands a level of emotional fortitude and courage which can exceed that required by more justice-based approaches.

The chapter introduces Addams' thinking concerning care as the basis of a social ethic, an approach to ethical relations which she argues should be at the heart of any collective human endeavor. It goes on to explore how her work could inform ethical leadership practice, both theoretically and by noticing how it is apparent within the Graduate School of Leadership and Change at Antioch University. First however, the chapter introduces Jane Addams and her work.

JANE ADDAMS

Jane Addams (1860–1935) was an American sociologist, peace activist and social reformer who was also the first American woman to win the Nobel Peace Prize in 1931. A forceful advocate of human rights, she was among the founders of the American Civil Workers' Union, the National Association for the Advancement of Colored People, as well as the Women's Peace Party. Although she was also a prolific writer concerning social theory (publishing 12 books and over 300 articles during her lifetime), she is best known for establishing (with Ellen Gates Starr) Hull House, a social settlement community in Chicago. Recognized as the leading social settlement of its time, Hull House became a thriving hub for exchanges between well-to-do Chicagoans, recent immigrants to the USA and those living in poverty in the surrounding neighborhood.

Born into a wealthy and politically active family (her father was a senator in Illinois and knew Abraham Lincoln), Addams was of the first generation of women to be university educated, graduating from the Rockford Female Seminary as valedictorian in 1881. After a trip to England in 1883 where she encountered the poor in London, she experienced a 'bifurcation of consciousness' that impacted on the direction her life would take (Lengermann and Niebrugge-Brantley, 1998). Faced with the terrible conditions people were enduring in the East End, she found herself retreating from her experience by comparing what she was seeing to literary accounts of such poverty. Reflecting on this reaction, she noticed how her education had taken her away from action, rather than towards it. She wrote that as a result of her pursuit of higher education she had 'lost the simple and most automatic response to the human appeal, that old healthful reaction resulting in activity' (Addams, 1910: 71).

The notion that care is not care unless it results in action is a central theme of Addams' subsequent writings. For her, rather than being a feeling of creaturely connection, it is the 'healthful response to action' which occurs when we encounter another human being or creature in need of assistance, comfort or attention. Furthermore, rather than being only appropriately bestowed within personal relations, for Addams such care is the basis of a social ethic. She went as far as to suggest that care is the very basis of democracy itself, writing,

> we are thus brought to a conception of Democracy not merely as a sentiment which desires the well-being of all men, nor yet as a creed which believes in the essential dignity and equality of all men, but as that which affords a rule of living well as a test of faith (Addams, 1907 [2012]: 6).

Addams' work offers the possibility of conceptualizing care ethics in a way that moves beyond the personal, to the organizational and societal domains. In doing so, Hamington (2001: 105) suggests that her pragmatic approach 'can infuse into care ethics a means for confronting the social and political issues while maintaining the emotive and relational dimensions that make it such an important contribution to moral philosophy'. In this way Addams offers not only an interpersonal philosophy of care ethics but a political one. Based in a radical understanding of the connectedness of all individuals she challenges us to look beyond our kinship bonds to accept that 'any person's problems and difficulties are indeed our own' (Addams, 1907 [2012]: 6).

As well as introducing a political dimension of care ethics, she also offers a means of resolving the problem of moral relativism, a criticism often waged at care ethics approaches. She does this by suggesting that rather than attending to universal principles, in bestowing care we should engage with a universal process. At the heart of this process is sympathetic understanding, a concept elaborated below. Finally, she conceptualizes the relationship between care and justice in a way that holds both within a dialectical dynamic, rather than suggesting one approach is sufficient without the other. The next section describes her approach in greater detail.

ADDAMS' APPROACH TO AN ETHIC OF CARE

The ability to care for others outside our immediate kinship group is based on a notion of radical interconnectedness. Reflecting on Addams' approach to care ethics Hamington (2001) argues that such interconnectedness is grounded in corporeal knowing; because we have experienced pain and discomfort in our own bodies, we can connect with others' suffering. Such embodied knowing prompts us to care beyond our immediate kinship groups to all other human beings and potentially to all other sentient beings as well.

Being able to care for those beyond one's own immediate relations is the basis of moral development, according to Addams, and is a fundamental social obligation. In order to care for others, we must engage 'sympathetic understanding', the capacity to perceive the world from another's vantage point. When acting from such a perspective, one attempts to 'do unto others as they, themselves would like to be treated', rather than 'doing unto others as you would have them do unto you'. For most people, this capacity has to be deliberately cultivated. Addams suggests that the best way of doing so is by actively seeking out those different from oneself, and engaging with them as friends in order to better understand their perspectives. This philosophy was central to the way Hull House operated, with the wealthy and poor of Chicago meeting there as neighbors, rather than as philanthropists and recipients of philanthropy.

Addams' appreciation of what it takes to truly understand the plight of another was informed by her direct contact with the poor living near Hull House. In her writing she often tells stories of how her own preconceptions about others revealed how little she truly knew of them. For instance, she recounts inviting a number of poor children to Hull House and offering them a bowl of candy. She was puzzled when, instead of accepting the candy happily, the children recoiled from it. She later discovered that the children worked in the factories in which the candy was produced, and thus did not want to go near it (perhaps they would have been punished for eating it while working?). Such events prompted Jane to reflect self-critically about how her own expectations inhibited her ability to genuinely care for another. The importance of understanding life from the perspective of those for whom one wished to care took on a new significance. In addition, she strived to perceive others as 'organic wholes' who were themselves situated within larger contexts. By many accounts, the ability to do so was one of Addams' distinct gifts (Leffers, 1993).

The Importance of Being Proactive

Addams took the view that in order to exercise care, one must proactively seek out those different from oneself. On this point her thinking is distinct from that of a more contemporary care ethicist, Nel Noddings (Hamington, 2001). Noddings (1984) suggests that the caring person will always respond to the needs of another as those needs are presented to her. This suggests a rather passive orientation, and Noddings herself intimates that the caring person might hope that 'stray cats' or 'distraught teenagers' would not come their way. For Addams, rather than waiting for those in need to fall into their path, the caring person actively seeks out those with needs. Consequently, consciously choosing an insular life is a dereliction of ethical obligation (Addams, 1907 [2012]).

This insistence that we should deliberately go beyond our kinship groups in order to expand our possibility for extending care links with Addams' view of ethics as an active endeavor. The manner by which that action is undertaken is also important. As one of the first professional social workers, many of

Addams' writings examine the relations between the charity visitor, who was typically 'a young college woman, well-bred and open minded' (Addams 1907 [2012]: 10), and her manner of caring. The measured care which such a well-intentioned person might give was contrasted to the greater emotional kindness which underpinned caring relations between neighborhood members. In relation to those receiving the care of the charity visitor she writes:

> When they see the delay and caution with which relief is given, it does not appear to them a conscientious scruple, but as the cold and calculated action of a selfish man. It is not the aid that they are accustomed to receive from their neighbors, and they do not understand why the impulse which drives people to 'be good to the poor' should be so severely supervised (Addams, 1907 [2012]: 11).

The passage intimates how power, a dynamic that is rarely broached within the context of care ethics, can influence interactions intended to be caring. Addams illustrates this point with the story of an industrial philanthropist, who not only provides men with work, but also builds a community for them to live in. So preoccupied with the loftiness of his own vision for how he can do good by these people, he 'ceases to measure the usefulness of the town by the standards of the men's needs' (Addams, 1907 [2012]: 46). He is affronted when, in the face of 'all that he has done for them', his workers participate in a strike. Addams comments on this writing: 'It is so easy for the good and powerful to think they can rise by fulfilling the dictates of conscience, by pursuing their own ideals, that they are prone to leave those ideals unconnected with the consent of their fellow men' (Addams, 1907 [2012]: 47).

In other words, from his position of privilege the industrialist can bequeath what he thinks is best, and the power differential is such that recipients of his well-intended care can't even tell him otherwise. Here Addams distinguishes between being good 'to' people rather than 'with' them. In noting this difference, Addams prefigures more contemporary debates among care ethicists about the importance of recognizing the perspective from which care is offered. 'Caring for', 'caring about' or 'taking care of' can each imply different power orientations between the carer and care's recipient. Addams asserts the importance of recognizing that without putting in the work of knowing those to whom one wishes to extend care, good intentions can go awry.

In summary, Addams' social ethic is based in a radical understanding of the interconnectedness of us all. Addams challenges us to proactively extend our knowledge of 'anonymous others' in order to foster sympathetic understanding for them, and to actively respond to their needs rather than expecting others to do so. Such sympathetic understanding was the starting point for being able to care 'with' others, rather than inflicting our own best intents on them. How might these ideas be applied to contemporary organizational contexts?

IMPLICATIONS FOR TODAY'S LEADERS

Addams publicly criticized a number of Chicago's politicians and wrote compellingly about how a social ethic infused by care should inform political, as well as industrial leaders. Hamington (2001) summarizes her thoughts about the role care could play within these contexts into four categories: active listening; participating; connected leadership; and activism. The next section of the chapter explores how these ideas apply to Antioch University's Graduate School of Leadership and Change and its Provost, Dr Laurien Alexandre.

THE GRADUATE SCHOOL OF LEADERSHIP AND CHANGE: ANTIOCH UNIVERSITY

As noted in Rita Gardiner's chapter (Chapter 15), a number of aspects of higher education institutions can result in their being uncaring contexts in which to work. Many universities still exhibit characteristics apparent in Heidegger's day: a bureaucratic way of operating underpinned by strict hierarchical structures and rigidly defined promotion routes, a strong emphasis on individual performance as determined by publications and teaching ratings, and rules concerning how faculty relate to students which emphasize universal ideals of fairness rather than attention to individual needs. There can seem to be little room for care (for one's colleagues, students, or even for one's self) in such highly competitive spaces.

Note my surprise, when upon joining Antioch University's Graduate School of Leadership and Change in the spring of 2018, I encountered something novel: a faculty whose members seemed to genuinely like (and care for!) one another. This was not only my observation, but was shared by students as well. At the final dinner for the School's students moving into the candidacy stage of their doctorates, a number of students gave impromptu speeches about just this fact. Many of them are faculty members in other universities and colleges and a recurring refrain among them was how they 'knew something was different about this place because the faculty weren't continually stabbing one another in the back!'. Although we all laughed at the time, in writing this chapter I began to question how such a culture of care is achieved within a sector notorious for the premium it places on individual performance and competitiveness. Here I'll focus on three aspects which align to create this sense of care: the larger University and its mission; the way in which Provost of the Graduate School, Dr Laurien Alexandre leads her faculty; and the School's structures.

Antioch University

Antioch University, with its five campuses in four states and the Graduate School's geographically dispersed program, is known for its commitment to social justice and activism for the common good. The abolitionist and educational reformer, Horace Mann, was the first president of Antioch College. His 1850s' commencement pronouncement, 'Be ashamed to die until you have won some victory for humanity,' remains its guiding principle. Antioch University has its roots in Antioch College's commitment to found the 'university without walls,' in the 1970s.

The kind of social justice Antioch strives for is not achieved through a sterile, hands-off approach. Its history includes the kind of engaged involvement promoted by Jane Addams. For instance during the 1960s Antioch students played a key role in boycotting the Gegner Barber Shop in Yellow Springs, Ohio due to its owner's refusal to cut African Americans' hair. Historically it has nourished activists and counts Coretta Scott King and the suffragette Olympia Brown among its graduates. More recently the Chancellor of Antioch University, William Groves, has joined other US university chancellors in publicly criticizing US policy of separating children from their parents at border crossings, and has also written against recent proposed changes to Title IX, which would weaken the rights of women and the LGBT community under its remit. By sharing these acts with the rest of the faculty, the Chancellor reinforces the university's continued commitment to engaged social justice. This mission and the way it is upheld by the university's leader serve as a container for a socially engaged institutional culture. My primary experience, however, is that of the Graduate School itself. To explore how care finds its way into that culture, I begin by focusing on its provost.

Dr Laurien Alexandre

Dr Laurien Alexandre is both the founding director of the doctoral program and founding provost of the Graduate School. The most significant activity undertaken by the school is its innovative PhD in Leadership and Change, initiated 20 years ago by Laurien and a small design team of faculty. The program enables experienced working professionals to pursue doctoral-level inquiries into the research and practice of leading positive change in workplaces and communities across the globe. On the vanguard of the education of scholar/practitioners, it has graduated nearly 250 doctoral students since it began. What is perhaps even more impressive is the high rate of completion. While it is common for up to 50 percent of those who begin PhDs in the United States not to complete (and some would put that figure higher in humanities and social sciences) Antioch's PhD in Leadership and Change has a completion rate approaching 75 percent. I would venture that one of the ingredients contributing to this success is the sense of care that imbues the program.

This care expresses itself in a number of ways: faculty advisors take their roles seriously and act as advocates for students as well as their supervisor; the program support includes a program manager who regularly goes beyond the call of duty to respond to faculty and student needs, a dedicated librarian whose care for students and their projects is legendary, and an educational technology staff who have created a virtual learning environment which truly enables student/faculty engagement. At the helm of this venture is Dr Laurien Alexandre, who is known for her distinctive way of leading the school. When I joined the faculty I was struck by how often I heard comments such as, 'Laurien's capacity to hold the diverse student body and really see each individual as a particular human being is extraordinary' from both students and faculty.

Indeed, as Laurien introduced me to various members of the team, I was struck by how easily she was able to recount significant aspects of biography, both mine and theirs. Her attention to the individual details of her faculty's lives is impressive: she sent flowers to my house the day my contract officially started; on the morning my husband was undergoing serious eye surgery she emailed us best wishes. She asked about the arrival of our dog through customs on the day we moved back to the States. Laurien's commitment to know those who work with her, as well as the students and alumni, demonstrates the kind of active listening, participation and connected leadership Addams writes about.

In wanting to include my experience of this caring leader and organization in this chapter, I was interested in talking with her about the difficulties inherent in this kind of leadership orientation. How does she balance the particularities of individual hopes/needs with the standards and systems inherent in a university system committed to principles of 'equity' and fairness? Our conversation soon led to the bane of many academic directors' lives: how to distribute workload (fairly) among faculty members. 'For me,' she noted,

> there was a realization that formulaic approaches to workload anchored in an antiquated notion of 'credit hour' established an artificial 'equality' or 'equity' approach. What if instead of aligning faculty with numbers of credits, we, as a Graduate School, ask the question, 'What does this person bring? What are their gifts and how do these talents contribute to the overall mission?' I need to think both of individuals but also of the overall unit – 'What does the unit need for its best performance?' Thinking this way allows for the recognition that different individuals contribute different things.

What is important here is the insight into how individuals' uniqueness can contribute to the overall purpose of the collective in ways that serve both the individual and the common good. In this way, Laurien demonstrates Addams' 'ability to see individuals as wholes that are also interconnected and inter-related parts of larger wholes' (Leffers, 1993: 69). One of the tensions inherent to this approach, however, is the need to have faculty who will 'buy-in' to this way of distributing work.

Another curiosity for me is Laurien's decision to act as academic advisor for the 20–30 members of each incoming cohort of doctoral students. I had never known of a provost being involved with students' progress at such an early stage (or indeed at any stage of an individual student's studies, unless there was an issue of misconduct). When describing her decision to take on this role, Laurien explained,

> First, I love working directly with students and helping individuals find their path. But there is another issue as well. My involvement shows from the outset that this is no traditional doctoral program, where it's impossible to get in touch with those who are the most powerful. I want to demonstrate in practice that we are all equally available, and equally caring.

This very public act of being present in the day-to-day role of student caretaking sets a particular tone of engagement, as well as creating a benchmark for the type of engagement faculty have with students.

Creating Structures that Support Care

Undoubtedly Laurien's personal style contributes to the quality of the Graduate School's culture. She characterizes herself as warm and engaging, she likes people, and is skilled at helping others feel at ease. But she stresses that these characteristics are only a starting point for creating a caring culture, noting that 'if one is operating within a highly competitive, cut-throat culture then one wouldn't experience the organization as caring, no matter how personable or caring the leader is.'

Elaborating on this point, Laurien stressed,

> I don't believe there is a 10-step model for bringing humanity to organizations. However, structures and ways of operating which reward behaviors that facilitate care can deliberately be established. For instance, students are evaluated on their level of engagement in peer learning and cohort accountability. During the annual faculty review process instead of asking only about peer-reviewed articles published and courses taught, we ask questions about how people have collaborated with other colleagues.

Additionally, faculty members are encouraged to offer peer reviews to one another during the annual review process. This provides a formal system by which colleagues can highlight their appreciation for one another as well as offer suggestions about how they might be more helpful. This process serves to disrupt power structures while also making faculty accountable to one another in a material way.

Certainly my day-to-day interactions with colleagues differ markedly from my previous experiences of academic faculties. For instance, I'm currently working on the PhD program's admission committee and another member of that committee has experienced technical problems in downloading applicants' files. No less than six email exchanges occurred between him and other academic members of the committee, helping to find a solution within half an hour of his first call for help. This is in sharp contrast to my first day in post at another university, where when I asked a colleague for help using the photocopier I was told 'that wasn't their job and they didn't have time anyway'.

In another rather radical organizational approach, the Graduate School pays all faculty the same salary, whether they are senior stars or recent hires. As Laurien notes, 'Paying everyone the same has turned out to be quite subversive and positive – doing so immediately moves us away from judging one another to recognizing each other's worth.' Certainly in my experience this transparency around pay offers one less issue for faculty to backstab or gossip about. In the end, Laurien explains 'caring is not a one-time achievement. It requires continual attention, experimentation and the willingness to try again.' This characterization echoes Addams' stance that caring is an engaged, proactive orientation rather than adherence to a universal principle. It requires a continual commitment to curiosity about the affect one is having on others, and the fortitude to admit when you've got it wrong and need to reconsider. These challenges make caring leadership anything but a soft option.

REFLECTIONS

In reflecting on Addams' 'social ethic' and how caring is enacted in practice, at least two further questions remain. How do care and justice (really) balance one another out in organizational settings? And, what is the toll such an approach takes on leaders who try to use it?

Balancing Care and Justice

Although she promoted sympathetic understanding and care as the basis for human interactions, Addams herself was clear that care needs to be balanced by justice in order for ethics to be realized. Suggesting that care and justice are oppositional rather than complementary ethical stances echoes Kohlberg's view that justice constitutes a higher order of morality than care. This is not necessarily a helpful way of thinking. Addams argues that:

> 'to love mercy' and at the same time 'to do justly' is the difficult task; to fulfil the first requirement alone is to fall into the error of indiscriminate giving with all of its disastrous results; to fulfil the second solely is to obtain the stern policy of with-holding, and it results in such a dreary lack of sympathy and understanding that the establishment of justice is impossible. (Addams, 1907 [2012]: 23–4)

It is more difficult to navigate a balancing point between the two than to align completely with one. Fashioning fair responses which attend to the needs of the whole while also accounting for the idiosyncrasies of particular individuals can be time consuming. Finding the 'path' between often requires creativity and the ability to work beyond habitual frames of thinking. Additionally, the person who steps beyond the strictures of fairness can be subject to criticism. It is much easier to rely on 'the rules': 'Of course I would help you out but the system won't let me do it'. This is a key challenge facing leaders aspiring to include care within their approach. Laurien alluded to 'getting it wrong' some-times by extending 'mercy' when instead boundaries needed to be adhered to. As proposed in this chapter's introduction, integrating fairness and care requires a fortitude and willingness to put oneself on the line that accepted approaches to justice do not exact.

This observation leads to the second concern: what toll does integrating care into one's approach take on leaders?

The Cost of Caring

In practicing her belief that care should extend beyond those with whom one is comfortable, Addams herself suffered adverse consequences. It is impor-tant to note that prior to the war, Addams had enjoyed an extremely positive reputation throughout the US and internationally. Her biographer Allen Davis asserted that 'probably no woman in any period in American history has been venerated and worshipped the way Jane Addams was in the period before World War I' (Davis, 1973: 200). However, her efforts to care for all of those suffering in the aftermath of the First World War, including starving Germans, resulted in her vilification by the American public. Labeled a 'German lover', she became the target of criticism and suffered a downturn in public opinion. Nevertheless, her efforts to care for those on the losing side of the conflict were a major reason why she was awarded the Nobel Prize for Peace four years prior to her death in 1931. Caring can be an unfashionable endeavor.

Nevertheless, Jane Addams argues that care should be at the heart of democ-racy itself. For her, democracy implies a system of relationships in which people genuinely care for one another and are willing to act on those caring sentiments (Hamington, 2001). As I read Addams' work I am struck by how relevant her writings are to our contemporary context. I wonder about how different our world would look if the social ethic she promotes were extended to those fleeing hostile lands (rather than building walls to keep them at bay) or to the Earth Herself as global climate change continues to take hold. Today more than ever it seems, leaders need to cultivate the courage to care exhibited by Jane Addams. Indeed, Addams teaches us that wherever we sit, seeking out the other, developing sympathetic understanding and striving to balance care and justice contribute to the possibility of a beneficial society for us all.

REFERENCES

Addams, J. (1907 [2012]). *Democracy and Social Ethics*. Middletown, DE: CreateSpace.

Addams, J. (1910). Charity and social justice. *North American Review*, **192**, 68–81.

Davis, A. (1973). *American Heroine*. Oxford: Oxford University Press.

Hamington, M. (2001). Jane Addams and a politics of embodied care. *Journal of Speculative Philosophy*, **15**(2), 105–21.

Hamington, M. (2007). Care ethics and international justice: The cosmopolitanism of Jane Addams and Kwame Anthony Appiah. *Social Philosophy Today*, **23**, 149–60.

Kohlberg, L. (1971). Stages of moral development. *Moral Education*, **1**(51), 23–92.

Leffers, M.R. (1993). Pragmatists Jane Addams and John Dewey inform the ethic of care. *Hypatia*, **8**(2), 64–77.

Lengermann, P.M. and Niebrugge-Brantley, J. (1998). *The Women Founders: Sociology and Social Theory 1830–1930*. London: McGraw-Hill.

Noddings, N. (1984). *Caring: A Feminine Approach to Ethics and Moral Education*. Berkeley, CA: University of California Press.

Index